Transforming Personality

Dr. Swami Parthasarathy, is eminent professor, noted author, orator, educationist, spiritual philosopher and philanthropist, and an eminent personality of management academia in India and abroad. He is the Chancellor cum Chairman, Sri Sharada Institute of Indian Management (SIIM) University and Chairman cum Managing Trustee of Sri SIIM-Research Foundation, New Delhi and Ramakrishna-Vivekanand International Foundation (RKVIF), New Delhi. He is also the Member of Joint Commission of BRICS Countries and the Chairman Asia-Pacific Development Initiative, a Joint Economic Forum of 25 Asia-Pacific Countries. He has also been nominated as Permanent Representing Member of India to UN-ECOC.

Dr. Parthasarathy is an MBA in International Business and Ph.D. from University of Chicago Booth School of Business. He has also been conferred with Seven Honorary D.Litt. from different Universities in India and abroad and is also a Distinguished Fellow of Indian Management Association. He has developed various management training modules, which are widely recognized by the corporate and academic world. An internationally noted writer, he has authored 28 books and 129 research papers. His famous title, "Forget Classroom Learning" carries the Foreword by the Apple Inc. Founder, Steve Jobs. Mr. Barak Obama, US President, referred his book "Transforming Personality" during his election campaign number of times. The book "Transforming Personality" was the best seller in European and North American Market in 2007.

Transforming Personality

Third Edition

DR. SWAMI PARTHASARATHY

ACADEMIC FOUNDATION
NEW DELHI

www.academicfoundation.org

Third edition published in 2017
by

ACADEMIC FOUNDATION
4772-73 / 23 Bharat Ram Road, (23 Ansari Road),
Darya Ganj, New Delhi - 110 002 (India).
Phones : 23245001 / 02 / 03 / 04.
Fax : +91-11-23245005.
E-mail : books@academicfoundation.com
www.academicfoundation.org

Disclaimer:
The findings/views/opinions expressed in this book are solely those of the author and do not necessarily reflect the views of the publisher.

Cataloging in Publication Data--DK
Courtesy: D.K. Agencies (P) Ltd. <docinfo@dkagencies.com>

Parthasarathy, A. (Avula), 1927- **author.**
Transforming personality / Dr. Swami Parthasarathy. -- Third edition.
pages cm
Includes bibliographical references.
ISBN 9789332704008

1. Self-actualization (Psychology) 2. Personality. I. Title.

BF637.S4A98 2017 DDC 158.1 23

Typeset, printed and bound by The Book Mint, New Delhi.
www.thebookmint.in

This new edition is dedicated at the
Holy Lotus Feet of my God & Guiding Spirit
their Holinesses Jagadgurus Sri Sri Bharathi Teerth Mahasannidhanam &
Sri Sri Vidhusekhara Bharathi Sannidhanam

Contents

Section 2

Section 3

Message from Swami Dayananda Saraswati

Personality development should not be left to nature. It has to be initiated and nurtured by parents in the formative stage and later by teachers in the school. This process goes on up to one's adulthood, and later the development is in one's own hands. The initiative has to be well guided, with clarity all the way. Swami (Dr.) Parthasarathy is presenting this book "Transforming Personality Emotional Intelligence to Spiritual Intelligence" which he calls a comprehensive programme for self-growth. His approach being holistic, he has taken help from different means and sources. I am sure this will be the base resource book for personality development, which he is planning to offer to people in various walks of life. It will also be a complete handbook for various programmes of personality development by which the personality can be developed successfully. I congratulate Dr. Parthasarathy for his outstanding contribution to this most important pursuit of self-growth.

Foreword

Life is a series of experiences that we congregate from different situations right from our birth to death; but when some experiences make our life `elevated' then the life becomes meaningful. Such experiences may come either through some practices or from a particular way of life, which would lead us to greater heights in life and ultimately culminate into a transformed state. To unveil our transformation, we need a practical guide, here Swami (Dr.) Parthasarathy, who would astoundingly transform the idea into a clear practical approach. At least in my life I cannot recollect coming across any such comprehensive guide. The expression in this book may be presented in an Indian way but, I am personally of the opinion, and even the world is well aware, that India is the land of rich ideas, especially when it comes to the matter of 'invention' of significance of life, spirituality and the practice for greater unfolding. When the author's life itself is the practical example then the writings become even more exulted. I, myself being one the eye witnesses of this conversion. I think in our country numerous people have gone through this book, but when a reader, like Mr. Barack Obama, refers to the book then it really matters.

I am quite sure that this work will significantly change so many human lives and pave their way to appropriate destinations. While reading the content, the western reader, specifically, will be able to acquaint himself with Indian ideas and ideals for changing life, which indicates the purport of life to a destination and beyond. I prescribe the book to all the people, irrespective of their walks of life, who keenly want to see a meaningful change in their lives. I also express my heart-felt gratitude and convey my heartiest congratulation to Dr. Parthasarathy for his contribution to the world of learning.

—Alden Winship Clausen
Former President of World Bank
New Jersey

Preface to the Third Edition

Third edition for the title: "Transforming Personality" and the second edition for "Forget Classroom Learning" and "Human Values in Modern Management" are published to present these three titles together in a new compendium form to the reader in a refurbished work of those titles. I am truly overwhelmed with the responses from the readers like Mr. Barack Obama, Mr. Ban Ki-moon, Prof. Colin Clouson-Thomas, Mr. Ravi Shankar Prasad and more such luminaries and other scholars, researchers and practising corporate managers across the globe. Reading these three books in a sequence shall undoubtedly enrich the human mind towards the culmination of human life.

As the world is graduating more and more from modernity to ultra-modernity, similarly human beings are advancing towards the realms of being superhuman. So the animal instincts of human race are getting more and more manifested into multidimensional face of new faculties of cruelty. The violence for ideology of misnomer religion, caste and colour has replaced the true fragrance and philosophy of religion. On one hand, the world is eradicating one form of slavery, on the other, introducing a new form. There is continual unimaginable erosion of 'values': the fourth faculty of humanity, which differentially identifies human beings from the animal world. There is growing evidence of complex obsession of misogynistic conduct and intolerance towards an individual's legitimate views, rights and choices. So we are at the crucial juncture where the planet is under serious threat from unprecedented humanitarian crisis arisen out of steep fall of human values.

Therefore, our effort of publication of this compendium is a humble prescription of solution to the global humanity towards the fundamental laws of human kind as our Vedic scriptures suggest us "*Atmano Mokshartham Jagadhitayo ca*" (Salvation of the Self and Welfare of the World). I am extremely grateful to Shri Sanu Kapila, and Shri Rituraj Kapila of Academic Foundation for undertaking this upheaval task. May the Almighty bless them with his choicest boons.

— Dr. Swami Parthasarathy,
FIMA, Ph.D. (UChicago), MBA (UChicago)

Preface to the Second Edition

People often listen to the talk on 'Personality Development', but never strive to seek answers to the questions which I pose to them. The questions are: (i) Whether personality can really be developed? (ii) Why we require so? (iii) And what an inferior personality is all about? Answers to these questions are basic to the understanding of the idea underlying 'Personality Development'.

The respective answers may be quite confusing, unprecedented or contradictory but in fact this is the absolute science; the perennial knowledge revealed in the time immemorial and communicated through the Indian traditional scriptures.

The expression 'Personality Development' itself is delusive. The common concept of personality development may connote importing a superior kind of personality where it is deficient. It is really astonishing to note as to how some kind of superior personality can be imposed upon inferiority. This is illogical, irrational and completely impossible. Rather, we should approach this in a scientific way which is very rational and logical in lieu of going the emotional way. I just would like to analyze it from the scientific standpoint — that infers that neither can you develop some thing, where there is a deficiency or absence of the particular substance nor can you create something out of nothing, which is a universal law. Accordingly, developing a superior personality from an inferior personality or to import developed personality into inferiority is absolutely a utopian idea. It's the Indian imperishable knowledge which also complements the physical science; defines that you can't import or add anything from outside. It's only that you can transform the already ingrained available material into new shape or form. Like an ugly black stone into beautiful black idol, a rough wooden log into a spectacular wooden statue or dirty mud into clay idol. Similarly, transformation in the case of a human being is the transformation of his/her inner sphere into an enlightened precious inner world, but not importing something from outside, only the material already available in the inner sphere gets transformed. It is discovering the developed personality already within you. Thus, building confidence is nothing but to discover your confidence, your inner strength derived from the awareness that we are having full existence of confidence. It is mere understanding and a cognitive change about your own self; one fine day, you discover yourself that you are already perfectly developed and confident. That means it is just the disappearance of your ignorance and your illusion about yourself. It is undeniably the cognitive change of an individual. So from this discussion we can safely conclude that we are already developed, confident and transformed but the problem is that we are unaware of this fact. It just requires self-effort to unfold and unveil the curtain of ignorance. The curtain of ignorance is just the ill and deficient understanding about our own self which we recurrently accept through our wrongly identified and mistaken practice. It just needs to be mandatorily corrected in order to see our real entity, which is perfectly developed and confident. This course of correction is nothing but a process of bringing in absolute change of perception about oneself.

This cognitive change is absolutely necessary for every human being to dwell upon one's real-self and to be able to know oneself correctly. By knowing our real entity, we will be able to perceive the world and be able to exhibit and demonstrate our ownself truly.

I hope this edition with this focus may really be insightful and an honest effort to purport the entire content as a crux and essence of the elaborate idea of practical science.

My oceanic thanks and gratitude go to the entire Macmillan family and especially to Sh. Sanjay Singh and Ashish for their constant cooperation.

—Dr. Swami Parthasarathy
New Delhi

Preface to the First Edition

A country may appear to be prosperous and advanced in every possible way; but if people of character, people of noble qualities, people with a kind heart are not present in large numbers, the decline and fall of that country is sure to come. Vast and varied geography and enchanting scenic beauty do not constitute a nation. It is the people who constitute a nation. This is a truth known to the wise. If the people are strong and dynamic, the country is powerful; if the people are cultured, the nation is civilised. Likewise, when the people are weak and uncultured, the nation also will be the same.

We know that the strength and glory of a nation depends on the sum total of the character of each individual constituting that nation. Now, what does it mean when we say a person has a powerful character or a powerful personality? Does it mean he has a strong body? Or that he has a tremendous intellect? Or that he has vast knowledge? All these are correct, no doubt, but these are all just certain aspects of personality, not the whole. What then is meant by a comprehensive, powerful personality? When we analyze this point, we find that a comprehensive, powerful personality comprises of six important aspects:

- Physical Strength
- Intellectual Strength
- Mental Strength
- Emotional Strength
- Moral Strength
- Spiritual Strength

If we have to say that a person's character is all-rounded, that his potential has been completely manifested, it means that all these four aspects—physical, intellectual, moral and spiritual—must be fully developed in him. If a person has a very strong physique, but no intellectual growth, he is no better than a strong bull. An intelligent man, who lacks moral development, is but a cunning fox! Without spiritual strength, all these strengths—physical, mental, moral—become like an edifice on sand, with no solid foundation and hence no certainty and permanence. In fact, they all become meaningless without spiritual development. Hence we have to clearly understand the significance of all these four aspects of our personality in a strong and meaningful manner.

Birth, growth and one fine day, death—this cycle is common to all living beings. In this cycle, birth and death are beyond our control. But with regard to growth, we have great freedom of choice; there is a lot we can do. But the masses give no thought to the growth of their personality. They make no special effort along these lines; they grow much as the birds and animals. Though born as human beings, many lead a dull life. Their entire existence is without any meaning, without any purpose. Just because such people form the majority, it does not mean their method is right. There is a method where, by disciplined effort, we can achieve systematic development of our personality and attain fulfilment in life. We just need to learn the technique of developing our personality in a comprehensive way. There is a technique for everything. Similarly, there is a science of developing our personality. Just think of the difference between simply scattering seeds on a piece of land and learning the technique of farming? How will it be if we simply place brick upon brick and try to build a house; and how will it be if we build a house under the technical assistance of an architect? Very similarly, if we try to develop our personality haphazardly, without guidance from an expert, without knowing the technique involved, in vain will be our efforts and our life will be without any meaning.

In this world, we can find many people who have developed themselves along particular lines, who have developed one or more of the above-mentioned strengths. But only those who have developed all the four aspects equally can be said to have developed a true personality, a complete and a meaningful personality. Let us study the nature of these four aspects and learn the technique of developing them in our personality.

I am really blessed by the grace of my guru, the world famous scholar-monk, Swami Dayananda Saraswati, who has transformed my personality and has bestowed his kind source and inspiration of this book for the masses, especially for the youth who keenly aspire to be great.

I am also grateful to Shri Pankaj Sharma, Shri Ravindar Singh and Shri J.P. Singh for their immense help in transcription; as also to Shri Anupamdeo Arya for his kind co-operation for providing me some data and information on Spiritual Intelligence. May the Divine Mother bestow her choicest blessings on them.

—Swami (Dr.) Parthasarathy

Section 1

1

Maturity and Human Life

Living is the Goal of Life

What is the goal of life? This is the question one often comes across. Some people ask the question for the sake of asking while others seem to be really concerned about what one is in for; what is the goal of life. You get different answers from different people. If you ask this question from a swami, the answer would probably be: 'To see God, to reach God.' A theologian may say: 'The goal of life is to repent for your original sin and all other sins and to go to heaven later.'

Death cannot be the goal of life. If death had to be the goal of life, I need not have been born at all. I do not remain after death in this form and I was not there before death in this form, and so I need not be born in order to achieve a state I already had even before I was born. So death cannot be the aim of my life. You cannot say heaven is the goal of my life because in that case, why should I be born here? The aim must be something in this life itself. Shall we say marriage is the aim of life? Well, it can be, but even married people also do not seem to have achieved the goal of life. Marriage can be something great or it can be a problem. Recently someone asked me whether marriage is a word or a sentence. It can be a very meaningful word or it can be a sentence of life! It all depends upon how you make it. Marriage has to be made. It is a means to something but not an end in itself. It can be a part of growing up.

Then what exactly is the aim of life? It can only be living. I am born not just for anything except to live, and that is what we find in every organism. A plant wants to live, a bug wants to live, an insect wants to live. Any organism that is born, wants to live. So living is the aim of life, nothing more.

The question is: What is living? Can we say that mere breathing is living?

To Live is to Grow

When a cow is physically, biologically adult, it does not have any problem psychologically. An adult cow is adult all the way. It does not have the problems of a human being. It does not have the complex that it is a bad cow or that it is a useless cow, that it is a white cow or a black cow. A cow does not have a complex that it is an ugly cow, and therefore there is no need for a plastic surgeon amongst cows! There is no beautician among cows either.

I grew up in a village and I know village psychology. Let us say there are two cows that belong to the same breed, are about the same age and yield essentially the same quantity of milk. Thus the different criteria that set the price of a cow are equally applicable to both the cows. The only difference is that one of the cows has shapely horns while the other has crooked horns! The cow with shapely horns fetches a better price than the one with crooked horns! Not because the latter is inferior in any way but because the buyer has a complex! He prefers to become the owner of a cow with shapely horns because the features of the cow somehow seem to reflect upon him! So he pays the price for his complex.

This complex is very costly. One pays with one's life for this complex. People, and especially we Indians, always worry about what others think of us. This is an unfortunate thing. It is one thing to take into account the opinion of others and to deliberate upon it, but it is quite another thing to worry about protecting one's image based on what others say. People even get married on account of what others say! What others would say is a problem for human beings; cows do not seem to have this problem.

A human being is born as a baby. The physical body has to grow, to metamorphose into an adult for which one need not do anything special. Nature takes care of it. The very nature that brought the body into being also takes care of its growth. The body should just keep living. If a boy survives for a few years, he finds he has to shave! One need not do anything to grow a beard, to become an adult. To become a graduate one should go to school, study, gain knowledge; one has to work for it. To learn swimming one must make an effort. But to become an adult, one need not do anything. You just keep living, eating, knocking about, and you will grow and become an adult ready for marriage! But is it that simple? Do you really live? I am afraid we do not really live. We only drag on because maturity is not merely biological or physical maturity. There must be emotional maturity. Emotional maturity seems to be a simple thing, but it is not.

You are your emotions. No matter what your learning or understanding is, it does not seem to have any bearing upon your day to day responses to the world. This gap between one's understanding and the actual day-to-day living is a problem. This gap is expressed by Duryodhana in this famous verse:

Janami dharmam na ca me pravrttih
Janamyadharmam na ca me nivrttih
Kenapi margena hrdi sthitena
Yatha niyuktosmi tatha karomi

[I know what is right, but I cannot pursue it. I know what is wrong, but I cannot desist from doing it. I do as directed by someone who seems to be within me.]

Arjuna also asks a question in the *Bhagavad Gita*, expressing the same idea:

Atha kena prayukto yam papam carati purusah
Anicchannapi varsneya baladiva niyojitah

[Now then O Varsneya (Krsna), impelled by what does this man commit sin even against his wish, as though being impelled by force?] (*Bhagavad Gita* III 36)

How is it that I behave in a given manner even though I am not convinced about it? Why does one act in an unbecoming manner, even though one has the knowledge of what is becoming and what is not?

This is Arjuna's question. The answer is that one requires to be emotionally mature in order to be able to act according to one's convictions.

A Child's Perception

The existence of emotional maturity is not denied. Modern psychology addresses the problems born of emotional immaturity. A man becomes criminal, not because criminality is in his blood but because of something he has in his mind. It is all buried in his childhood. It is really the childhood that makes a person what he or she is. This is a very unfortunate situation because no one can be born an adult, with an adult mind. No one can escape from a child's perception.

A child's perception is a child's perception. We cannot call it childish even though it is. A child feels insecure; it is insecure on its legs, insecure about everything. Everything seems to be big and overwhelming. When a Swami with a long beard comes home, the child, frightened, seeks security in the parents' lap. If a child is left with a baby-sitter, it feels abandoned—it does not want to be away from its parents. Have you seen a child carrying a piece of his mother's sari wherever he goes? That is because the child finds some security in it.

If I was insecure as a child, holding on to my mother's sari or whatever, how secure am I now, when I have grown up? I was insecure as a child, and I do not fare much better as an adult also. The reasons for insecurity may be different—now I feel insecure with reference to my job, my relationships, my money, my retirement and so on. What I am worried about may be different but the insecurity continues.

Look at this. A child is given a clay doll and is playing with it. The doll falls and breaks into pieces. The child cries. Why? Because emotionally he is not an adult. He is only a child. He refuses to accept the fact that the clay doll is breakable and that it will break some time. The child cries when a doll breaks because he cannot accept the fact. I will not call that child childish because he is just a child. He has yet to become emotionally adult to accept and assimilate facts.

The father, the grown up adult, comes and tells the child: 'Hey, come on now. Don't cry. After all, it is only a clay doll. I will get you another one.' But the child insists: 'I want the same doll. Why should my doll break? Why not my brother's doll? Why should it happen to me and not to him?' The father, the wise man, says: 'That doll is also made of clay and that will also break some day.'

I am the younger of the two brothers. One day, mother gave me a piece of chocolate candy. I was very happy because normally she did not give me candy unless I asked for it. But even as I was unwrapping my candy, I saw mother giving two pieces of the same candy to my brother who was just a couple of years older than me.

I asked my mother to give me another chocolate, but she refused saying that I was too young. I got furious. I threw away the one chocolate in my hand. Why should he be given two? Why not I also? Why am I not treated the same way? I could not understand mother's thinking. I cried and made a scene.

Twenty-five years later, now working in an office, I was happy when I got an extra increment. But soon I found that my colleague had got two extra increments. I could not stand this discrimination. I went to our superior and demanded an explanation. The superior explained that the other person had worked harder than me, but I could not accept it. I resigned the job and got into a lot of trouble. It was the same old chocolate habit!

As a child, when my schoolmate had something I did not have, I felt jealous of him. When I had something that someone else did not have, I held on to it even though I may not have wanted it, because it was 'mine.' These are 'my' marbles, 'my' toys, and nobody should touch them. These are 'his' toys and I should get as many of them as possible, but I cannot part with mine. This was all understandable because I was just a child. People around me understood this and I was excused because I was a child. No one criticises a child because a child is accepted as a child. People are kind and loving and understanding, hoping that one day the child will become an adult, not merely physically but emotionally too.

Growth Has to be Initiated

But how many of us have really become adults? What is it that you can really stand up emotionally? Things have a knack of being what they are and in spite of all your will and effort, they go to pieces. Since I am grown up now, I do not weep when a toy breaks. But suppose what breaks happens to be a curio which I received as a gift from someone, and which I have been preserving? When that breaks, my heart also breaks, because I am still a child. If a toy does not upset me, it can be something else or someone else. If someone near and dear passes away, it is not easy for me to accept and assimilate that fact. It is a fact that someone has passed away. But can I accept that fact? I lose my job or even lose hair or find my hair turning grey. A number of unpleasant things keep happening as I proceed with my life, but how many of them do I accept gracefully without a murmur? I hardly see any one accepting such events. I find very few who are adults emotionally.

We do not seem to grow, we seem to remain the same. No matter what our intellectual accomplishments are, emotionally we seem to remain immature and insecure. We seem to be helpless. No one can consciously get angry—you will find this out; consciously try to get angry; you will not be able to. But you do find yourself getting angry because anger happens. And anger does not go away because you do this or that—not even if you become *a Swami*! Anger happens; it comes to you, and that means you are helpless. No one wants to become sad, but one finds oneself sad. No one wants to become depressed but depressed one finds oneself to be.

This helplessness is what we call emotional immaturity. Physically, biologically a person is an adult, but emotionally, he or she is not. A cow is programmed to be a adult all the way—there is no emotionally immature cow, there is no immoral cow. But a human being is not programmed to automatically become emotionally adult, because he has the faculty of choice. He is a self-conscious being and, therefore, this particular growth has to be initiated by himself; it is centred on self-will.

As a person, I have an image of myself and this image is a problem. I have created an image for myself even as a child. I found the world too much for me as a child. I felt I was not loved and cared for. I found parents quarrelling with each other and I was caught in between. I thought I was responsible for their quarrel. This is a typical child's way of looking at things. If the father is an alcoholic, his behaviour in the morning and in the evening is very different and the child gets confused. He is unable to understand what is normal. A child's perception is all right as a child, but it is not valid for an adult. The world of an adult is entirely different, but the child's perception forms the very personality, the self-image of the adult and that vitiates the perception of the adult and his or her responses to the situation. Unless you pay attention to some of these problems they will not disappear; they will remain as they are now, no matter what you learn, what you become. The emotional insecurity clings to you.

Can you avoid situations in life? Can you command an agreeable situation all the time? Do you call all the shots in your life? You do not. Situations keep changing like traffic; sometimes unpleasant, sometimes messy—you do not know how to get out of them. Occasionally, there are pleasant situations too. This life is nothing but changing, varying situations. You have to face them and you are the only one who can face them. Even if there are people to help you, you have to ask for their help and you cannot take any more help than your capacity enables you to. When you get married, a number of people come to attend the wedding and it looks as though they are all with you. But once the ceremony is over, they all go away and you are left with your partner in a small apartment. Thereafter, you have to make your own life.

There are different areas we have to look into to find out whether our understanding, our attitudes, are mature. One has to learn how to drop things, how to face situations, how to accept situations, in the light of *Vedanta*. Then you find that *Vedanta* is alive. *Vedanta* is not a topic in books. It is just you, it is your vision, it is your responses to the situations. *Vedanta* helps change your scale of vision. Your emphasis changes and thus small things remain small because you are concerned with something bigger. Thus *Vedanta* does bring about a cognitive change. Your cognition changes and with that a number of changes can take place.

I am not talking about psychiatric patients who are abnormal psychological cases. I am talking about 'normal' people who have certain 'normal' psychological problems. There are many people who are abnormally abnormal. Vedanta does not deal with them. We are dealing with normally abnormal people; those who get angry now and then, become depressed now and then; people who are reasonably angry, reasonably sad, reasonably frustrated, reasonably depressed! I am addressing these people. If you are unreasonably sad, it is better that you do not go to a *Swami* because he will confuse you even more!

To begin living my life, I must be a complete person, a mature person. Completeness is only in terms of emotional maturity. Once I become emotionally mature, from that time onwards I begin to live; my seeking has a direction, my struggle gains a direction. Otherwise my struggle, my spiritual seeking, all these remain unconnected. They belong to the person who is currently facing the situations and who is the good old emotionally immature person. Please do not mistake me, when I use the term 'emotionally immature', it is not meant to condemn you. There is a general tendency that we convert everything into a self-condemning device, but I do not want you to condemn yourself and see yourself as emotionally immature. I just want you to see what immaturity is. To judge oneself as immature is another form of immaturity. It is not so much judgment as it is understanding of what I am saying.

Acceptance of Fact is Maturity

The physical body of a human being, in time, becomes adult but physical adulthood does not necessarily imply maturity of the mind. The thinking person that a human is, he or she has to respond to the world emotionally and emotional response can be mature or immature depending upon the understanding one has gained while going through the various experiences in day-to-day living.

Pain can be an unpleasant factor that remains unpleasant all your life, held in memory, or it can be an experience out of which you can grow to become greater than the pain. It is childish to expect that life should be without pain. It is equally childish to conclude that there is no possibility of being happy in one's life. A person who commits suicide has concluded that there is no way of his or her becoming happy in future. It is this conclusion that makes the person raise his or her head against the self. If you analyse this conclusion, you find it is childish.

There are always pleasant and unpleasant situations in life. Such situations existed in *Satyayuga* and *Tretayuga* and in *Dvaparayuga* and these are present in *Kaliyuga* too. Human life is always fraught with situations that are both pleasant and unpleasant. But people want things to be always pleasant. Most of our responses to situations are reactions because there is no acceptance of facts. When you respond to a situation in terms of anger or jealousy or frustration or hatred, you do not really respond to the fact. You basically refuse to accept the fact, don't you?

A stoic philosopher, I am told, was a businessman too. He was waiting for the safe arrival of a large sailing ship carrying his wife and children and all his wealth. One day, he heard a knock on his door and found a breathless messenger who announced:

'Sir, your ship has sunk.'

'What?'

'Your ship has sunk!'

'So what?'

'Sir, you have lost all your wealth.'

'What?'

'You are a pauper.'

'So what?'

'Sir, you have lost your wife and children.'

'What?'

'You are a childless widower.'

'So what?'

Look at these two types of responses from the same person. The first response is an excited, 'What?' The second is a cool, 'So what?' The difference is obvious. When he said 'What?' it is not that he had not understood what he was told or that he was asking for clarification. The messenger had announced the news in clear words and it was very clear to him that the ship had sunk, and still when he said, 'What?' it means, 'Oh, no! Not really!' Thus, 'What?' is the response of the non-acceptance of a fact. An ordinary person will keep on building up on the non-acceptance. There is a sense of loss and one sees one's self as a person without the family and all that money brings.

One would have to start all over again and there is no certainty of whether one will be successful. One sees a variety of things associated with the loss of family, with the loss of money and becomes sadder and sadder. It is all due to the resistance to accept the fact that the ship had sunk. The philosopher also said, 'What?' as an ordinary person would say. But he was a thinking person, a mature person and therefore the next response was, `So what?' That is the response from a person who has accepted the fact. 'What?' is the response from a person who has not accepted the fact, who does not want to accept the fact. But it is childish not to accept a fact because a fact is a fact whether you accept it or not.

All you accomplish by not accepting a fact is an emotional build up which results in sorrow, frustration, despair; a whole chain of reactions and then a series of actions. You may require the whole of society to come and console you. Many years may roll by and still there is a chance that the fact is not accepted.

There is a great distance between these two types of responses. It may take a hundred years for some people to bridge this distance. It may take twenty years for some others. It may not happen in this birth in case of many—it may take several births! But, for this philosopher, it involved only a few seconds. If something can go wrong, it will go wrong—that is Murphy's Law. If a ship can sink, it may sink. If it does not, be grateful. This philosopher was able to assimilate, within a few seconds, the fact that things had gone wrong, and he accepted the fact.

Lord Krishna says in the *Gita*:

Tasmadapariharyerthe na tvam socitumarhasi

[Therefore you ought not to grieve over an irreparable fact] (*Bhagavad Gita* II 27)

If there is a situation you can do something about, it calls for action. If it is a situation, like the sinking of a ship, like death, which you cannot do anything about, you have to accept it. The sun is set and you cannot bring it back. So, you have to accept it.

One who accepts facts, who faces facts is a practical person, in other words, a mature person. One who has lived one's life growing, getting something out of every experience, is a mature person ready to accept facts. Therefore, accepting facts is characteristic of a mature person. Acceptance of facts calls for action where the situation can be changed. Regarding the situation that cannot be changed, Lord Krishna says:

Tamstitiksasya Bharata

[May you bear with them 0 Bharata]

(*Bhagavad Gita* II 14)

If a situation is irreparable, something that cannot be altered by you, you have to bear with it. You have to have *titiksa*, forbearance. So, *titiksa* is nothing but maturity. If you analyse any virtue, it is nothing but the disposition of a mature mind. The first thing about a mature person is the capacity to accept facts and do what is to be done. We find that the *Gita*, which talks about a variety of things leading up to the nature of Truth, deals with facts and our way of responding to them. There are certain things which are simply to be understood. There are others where, after understanding, we have to do something. When the *Gita* talks about the Truth, about the nature of the self, the world and God, that is something to be understood, while a situation like the war in which Arjuna found himself, calls for a certain mature understanding followed by appropriate action. When the teaching was complete, Lord Krsna gave Arjuna a free hand:

Yathecchasi tatha kuru [Do as you please]

But this was only after the Lord was sure that Arjuna could not but do the right thing. That is the confidence of a teacher who has covered all the necessary aspects of the subject matter and also observed understanding in the eyes of the disciple. The confusion and the contortions born out of it, all seem to have disappeared. The Lord is sure that the teaching has gone home, and fulfilling the expectations of the teacher, the disciple says:

Nasto mohah smrtirlabdha

[The confusion is gone, by attainment of clear understanding] (*Bhagavad Gita* XVIII 73)

Arjuna says that his understanding is clear, that he understands the facts as they are and will do what is to be done.

Note the difference between action and reaction. Arjuna's identification with his opponents as, 'mine', etc., his fears, his incapacity to appreciate facts, all these were expressions of an immature mind. Even though Arjuna was a mature person in many other respects, in this respect he was not. 'These are all my people. How can I fight with them? I know I am supposed to protect *dharma*, but when my own people have taken the side of *adharma*, how can I fight them?'

This attachment was his problem and that went away as a result of the teaching. He understood the whole situation clearly and therefore, in response to the Lord's command: 'Therefore, O Bharata, may you fight.' Arjuna said, `I shall follow your instructions.' Then he took up his *Gandiva* and fought the battle.

Maturity is the End

Everyone has to become mature. Growth is maturity and we are all designed for the purpose. We must fulfil the design of growing by becoming mature. Every wise man is a mature person. Discovering God, discovering yourself is nothing but maturity. There is nothing but maturity as the end in life. Unless a person is pathologically defective, every person is designed to be mature. The system of *varna* and *asrama* that the Vedas designed for us, is meant to make a person mature. All *varnasrama-dharma*, all ethical values, all forms of worship, prayers, etc., and even the study of Vedanta are meant purely to make you a mature person.

A mature person is one who first accepts facts and then becomes alive to facts. When you re-look at what you consider a fact now, you find that it is nothing but some other fact and again you find that that fact has its being in some other fact. And so what is the fact? If a person is aware of that, he or she is mature in the true sense. Such a person is called *sthitaprajna*, a wise person.

The qualifications, namely, *amanitvam, adambhitvam, ahimsa,* etc., which a seeker of knowledge is advised to cultivate, are called jnanam. The word *jnanam* is used here in the sense of that by which something is known. That means the mind. These qualifications are just the mind. What kind of a mind? A mature mind, *manitvam*, vanity is an immature mind; *amanitvam*, humility is a mature mind.

Vanity, pretentiousness, cruelty, all these exhibit an immature mind. Every black-marketer is immature.

Hitler was an emotionally immature person. A person who has developed a national ego or a community ego is an immature person. Every ego is immature, whether it is a religious ego or a social ego or a national ego or a community ego. There is nothing but clashes where there is ego. There is no problem in the world except immaturity. We can deal with all the problems if we are mature, and so, growing is the solution.

Maturity is not meant only for a few chosen people or the *avataras*, etc. It is meant for every person because every human being is designed to grow, to become mature in all ways—physically, emotionally and with respect to understanding. You will be confused if your understanding is confused and you will be mature if your understanding is right. That is what Vedanta does, it gives you the right understanding, makes you a mature person. A mature person is *krtakrtya*, the one who has done all that has to be done in life. Whatever that person does thereafter is a blessing for others because he or she is already blessed. Lord Krishna says in the *Bhagavad Gita*:

Na me parthasti kartavyam trisu lokesu kincana
Nanavaptamavaptavyam varta eva ca karmani

[In all the three worlds, O Partha, there is nothing for me to really do (because) there is nothing unaccomplished that has to be accomplished by me. Still I remain engaged in action]

(*Bhagavad Gita* III 22)

I am free because I know myself to be complete. There is nothing for me to accomplish but you still see me engaged in action as even now I am driving your chariot. In action I remain, meaning I do whatever has to be done. This is the mature state.

If *samsara* gives you a particular life, a life of struggle and conflicts, it can also give you relative maturity. The *Upanishad* says:

Pariksya lokan karmacitan brahmano nirvedamayat

[Having analysed his experiences, the *Brahmana* (contemplative person) becomes dispassionate]

(*Mundakopanisad* 1 ii 12)

An experience is also called *loka*. Having examined the experiences of life, the thinking person becomes dispassionate, meaning objective, ready to see things as they are. He neither adds anything to what he sees nor reduces anything from it. He does not dismiss a situation saying, 'There is no problem,' nor does he see the problem more or less than what the situation reveals. That is mature vision. That is what everyone has to grow into and so, the Vedic vision of life is to make you grow, and grow to such an extent that you can grow no more. Then the growth will only be in terms of *aparavidya*, worldly knowledge. You can learn this or that. You can learn electronics, you can learn languages. That is all for fun. You cannot grow any more. Therefore, the goal of life is to grow because one is born a child.

2

Importance of Emotions

Here are a few of the reasons why our emotions are important in our lives. Incidentally, the first few chapters of Goleman's 1995 book, Emotional Intelligence, contains a good presentation on evolution and emotions.

Survival

Nature developed our emotions over millions of years of evolution. As a result, our emotions have the potential to serve us today as a subtle and sophisticated internal guidance system. Our emotions alert us when natural human needs are not being met. For example, when we feel lonely, our need for connection with other people is not met. When we feel afraid, our need for safety is not met. When we feel rejected, it is our need for acceptance which is not met.

Decision Making

Our emotions are a valuable source of information. Our emotions help us make decisions. Studies show that when a person's emotional connections are severed in the brain, he cannot make even simple decisions. Why? Because he doesn't know how he will feel about his choices.

Boundary Setting

When we feel uncomfortable with a person's behaviour, our emotions alert us. If we learn to trust our emotions and feel confident expressing ourselves, we can let the person know we feel uncomfortable as soon as we are aware of our feeling. This will help us set our boundaries which are necessary to protect our physical and mental health.

Communication

Our emotions help us communicate with others. Our facial expressions, for example, can convey a wide range of emotions. If we look sad or hurt, we are signalling to others that we need their help. If we are verbally skilled we will be able to express more of our emotional needs and thereby have a better chance of filling them. If we are effective at listening to the emotional troubles of others, we are better able to help them feel understood, important and cared about.

Happiness

The only real way to know that we are happy is when we feel happy. When we feel happy, we feel content and fulfilled. This feeling comes from having our needs met, particularly our emotional needs. We can be warm, dry and full of food, but still unhappy. Our emotions and our feelings let us know when we are unhappy and when something is missing or needed. The better we can identify our emotions, the easier it will be to determine what is needed to be happy.

Unity

Our emotions are perhaps the greatest potential source of uniting all members of the human species. Clearly, our various religious, cultural and political beliefs have not united us. Far too often, in fact, they have tragically, even fatally, divided us. Emotions, on the other hand, are universal. Charles Darwin wrote about this years ago in one of his lesser-known books called *The Expression of Emotion In Man and Animal*. The emotions of empathy, compassion, cooperation, and forgiveness, for instance, all have the potential to unite us as a species. It seems fair to say that, generally speaking: *Beliefs' divide us. Emotions unite us.*

Human Emotional Needs

All humans have some basic emotional needs. These needs can be expressed as feelings, for example the need to feel accepted, respected and important. While all humans share these needs, each differs in the strength of the need, just as some of us need more water, more food or more sleep. One person may need more freedom and independence, another may need more security and social connections. One may have a greater curiosity and a greater need for understanding, while another is content to accept whatever he has been told.

One of the major problems I have observed in schools is the treatment of all children as if their emotional and psychological needs were identical. The result is many children's needs remains unsatisfied. They then become frustrated, as any of us do when our needs are not met. They act out their frustration in various ways which are typically seen as 'misbehaviour'. This is especially evident when all children are expected to do the same thing for the same length of time. The better we identify their unique needs and satisfy them, the fewer behavioural problems will crop up. It is also evident when children are made to do things which are not interesting to them, or when they are not challenged enough with things which are relevant to their lives. One of the things teenagers who cut classes seem to have in common is that they are extremely bored at school as well as emotionally neglected, over-controlled or abused at home.

In dysfunctional families it is most often the emotional needs which are not met. Children and teenagers are getting enough to eat and they have a roof over their heads, but their emotional needs are not being met.

It is helpful to become more aware of these emotional needs as a first step towards helping to fill them.

Primary and Secondary Emotions

Some authors use the terms primary and secondary emotions. I find this distinction quite helpful. A primary emotion is what we feel first. The secondary emotion is what it leads to.

Anger is a good example of a secondary emotion. As I discuss in my section on anger, there are many possible primary emotions which, when they are intense enough, can lead to anger. We might feel insulted, pressured, cheated, etc. If these feelings are at a low level we are not likely to say we feel angry. But if they are intense, we normally say we feel 'angry'.

Depression is another example of a secondary emotion. We might call it a 'catch-all' term. Depression can include feeling discouraged, hopeless, lonely, isolated, misunderstood, overwhelmed, attacked, invalidated, unsupported, etc. Normally it includes several feelings. These more specific feelings are what I would call primary emotions.

Secondary, 'catch-all' terms like anger and depression do not help us much when it comes to identifying our unmet emotional needs (UENs). When all I can say is 'I feel angry,' neither I nor any one else knows what would help me feel better. But if I say I feel pressured or trapped or disrespected, it is much more clear what my UEN is and what would help me feel better. A simple, but effective technique, then, is to identify the primary emotion.

Managing Negative Emotions

General Guidelines

I have been trying to develop some general guidelines for managing negative emotions. Here is what I have come up so far.

First, identify the feeling.

Next, ask if it is a healthy feeling.

Then list your options and choose the one which is most likely to lead to your long-term happiness.

After taking the first two steps, the next step is to ask what would help you feel better. I try to remember to focus only on answers which are in my control, since it would be easy. Even though it may not be to helpful, it would be better than thinking of other ways things could change so I would feel better.

Another question is to ask how you want to feel. This helps you direct your thoughts in a positive direction.

To summarise, here are some questions that I believe are very helpful: How am I feeling?

- Is it a healthy feeling?
- How do I want to feel?
- What would help me feel better (that I can control)?

Anger Management/Feeling Destructive in Germany—A True Story

I once went to Germany to visit a lady for what I thought would be a romantic vacation. When I got there she met me at the station with her ex-boyfriend. I asked why he was there and she said they had just reunited and she wasn't going with me to Paris for Christmas and New Year as we had planned. I remember lying in bed that night. I picked up a small souvenir glass that I had brought for her mother's collection. I remember thinking that I wanted to smash it against the wall. I asked myself what I was feeling as I stared at the glass clenched in my hand. The word that came to mind was 'destructive.' I said to myself: 'that is not a healthy feeling'. I took a deep breath, exhaled slowly, and put the glass down.

Expressing Negative Feelings

Here are a few suggestions for communicating your negative feelings:

- Don't be dramatic.
- Don't wait till things build up.
- Be brief.
- Don't blame or lay guilt trips.
- Talk about how you feel.
- Ask how the other person feels.
- Offer a way to save face. (For example, 'Perhaps I misunderstood you,' or 'I know your intentions were good.)

Resentment

- Resentment as re-feeling
- Resentment as a secondary emotion
- What are some causes of resentment?
- Managing resentment

Understanding Resentment

1. Nature's Purpose for Resentment
   In certain languages, Spanish and French for example, *sentir* means to feel, so *re-sentir*, or resent, means literally to feel again. Nature evidently has a purpose for us 're-feeling'

something. We may assume that nature wants us to continue feeling something or to feel it again so something positive will be gained. The purpose of resentment might be so we can:

- Keep feeling something till we take responsibility for something to which we contributed and thereby learn, grow and become a more valuable member of the species.
- Keep feeling something till we take some action to help remedy a socially unhealthy situation.

2. Resentment as a Secondary Emotion

Resentment seems to be *a secondary emotion*. By this I mean we usually experience a more primary feeling first. A person could feel resentful for many reasons, just as a person could feel angry for many reasons. Here are some examples.

- If someone ignores me when I ask them a question I first feel a little ignored. If they continue to ignore me I might say I feel resentful towards them for ignoring me.
- If someone tries to tell me how to run my life, the more primary or specific feeling might be feeling controlled.

A person could feel resentful towards authority if he has repeatedly felt controlled and forced by authority figures in the past. A child who has felt controlled, pressured and forced to do things by his mother, father or both, and then who felt pressured, controlled and forced by his teachers and school authorities may later feel resentful of anyone in a position of authority as soon as those earlier feelings are triggered or re-stimulated.

But can resentment also be instantaneous? If a person insults you, you might say 'I resent that comment'. This is another way of saying you don't appreciate it. To say 'I resent that' seems to me to be a more intense and threatening statement than saying 'I feel insulted'. One could also say, 'I feel resentment when you say that,' but not many people talk like that so you will sound strange if you say that. Even if you say, 'I feel insulted' you will sound strange, since so few people express their feelings directly with words.

In any case, it seems helpful to identify the more primary feelings which lead to resentment, just as it is helpful to identify the more primary feelings which lead to anger. It is more helpful, for instance, to tell someone 'I feel ignored' than to say 'I feel resentful towards you' or 'angry at you'. It is more helpful for two reasons:

1. It more clearly indicates what is causing you the pain.
2. It may be less threatening to say 'I feel ignored' than to say either 'I feel resentful,' or 'I feel angry.'

Because so many people have experienced so many negative emotions such as feeling afraid, insecure, controlled, pressured, teased, laughed at, judged and rejected, there are a lot of people who feel resentful, afraid and insecure. When these people come in contact with each other it is easy for emotions to become intensified. That is one reason why it is so important to understand emotions. With more understanding, people can learn less threatening and less hurtful ways of saying things.

Another note about resentment is that it is probably just before hatred on the love-hate continuum.

A simplified version of this is:

Love > Appreciation > Resentment > Hatred

If we like what someone did, we feel appreciation. If we really, really, appreciate it, we may feel love for them. If we don't like what they did, we may feel resentment. If we really, really, don't like it, we may feel hatred.

I'd say there is an imbalance of resentment and hatred in the world. If so, this would imply that we all could benefit from trying to create feelings of appreciation and love.

Note: Writing this led me to think that part of a test of emotional understanding is understanding which words and statements evoke which feelings and their intensity. For example, is a person likely to feel more threatened if I say:

'I resent that'

Or

'I feel insulted'

Some Causes of Resentment

It seems there are fairly universal causes of resentment. Most of us are likely to feel resentful when:

- Others try to tell us what to do, how to run our lives, what we need, what they think is best for us.
- Others tell us what they think we should do, how they think. we should feel, how they think we should act.
- Others feel and act superior to us.
- Others act in hypocritical ways.
- Others deprive us of our needs.
- We see those in power abusing their power and hurting others who are less powerful.
- We feel falsely accused, judged, prejudged, discriminated against, labelled, ignored, attacked, hunted, persecuted, underestimated, invalidated.
- We feel lied to or lied about.

Managing Resentment

One of my most helpful insights, which I call the AR3 principle, is: Accepting Responsibility Releases Resentment.

Sometimes when I find myself feeling resentful, or bitter, which is often a more intense indication of resentment, I remind myself of this. I then begin to search for ways in which I was responsible for contributing to the development of the situation. It has been extraordinarily helpful in avoiding placing 'blame' on other people and on focussing my attention on my own areas which need improvement, growth and learning.

One useful way for me to reduce my resentment is to focus on how I contributed to the situation and what I could have done to prevent it. In other words, to take responsibility. I learned this after one particularly painful relationship.

I don't believe in 'magic,' but the word 'magical' comes to mind. The power of these words, when applied, is indeed seemingly supernatural. Yet, nature has evolved certain truths, certain relationships in her complex web of life. These truths when discovered, seem like magic at first only because so few people have discovered them for themselves.

Another AR3 principle I developed is *Accepting Reality Releases Resentment*. This principle seems to help when we have done very little to contribute to a situation and there is very little we can do about it.

Something else I have found helpful is to either learn something from what has happened or to take some constructive action.

Here is an excerpt from an article about David Caruso and his resentment towards me for writing about him. When I say resentment I am talking about a feeling or a combination of feelings that are either

(a) poisoning us, or
(b) trying to teach us something, or
(c) trying to help us or help others.

Let me try to Explain

By poisoning I mean negative feelings that are not helping us in any way. They are simply eating us away from inside. They are causing us to be defensive, hostile, sarcastic, bitter. All of this is physically unhealthy and toxic for us to spread around. We could even say it is contagious and we are spreading unhealthy emotions. Or we could say we are spreading emotional pollution. David lives, by the way, in a country, which I suspect already, has one of the world's highest levels of this 'emotional pollution'. I have no doubt that it is partly a result of this emotional pollution that David has started having feelings of regret, resentment and defensiveness. These feelings are all-contagious and widespread in the U.S.A. I think it would be fair to say they are found in epidemic levels, in fact.

But getting back to the three possible effects of resentment.

The second effect of, or we could say, purpose of, resentment may be to teach us something. If I feel resentful about something and I look for a lesson from that experience, my resentment will diminish quickly. But let me clarify that. Let me say If I look for a positive lesson'. I say this because David could be telling himself, 'I learned not to trust Steve Hein' or I learnt not to invite people I don't know into my home.' But I would say that these are not particularly positive or helpful lessons. I suspect that these kinds of lessons will not do much to reduce David's feelings of resentment. In fact, they might just add fuel to them. And at the very least, they will stop David from feeling open to learning from me in the future.

This is one of my biggest sources of pain, actually. The knowledge that David will now be less likely to learn from me, first of all, and second, that he will be less likely to support or endorse my work. But my work is doing all right by itself, so what hurts me more is knowing that I have lost, perhaps, my ability to influence David in a way which I truly believe is:

(a) healthy for him, and

(b) helpful to humanity.

The last of the three effects or purposes of resentment is to help others. For example, when we see injustice and it bothers us and keeps bothering us and we keep seeing it again and again, our feelings turn to resentment. This resentment could drive us to take some action to try to correct the injustice, which would be a positive reaction for everyone.

There is something else I want to say about resentment. Resentment itself is a secondary feeling. The first time we feel something which pains us, we don't feel resentful. We feel the original pain. For example, the first time someone insults us, we feel insulted. If that person had never done anything to cause us pain, and if we had never been insulted before, and the person quickly apologises, we are not going to feel resentful.

Resentment is something, which builds up. It is therefore a higher level feeling, and thus more powerful. Resentment can lead to hatred and the hatred can then lead to motivation to kill and destroy. What is needed for this emotional chain of events is repeated feelings of injustice and other forms of pain without any relief or personal self-growth. And this is exactly what has happened in the case of terrorism.

If we learn to manage resentment, we will prevent hatred and its natural consequences: death and destruction. We will, in other words, learn to prevent terrorism and killings which follow by those who believe they are fighting a justifiable 'war on terrorism.'

So I would suggest that when we feel resentful, it is a sign that we need to keep studying resentment, and keep studying how to manage it so that we can prevent it from building and leading to even more toxic emotions. We also need to study how we can stop creating more of it.

I want to emphasize that the best time to study resentment is when we are actually feeling it. As I have written, true understanding requires feeling. We cannot just read about resentment. We have to feel it, and while feeling it, look deeper—look for the underlying feelings, the primary feelings. Then we have a chance to learn from it and become wiser with our new knowledge and understanding. And with this new wisdom, we can help others and ourselves while preventing the resentment from poisoning either us or those around us.

Disappointment

There seem to be at least two ways the word 'disappointment' is used. For example, one day at a friend's place, I opened a CD case expecting to find the CD inside, but the case was empty. I felt a combination of sadness and surprise, which fits some academic definitions of disappointment. But I did not feel judgmental or disapproving, as a parent might feel when their child gets suspended from school. The parent might, for example, say, 'I can't believe you got suspended, what is wrong with you?' In this case we might say disappointment is a combination of disapproval and disbelief.

I find it helpful to look at disappointment as something we do to ourselves. I say this because it seems to arise out of our own expectations or demands about how we think the world should be or how we think people should act. In other words, I look at 'disappointment' as an inaccurate view of reality. Looking at it this way could help us accept that we didn't really understand things as well as we thought we did and that our expectations were unrealistic.

By looking at it this way, it is easier for us to take responsibility for it and thus, reduce the negative feelings which usually accompany it. It also helps us avoid laying guilt trips on others as I explain below.

Instead of using the word 'disappointed,' I sometimes try to substitute the word 'disillusioned.' This helps remind me that I had created an illusion in my own mind about something which did not occur. Calling something an illusion suggests that my interpretation of reality was inaccurate. So when things don't go the way I expected or wanted them to go, it seems to help if I take the perspective that I created a false image of reality in my mind and I need to quickly adjust myself to the actual reality. The sooner I do this the faster I get over the negative feeling of what I used to call disappointment.

Many people use the expression 'disappointment' as a way of laying a guilt trip on someone else. Consider the parent who tells the child 'I am utterly disappointed in you,' or, 'you really disappointed me'. Think for a moment how you feel when someone says such things to you. You might feel guilty, blamed, inadequate, unworthy or ashamed.

A woman once said she felt devastated when her father said to her, 'You have utterly disappointed us'.

Is this how we want our children to feel? The father who feels disappointed does not stop to consider that it was the father himself who did not know his child as well as he thought. Turning it into an opportunity to lecture the child will hurt the child's self-esteem by causing him to feel 'faithful'. The parent who uses disappointment to lay guilt doesn't consider the long-term damages to the child's self-esteem. The parent is simply using guilt as an expedient way to emotionally manipulate the child as a form of control. Disappointment in another person is basically a form of rejection and disapproval. It can be powerful in its toxic affect on the self-esteem.

Another problem arises when you tell someone you feel disappointed in them is that it encourages them to avoid sharing things truthfully with you. It helps others feel judged as well as disapproved of.

Note that it is the person in power who creates the expectations. They are the ones who say, 'I am disappointed.' I noticed this in Australia when the government said they were 'disappointed' that the aboriginals put up metal structure on the land where they had created the Aboriginal Tent Embassy. The Australian police soon came and tore it down.

Bitterness

A more intense form of disappointment is sometimes bitterness, which tells us that not only did we expect something, but we started to count on it or depend on it.

A healthier reaction would be to let the feeling provide an opportunity to get to know the other person or the child better. By showing sincere curiosity and a desire for knowledge instead of disappointment, we open the door to understanding and bonding. In other words, we might say to ourselves, 'Hmm, I expected x to happen, in fact I really wanted x to happen. I was even counting on it. I am sad, or hurt or frustrated that it didn't happen. I wonder why it didn't happen. What can I learn from this?' Such curiosity opens the door to seeking knowledge and helps get our thinking back in line with reality. In other words, situations where we initially feel disappointed can lead to wisdom if we allow ourselves to learn. In the case of the parent and child, the parent might learn about the circumstances surrounding the child's life, and the way the child makes decisions based on his or her values, beliefs and needs. The same idea applies to friends or romantic partners.

Here is an example of how a mother might react when she initially starts to feel 'disappointed.'

'Jessica, I feel sad and confused about what you did. Can you help me understand?'

The mother might also ask: 'How were you feeling when you did so and so?' or 'How do you feel about it now?'

This question, if asked without causing the child to feel interrogated or afraid, is much healthier than an expression of disappointment.[1]

1. For a good discussion of emotional manipulation, see Chapter 1 in Smith, M J, When I Say No I Feel Guilty. Bantam, 1975.

Discouragement, Hopelessness

I am afraid this will sound simplistic, but when you are feeling discouraged and hopeless, you could look at it as a sign that you need to find some source (or create one within yourself) of encouragement and hope. Maybe a technique would be helpful, like making a list of some things which are encouraging. Or forcing yourself to find just one encouraging thing amid your present feelings of discouragement. Maybe just find some uplifting books or articles or read a story on what someone is doing somewhere to help people. There is a huge selection of inspirational books and tapes. Some of them have helped me both during a current down period in my life and also in a longer term sense because I have the memory of some thing. they said which helped.

Another option is to seek out some optimistic, but validating people. Perhaps just tell a friend who knows you well that you are feeling discouraged and hopeless. Perhaps they will remind you of some encouraging truths.

I remember a few times I was feeling discouraged and I was able to remember some encouraging things. And it helped me to know that I have felt extremely discouraged and hopeless, even suicidal, but I have bounced back from those feelings. And I believe those feelings helped me focus on what was truly important to me.

If nothing else, write to yourself and say: I AM FEELING HOPELESS!

Or scream it out if you must, or cry it out—your body or your amygdala is sending you a message. Let it know that you have received it. I am not sure how the process works but it seems that once the message is fully accepted, validated and understood, it can be integrated by survival forces of the brain which go to work on solving the problem.

Once you have completely accepted that you feel hopeless, you can begin to take action to feel more hopeful. You can search for inspiring websites, books, tapes, etc. You can actively think of people who you admire, who are contributing to the world in the way you believe is needed.

When you are feeling hopeless, it can be looked at as a clear sign that you need to feel more hopeful, (or more optimistic, more encouraged, etc.) in order to get back into a healthier state. I believe our survival instinct itself is a source of hope. If I truly had no hope, why would I even bother to eat? As long as your body is feeling hungry, sleepy, etc., I believe there is hope. As I see it, as long as there is one male and one female alive on the earth, there is hope for the human species. Imagine that the current members of the species have somehow managed to kill everyone of your gender except you. Now imagine you have 10 seconds to chose a partner before all the other members of the opposite sex are killed. Now, ten seconds later, it is just the two of you. Would you still feel hopeless? Or would you get to work on rebuilding the species?

Feeling Destructive

The amygdala is capable of initiating a sequence of chemical reactions which create extreme energy. Some people's brains, for whatever reason, create these intense chemical reactions extremely quickly. In a life-or-death situation, this could prove to be the critical difference. But we are not often in life-and death situations. Yet we still sometimes feel the same urges, such as the urge to completely destroy our attacker.

The challenge is how to use the energy in a constructive way. When I have felt destructive in the past, it has proved helpful to ask: What do I really want to destroy? A person? A relationship? Myself? Asking these questions helps me realise that I don't want to hurt others or myself. Nor do I want to damage relationships, even though they may be bringing me pain at that moment. But what I do want to destroy are the dysfunctional systems which perpetuate the hurting and killing which have been going on for centuries. I want to prove that there is a better way. I want to show the world that there are more options than repeating the mistakes of the past. I try to focus my energy in this kind of positive direction. This takes practice, especially when one comes from a dysfunctional family, but I believe we can all make improvements in how we handle our destructive urges by re-focusing our energy into more productive outlets.

If you have so much energy that you really have to release it in a physical way, try finding something like a cardboard box or an empty cereal box and smash it, tear it to bits with your hands. If you often experience strong destructive feelings, in fact, keep a supply of boxes handy! After you have released your energy physically, chances are your mind will guide you to what is important to think about, as the emotional intelligence model suggests.

Resiliency

Goleman said that resiliency was part of emotional intelligence. Mayer and Salovey, however, do not include resiliency, so I assume they would call it a `personality trait'. Whatever category you want to put it under, it is clear that resiliency helps us survive and 'thrive'. I recently discovered a website called thrivenet, which includes a wealth of information on resiliency. The site is based on the work of Al Siebert who has studied what he calls 'survivors'. Interestingly, his list of the characteristics of resilient people is quite similar to what I call high EQ people.

Forgiveness

I am not a big believer in what some others have called 'quick forgiveness'. Generally, I believe if someone has harmed us or the species, there is some restitution needed, or at least some acknowledgement, acceptance of responsibility or apology. I have not done much work on forgiveness. For me, I am able to forgive when someone apologises, but not when they do not do any of the above. I think there is some value in not forgiving, but on the other hand I see that bitterness is toxic and acceptance leads to inner peace and better physical health.

3

The Individual Perception

To live my life is to be alive to facts, alive to realities. I see before me a world for which I am not responsible. I am given a physical body, a set of sense organs, a mind. If I had a say over any of these, perhaps, I would have defined them differently, but I have no say. Everyone is given this set up called the world. Mark the word 'given'. This is my father; given. This is my mother; given. This is my neighbour; given. I find myself being related differently to different people; given. This creation is a set up. It is not created by me. It is something that is there and I happen to confront it.

The world is available for public gaze. But do I look at the world as the world is supposed to be looked at? Do I look at the world as it is or do I look at the world that I have created out of my own imagination, set by my own mind, my own limitations, fears, anxieties, insecurities? In fact, every one of us lives in his or her own world, a world which one projects, a world which is set by one's own mind.

One does not see more than what one knows; one's fears and anxieties set one's perceptions and therefore a world which is simple and harmless can be seen as a world that is harmful, that seems to have conspired against oneself. Thus one comes to condemn the world. Another person who is in the same set up looks at the world in an entirely different way. The same person may look at the same world quite differently at different times. Why? Because one does not see anything more than what one's mind allows one to see.

Individual Creation

In the *Gita*, we have a clear presentation of this individual perception of the world as that which is coloured and distorted by two factors: *raga* and *dvesa*, meaning likes and dislikes. The psychological aspect of the spiritual person is presented in these two terms: *raga* and *dvesa*. I have *raga* for an object when I consider it desirable, because in its presence I expect myself to be happier, more secure than I am at present. *Dvesa* is just the opposite—the dislike for an object in the presence or experience or possession of which I feel there is a threat to my happiness, my security. I want to acquire and possess a thing for which I have *raga* and want to avoid or get rid of that for which I have *dvesa*. Therefore, my whole life is nothing but an expression of this *raga* and *dvesa*. You may want to get away from your home because there is some problem there. That is *dvesa*. Then you have a choice as to where you can go, and you decide to listen to a Swami because of some kind of *raga*—you have a value for listening to these talks. Your whole life, your day-to-day struggle is nothing but an expression of *raga* and *dvesa*.

I have looked into modern psychology and I find that this discussion in the *Gita* is adequate for a normal person. Please understand that I am not talking about clinical psychotherapy, which is quite different. I am talking about the psychological disposition of a person that is dealt within these two terms: *raga* and *dvesa*. This discussion in the *Gita* is adequate to discover and live a life of maturity.

When there is *raga* for a thing, you want to acquire it if you do not presently have it. It may be money, it may be a house, it may be a place you want to reach. There are a number of things you do not have now which you wish to possess. And there are a number of things you have now which you what to retain—you want to retain your health, your money, your job, the hair on your head, etc. You want to retain your usefulness. This attempt to acquire what you do not have is called *yoga* and to retain or protect what you have is called *ksema*. The *raga* results in *yoga* and *ksema*—attainment of what you do not have and protection of what you have.

This is your struggle. Not only acquiring what you do not have involves struggle, but retaining what you have also involves struggle. To retain something is also not easy. You have to work for it. Suppose you have reduced your weight to a certain level; now to retain this level, my God, you have to work hard! People do jogging, exercises and what not! You have to work hard to retain your job. Thus, both acquiring and retaining call for hard work.

Again, to avoid, to stall or to get rid of what you do not like also calls for hard work. It is not that you can necessarily accomplish what you desire or what you want to avoid. Who wants a headache? But headaches come. You are supposed to observe precautions to avoid disease. Thus, a lot of money and efforts are involved in order to avoid disease, too. You have to work hard to get rid of things. Washing clothes, cleaning the floor, clearing the garbage, etc. are nothing but efforts for getting rid of things.

Thus, the whole life is a struggle to fulfil *raga* and *dvesa*. There is nothing right or wrong in this, please understand. All that I am saying is that this is what life is. These likes and dislikes themselves are acquired while growing up in a given environment, consisting of culture, religion, family, education, etc. Environment has a great influence upon a person. What is happening elsewhere in the world also reaches you. I wonder about the means of communication that bring the fads and frauds from Berkeley to New York in some months and then to Ahmedabad and Baroda in one year and then to Bombay! When something happens somewhere in terms of fashion or in terms of music, it seems to reach here. Then there is this campus connection; what happens in one university campus seems to reach another in a very short time. Thus, one often picks up likes and dislikes without volition or effort on one's part. The family, the culture, the society, all give rise to likes and dislikes and some of them have a binding status. They colour one's vision.

In the process of achieving your likes or avoiding what you dislike you also pick up fears, anxiety, etc., because you cannot always fulfil your likes and dislikes.

Is there any one here who can say that for any one single day one fulfilled all one's likes and dislikes, that one was totally free from them even for one day? Should you not have a day of twelve waking hours during which you are totally free from likes and dislikes, meaning free from desires arising from likes and dislikes?

I do not remember that as a child, I had even one day free from all desires. I wanted to eat something and I was told it was not good for my health. If I had my way, I would have cleared the entire toy shop and brought it home! I did not have all the toys I wanted, I could not get all the crackers I wanted to buy, I could not get all the candies I wanted to eat! I always had to settle for less than what I wanted and thus when I was a child, many of my likes always remained unfulfilled. And when I grew up to be a boy, then also, many of my desires remained unfulfilled. Who does not want to finish first in every sports event? Who does not want to stand first in all the examinations? But no one ever achieves that. You always settle for something less, something less, something less. You find the competition is too much and you are humiliated again and again. As a young man, of course you have many wants that are not fulfilled. Was there ever a period of twelve waking hours—I am not talking of sleep because in sleep you are totally free from desires—when you were totally free from likes and dislikes? Never, This is you.

Many of the unfulfilled likes and dislikes remain with you; some of them mutilated, injured, hurt, some of them bleeding, some of them breeding! They distort your perception. The world is not going to be seen by you as it is. There is fear, anxiety, insecurity, concern in you and all these vitiate your perception. Thus, you do not confront *isvara-srsti*, the world created by the Lord, but you confront *jiva-srsti*, the world created by your own perceptions. You can face problems if they are facts, but the fears, anxieties, worries, etc., are all created by your own perceptions, they are your own way of looking at things. In other words, you hardly face facts. You face what you think are facts. This is the problem of what they call empiricality and subjectivity.

That one plus one is equal to two, is empirically true. That this is a flower, is empirically true. That this is a rose, is empirically true. But the way you look at it, is a different matter. Your subjectivity is generally absent when you are with nature—mountains, sky, stars, moon, etc. When you look at the sky, you do not want it to be different from what it is. You accept the sky as it is; you do not want it to be green, for example. Then there is empiricality, objectivity, there is an appreciation of what it is. The sky, the stars, the mountains, the birds, the bushes, the trees, the flowers are all taken as they are; you do not want them to be different from what they are. You find that your subjectivity is absent when you are with nature. That means that you do not interpret things. You are all right as long as you do not interpret. Everything seems to be bright and beautiful as long as your frightened mind, your anxious mind, your desiring mind does not come into play and vitiates the perception.

When you pick up your infant son or daughter, you are happy; you do not think about its future, its health, etc. You enjoy the baby as it is when there is no concern about it. But the situation changes the moment you get concerned about the baby. You may want the baby to be more active, you may wish that it should not cry and so on. Then it is entirely different, you cannot enjoy the baby.

Thus, when it comes to certain situations when people are involved, when my own life is involved, then I do not really face facts. I rather face situations as projected by my mind that is controlled by its own likes and dislikes. An appreciation, an understanding of these likes and dislikes and the capacity to manage them, to remain free from their sway, is what emotional maturity is all about, that is what the *Gita* talks about. That is why I find the *Gita* totally adequate. We do not require any other psychological approach.

When I come under the spell of fears, etc., caused by *raga* and *dvesa*, there is only the *jiva-srsti*, individual creation, and not the isvara-srsti, creation of the Lord. *Isvara-srsti* is what is given, the empirical world. When I allow my vision to be vitiated by my own fears, etc., then I live in a world of my own.

Let us say I incur a heavy loss in business. The stock market has crashed and there is a disaster. Then it becomes important as to how objectively I am able to look at the situation. Such a situation calls for action on my part. I should be objective. Similarly, when there is a situation involving bereavement, dishonour, some loss of security, etc., then it is important that I be objective, as I am when I see a mountain.

Objectivity is Maturity

We are quite objective when some else has a problem. Then we become philosophers, great counsellors. If your friend is bereaved, you go to him and console him, 'Oh, well, death is a fact of life. Death is always round the corner and everyone has to face it one day or the other.' As the *Gita* says, 'The soul gives up the old body and takes up a new one, just as a person gives up old garments and takes up new ones. So the soul is not dead, it continues to exist.' You thus console, and the other person also feels consoled as he has been waiting to hear something like this. But later, you lose your wife. Now you need to be consoled and the other fellow comes and consoles you! You have no problem whatever when the pinch is in someone else's shoes. You are able to give advice all right. Then the *Gita* is at the tip of your tongue. You know exactly what is right and what is wrong.

You are absolutely ethical as far as the behaviour of other people is concerned. You should not be hurt by anybody, you should not get robbed, no one should be angry with you, no one should hate you, no one should be jealous of you, and so on. Other people should be sharing, friendly, compassionate, sympathetic. Even God should always be merciful to you, compassionate to you! You know exactly how others should behave with you. Who does not know that? Everyone does. But it is a different case when it comes to your own life, you own situation. You are quite objective, when you look at a mountain. But suppose you have a property on that mountain and you find that you are losing a small part of it every year because of landslides, then you become a mountain of sorrow whenever you look at that mountain! It is beautiful to see landslide when you are not underneath it! You are objective as long as you are not affected.

As I said earlier, you are a *jnani*, a wise person with respect for a clay doll—you are quite objective when your child's doll breaks and are able to buy a new one for him—you are a *sannyasi*, a mature person! Lord Krsna says:

Jneyab sa nityasannyasi yo na dvesti na kankasati

[Understand that person to be always *sannyasi*, who is not under the sway of *raga* and *dvesa*]

(*Bhagavad Gita* V 3)

You are a *sannyasi*, with reference to a clay doll because you neither have *raga* nor *dvesa* for it. You are neither tempted by the doll nor are you afraid of it. You may buy a doll and play with it to please your child, but you are above the doll. You do not become sad if the doll breaks. But the child cries when that happens. Why? Because it has not yet become mature like you. Similarly, you are mature with respect to marbles. Once upon a time, as a child, marbles were important to you. You perhaps counted them every night to make sure that you had not lost any during the day's play. Now you are a grandfather and if your grandson comes to you and asks if you would play marbles with him, you have no such problem of either getting tempted by the marbles or having a need to avoid them. You are neither overjoyed when you win some marbles while playing with your grandson, nor is there a sense of loss if you lose in the game, because you are mature with reference to marbles.

Suppose, you happen to go to a rich man. You notice a number of marbles scattered on the floor, while you are waiting alone in the other room. You are quite unaffected because marbles are not going to make your life better than what it is nor are they going to create any problem for you and so, you have neither an attachment for marbles nor an aversion towards them. But suppose, you happen to see gold marbles! You have your own doubts as to whether they are really made of gold or whether they just look like it. So you pick up a couple of them and from their weight, etc., are convinced that they are really made of gold! My God, is this fellow so rich that his child plays with gold marbles! There is *sannyasa* with respect to marbles but not with respect to gold! This is a different thing altogether.

All of us are mature with reference to a few things. If we can be mature with reference to everything else, that is the maturity *Vedanta* talks about.

Reaction is a Happening

There will be only reactions on my part if I do not accept facts. A reaction is a happening; it is a mechanical thing that happens to a person. A reaction is not something that is commanded by you. It does not have the stamp and seal of your conscious approval. It just happens to you. It is like an electric motor that is set to revolve at a given speed and keeps rotating at that speed. It is moving mechanically; it is not conscious that it is rotating at a given speed. It does not think.

If it could think, if it had freedom, perhaps it would not go on revolving at the same speed all the time. Sometimes it may revolve faster, sometimes slower. But it is not conscious that it is revolving at a given speed, the act of revolving just happens. We would say that the motor is not acting, it is reacting. It revolves at a given speed not out of its own will; it is set to function in that way and so it is a reaction. So also whenever you are not conscious of something that happens to you, it is mechanical, it is a reaction.

When the clouds gather and the situation is conducive, rain happens. It is not by choice. It is not that since Baroda did not have rains for a long time that the clouds decided to come here and rain. Clouds have no choice. Thus rain happens as a result of certain conducive conditions. So too, a reaction happens. Anger, frustration, jealously, sadness, despair—these are all reactions, and they happen.

It is unfortunate that some people think anger is necessary to get things done. This man gets angry whenever things do not go his way. But that is bad management, because no one respects anger. It is not because of the person's anger, but because of his or her power or position that people comply with the person's wishes. Such people have certain buttons and people around know these buttons. In an office, the subordinates know the buttons of the superiors and they take care to avoid certain topics and issues.

Every wife knows the vulnerable areas of her husband and she warns her children also, 'Don't say this to your father. He will get angry.' She has figured out over the years what these buttons are. Even children figure out these with reference to their parents. When the father is really angry, they will not be around for three hours because they have found that it takes that long for the father to cool down. It is childish to entertain a value for anger. As a child, you became angry whenever you were not given one more piece of candy. You screamed and pulled your hair and ultimately your mother gave you that extra candy. You found that anger worked and so, from then on, you became angry whenever you wanted things your way. But anger is a happening; you cannot consciously become angry because it is a reaction.

You are a conscious person having free will, freedom of choice. You are not like a toy car set to respond in a certain manner. A toy car may be programmed such that it turns right whenever it meets an obstruction. You release the car, it moves forward and turns right when it comes across an obstruction. Then it moves in that direction and again turns right when it comes up against another obstruction. Then it moves in that direction and again turns right when another obstruction is met with. It can only turn right, it cannot turn left or move backwards. Why? Because it is automatic. It is programmed, it is mechanical.

But you are not like this toy car. You are like a motor car that has a steering wheel and a gear. With the car, you can turn right, you can turn left, you can move forward or backward. You can do a variety of things with a motor car. So also, as a human being, you have the freedom to do a variety of things. If, for example, I ask you to clap, you may clap, you may not clap, you may clap later on! You have the freedom to act, not to act or act in whichever manner you wish. But this faculty of choice, this free will does not come into play when you get angry or sad or frustrated because these are all happenings, they are mechanical. You say and do things in anger which you regret later. If someone has a value for anger, I sympathise with that person. Lord Krishna says:

Kama esa krodhd esa rajogunasamudbhavab
Mahasano mahapapma viddhyenamiha vairinam

[This desire, this anger, born of *rajoguna* is a great devourer, a great sinner. Know this to be the enemy here]

(*Bhagavad Gita* III 37)

The Lord calls an angry person a great sinner. An angry person even abuses his teacher; a person may do anything out of anger. He does not care for anybody, he can shoot another person, he can even shoot himself. Therefore know anger to be your enemy. It is not outside; it is right within you. Your own mind can turn into an enemy for you.

If anger is a happening, a reaction, so is sadness because no one wants to be sad. And similarly, emotions such as hatred, jealousy, etc., which you do not approve in others and in yourself too, are all reactions.

You do not want to be sad, but you become sad. Now this must be understood that you can never become sad without thinking. A single thought cannot make you sad. The light just went off here. It can be a matter of complaint, frustration and anger. Or you can accept the fact and sit quietly and meditate. Some action had to be taken and we did what we could do. That is what I would call acceptance. Acceptance of a situation does not mean you just sit and watch without doing anything. Acceptance is doing what is to be done without being swept off. An event as such cannot cause sadness. It is only when I refuse to accept a fact and start imagining things like the possible consequences in future, etc., that there is a build-up which results in sadness. A particular form of thinking is triggered off by an event and sadness happens. That is because you are already sad.

Everyone is sad in one form or another because there have been a number of likes and dislikes that have remained unfulfilled. We think we have grown out of them but very often, that is not the case. We have only given up our pursuit of them because we know we cannot fulfil them. So they remain at the very nucleus of our personality, giving rise to sadness, etc. Generally a great or major event is not necessary to make a person sad. It is a process of thinking which happens over which one has no control at all. Thus, sadness is mechanical.

Similarly frustration, jealously, despair, hatred, all these things happen. What you do not like happens to you but what you like has to be consciously effected. Since we are generally mechanical in our thinking, these reactions keep on happening and presently it looks as though the moments of joy are also a happening because they are few and far between. In fact, happiness is not mechanical, it is a conscious process. You are happy when you are aware of the situation, as for example when you are listening to music. You are aware of the situation, and the situation and you become one with it. There is no let or hindrance between the person who is happy and the situation he or she is enjoying; both become one unit, a whole piece. In mechanical thinking, on the other hand, you have no control whatsoever.

But today, even the moments of happiness also seem like a happening, they have to be shaped by the hands of chance. It looks as though we have no control over the moments of happiness also. But that is not so because one is conscious of oneself and of the situation when one is happy. One has to realise the difference between an action when one is happy. One has to realise the difference between an action and a reaction very intimately. Sorrow is a reaction. Anger, jealousy, hatred, depression, frustration—these are all reactions. Non-accommodation is also a reaction. If there is so much as a murmur, a patch of sorrow or anger, there is a reaction involved. You can manage a situation if you understand the difference between an action and a reaction.

Seek Help

You cannot manage a situation unless you know exactly what is happening. The inner responses are just allowed to happen for want of proper insight and knowledge. We need to have the capacity to manage every happening properly so that we do not deliver ourselves to the hands of likes and dislikes, to the hands of anger, frustration, etc. If anger happens we should be able to see it, recognise its pattern, its roots. That is the capacity we are working for now.

Presently I am absolutely helpless in the event of a reaction. I seem to have no power over anger. Please understand that it takes a lot of courage to accept helplessness. Unless I have the courage to accept helplessness I can never grow out of it. I will not seek help even if it is available. It is like the man who was an alcoholic. When someone asked him, 'Why do you take alcohol every day?' he would reply, 'I am not an alcoholic. I can give up alcohol any day.' This response is more from the alcohol than from the person! A man who wants to give up alcohol has to first accept the fact that he has no control over alcohol. Similarly, I must intimately know that I have no power over my anger, my sorrow, depression, frustration.

Some people advise, 'Don't get depressed'. Very often, religious teachers become advisers. Nobody seems to really understand what is going on. A person does not get depressed by choice, it just happens and therefore that person has no choice but to get depressed. When we advise someone not to get angry, he gets more angry because it is not that a person wants to be angry. Anger happens. So realise this: you have no power over anger, over sorrow, over mechanical thinking. Why? Because they are mechanical. If you had control over them, you would not have them in the first place. If this is understood, there is something open for you.

When I say that everything is given to us, a question naturally arises: Is there a Giver, and if there is, what is His nature? When I am helpless in controlling my reactions, I can approach the Giver for help because everybody else is in the same situation as I am in. I am sad and another person is also sad and two sad persons coming together do not make a happy lot! If a drowning person gets hold of another drowning one, both get drowned in the process. Therefore, I should approach the Giver and seek help: '0 Lord, I am helpless. Please give me the maturity to accept gracefully what I cannot change, and the will and effort to change what I can, and the wisdom to know the difference'.

All of our problems are because of our refusal to accept facts. Very often we worry about things we cannot change. We do not know what can be changed and what cannot be. If we know that, we could spare our efforts and divert our energy. Our efforts can gain a direction.

4

The Giver

What characterises one's inner maturity is the degree of objectivity with respect to one's virtues as well as one's limitations. It takes a lot of courage to own up one's limitations. I find I do not have power over anger, over sorrow, over all those conditions of the mind which I do not want to have but which I find myself possessing. Therefore, it is clear that I do not call all the shots. This realisation, this mature recognition implies naturally an appreciation of the source which I can resort to, I can take refuge in. When I find that I have run out of my abilities, my resources, I apply for help to the source which can help. This is true in our day to day life also; for example, when one runs out of financial resources, one seeks help of financial institutions. So too I seek help from the source which can help, which should be free from the limitations I have because there cannot be begging among beggars. That source is *isvara*, God.

Here again I must draw your attention to what is mature and what is not. There is the God of a mature person and the God of one who has not yet become mature.

The World is a Creation

When I look at this world, I find a scheme of things which is related to a certain order. Whenever there is an assembly, made up of a number of components put together intelligently, serving a certain purpose, we call that assembly a creation. "When things are not put together chaotically—like one's throwing things in a garbage can—but put together in a meaningful way, such that together all things become a totality, that single total entity is called creation. The chair on which you are sitting is a creation." A chair is an assembly, consisting of a number of components put together meaningfully and serving a certain purpose and therefore it is a creation.

Similarly, a car is an intelligent assembly; it consists of a number of components such as engine, radiator, tyres, gears and so on. A heap of these components would not make a car. When they are intelligently assembled such that the engine is where it should be and the wheels are where they should be, what should be moving moves and what should be stationary is so; there you have an assembly to serve the purpose it is designed for.

Thus a car is a creation. A clock is a creation. Your shirt is a creation. A nucleus is a creation. A solar system is a creation. All the laws of nature are creation.

This physical body is a creation, a marvellous creation. You look at any part of the body and you will be convinced of this fact. These arms have the right number of joints, otherwise they would not be able to perform the functions they are performing now. Eyes, ears, heart, legs—these are not ordinary designs. Look at the function of the heart. It is a simple pump that continuously performs its function for a number of years. It takes a great deal of engineering and a great deal of money to make an artificial heart. And again, the different parts of the body are exactly where they should be. The eyes are exactly where they should be and so are the ears. At one point, I thought that the location of the nose can be changed. May be, it would be better to place it on the top of the head. There would be certain advantages in placing it there. For one thing, I would be saved from picking up bugs when someone sneezes in front of me.

Secondly, the smoke from some other nose would not enter my nose because it would go up directly. But then, thinking further, I realised that I would not be able to distinguish between a cup of coffee from a cup of tea, because both look alike; smell would enable me to make a distinction, but for smelling, I must lift the cup to the top of my head and then also, the vapour from the cup would not enter my nose because vapour goes up! I must pour the liquid into my nose to smell it! Therefore, I came to the conclusion that even the nose is best placed where it is so that I can pick up the smell at the same time I am drinking coffee or eating food. Thus, the more we think, the more we see the meaningful order in creation.

I find that everything is a marvel when I look into it. Every cell is a marvel. Even man-made things such as rockets, computers, etc., are all marvels and I have been given an intellect to discover and enjoy the marvels.

The Creator Must be Omniscient and Omnipotent

Thus, this world is an intelligent assembly, serving a definite purpose and therefore it is a creation. It is an intelligent creation, which implies knowledge. The maker of a given thing must have the knowledge of the thing. Whether it is a pot or a cloth or bread or what you call *srikhand*, you must know all about it before you can make it. Whether it turns out to be the way you wanted it or not depends upon your experience, skill, resources, etc., but you must necessarily know about it before you start making it. Even a modern artist knows what he is going to make. Even though the product may not look like it has been planned, he definitely had a plan before starting to make it. He takes some paint and throws it on the canvas and a certain pattern emerges from that. If you take the same paint and throw it, you will not get that pattern out of it!

The logic is: *yo yatkarta sa tajjnab*—the creator of a given thing has the knowledge of that thing. The creator of a pot has the knowledge of the pot. When we extend this logic to the creation of the universe, it can be said: *sarvasya karta sarvajnab*—the creator of everything must have the knowledge of everything; he must be *sarvajna*, omniscient.

Over and above knowledge, the creator must also have the skill and energy to create. So, the creator of the universe must have all the power and skill to create everything. In other words, the creator must be omnipotent, *sarvasaktiman*.

Once we accept that there is a creator of this universe, then it follows that the creator must be omniscient and omnipotent. And knowledge and skill always rest in a conscious being and so the creator of the universe must be a conscious being who must be omniscient and omnipotent.

Thus, the argument in arriving at the aspects of the creator is that this universe is a creation because it is an assembly, *samhati*, intelligently put together, serving a certain purpose. Since it is an intelligent design which implies both knowledge and power, the creator must be a conscious being who must be both omniscient and omnipotent, that is, almighty.

Therefore, appreciation of creator, or *isvara*, is not the belief of some fool or some ignorant person or the privilege of some intelligent person or something. It is a part of growing up. It is a mature way of looking at things. You do not just take things for granted. Since an intellect is given to you, it is only proper to appreciate a being who is the creator of this universe.

Where is God?

Now the question naturally arises with respect to the creator: Where is this creator? The answer to this question brings about further maturity.

It is quite clear that the creator is not here nor anywhere around and therefore, we assign him a place that is beyond our our reach, beyond the reach of our eyes, ears, or thoughts. We call that place heaven, where our sense perception, our inference, our presumption have no access.

Some people call it *vaikuntha*, some call it *kailasa*. Let us call it heaven. And where is it? Up there. That is why people look up, throw their arms up when they pray to God. No one ever looks down while addressing God.

Most of the people who believe in God accept that he is in heaven. Then there is a further question. If God in heaven created this world, then who created heaven? We have to say God. Since heaven is also a part of creation, it could not have been there before creation, so the next question is: Where was God before the creation of heaven? The only place that is left, is hell which amounts to saying that God in hell created heaven!

This is absurd. Every growing child raises this question. As a child grows, it looks around and this question naturally arises as to where is God, the creator of this universe. No satisfactory answer comes forth and when the child grows older, the question is dropped. The question remains unanswered and that is a part of one's problem too because one is as good as one's understanding. If one is not at home with one's understanding, how is one going to be at home with oneself, how is one going to accept oneself?

The Maker and Material are One

The question as to where God is, does not get resolved unless we look at the whole thing as the *Vedas* do. When we inquire into creation and its cause, we should not confine ourselves to a part, but should look at the whole. We cannot get the right answers if we ask wrong questions because the answer we get is always in keeping with the question and so, if we ask a right question, there will be a right answer.

When we inquire into the nature of the cause for creation, we find there must be two causes for any creation: the maker and the material. The maker, the one who is responsible for creation, is called the efficient cause or *nimitta-karana*. And there also must be some material out of which any given thing can be created. For creation of a pot, for example, there must be a pot maker, the efficient cause, and also some material, such as clay or copper or brass, out of which the pot is to be made. For baking bread, there must be a baker and also the flour out of which the bread can be baked. With reference to the creation of the universe, if *isvara*, God is the maker, the efficient cause, the question is: What is the material out of which God created this world? When we are inquiring into the nature of the cause of the creation, we must take into account the material also.

Where did the Lord find the material? Here, we must also bear in mind that both the space and the time are part of creation and so, before creation, there was nothing outside the creation because 'outside' is a concept in space which was not yet created. Therefore, there is nothing outside the Lord before creation and so the material should also be within the Lord. That is why He is called the Lord. Therefore, not only is the Lord the maker, but He is the material too. *Tasmadva etasmadamana akasab sambhutab*—from the Lord that is this Self, is born fire, from fire, water; from water, earth was born.

The Vedas give us this model of the five elements for the creation of the world. The world is nothing but these five elements and their combinations.

While explaining how the maker and the material of this universe are one, the *Vedas* give us the illustration of a spider: *Yathornanabhil srjate grhnate ca*—just as a spider creates (a web) and withdraws it too. The spider is the efficient cause of the web because it has the intelligence and the skill to create the web. It chooses the right place for the web where it would not be swept away by the lady of the house and where it can get its prey. This shows that the spider has intelligence. And the material for the web is the secretion of a gland which it finds within itself. So too, the Lord projects this creation and withdraws it unto Himself at the time of dissolution.

Dreaming is an even better model to explain the creation of the world where the Lord is both the maker and the material. In a dream, you create a world merely by *Isankalpa*, by thought. You think of a mountain, the mountain is. You think of anything, that thing is, You have prior knowledge of what you create in a dream because you cannot dream of something that is totally unknown to you. Things may get jumbled up all right; for example, you may create a man with horns in your dream. But there also, both the man and the horns are known to you: somehow they get mixed up and you have a man with horns. And there you are the maker of the dream world of which you have the knowledge. And where do you go for the material of the dream objects?

You are the material. Your memory is the material. Hence you are both the maker and the material for the dream creation. You create a wondrous mountain and the sky and the stars, and there are many people standing below on the earth, looking at the stars and wondering as to who has created this wonderful world. They are all praising creation, some of them writing poetry. And all the time you are the maker, *isvara* of that creation. No one in your dream world knows who you are!

Now, what was there before the dream creation? You cannot say there was nothing, that there was non-existence before the creation of the dream. You were very much there. You were sleeping before the dream. From sleep you enter the dream, which is a half-waking state. So you were there before the dream. True, there was no time, no space, no object, no situation before the creation of the dream world because one of these exists in sleep. But you were very much there. Hence the self was there before creation.

Similarly, for the empirical world also, the Lord is both the creator and the material. That is the mature vision about God, the Lord.

If the Lord is both the maker and the material, please tell me: What is the distance between the Lord and the creation? Can any one establish a distance between the product and the material from which it is made? What is the distance between the shirt you are wearing and the fabric from which it is made? Can you imagine a shirt without a fabric or without some substance? There is no product without a material. Where the product is, there the material must be. The product need not be where the material is, but the material must be where the product is. A creation can never be separate from its material cause.

Now if space is a part of creation, space cannot be separate from the material. And the Lord is the material for this universe. And so, what is space? The Lord. Time is also the Lord. Air, water, fire, earth—all of these are the Lord. Sun, moon, stars, planets, are all the Lord. The heavens, all the worlds above and below, all of them are the Lord. And this physical body that is made of the five elements is again the Lord. The breath is the Lord, the sense organs are the Lord, the mind is the Lord and the consciousness behind them all is also the Lord.

Then where are you? You asked a question: Where is God? I am asking: Where are you? When you ask the question as to where the Lord is, you have already assumed that He is not here. But can you establish your existence isolated from everything else? The physical world includes your body and if the world is the Lord, you body is also the Lord. Then where are you as a separate entity?

God is to be Understood, Not Believed

Isvara is not a matter for belief. He is the matter for understanding. This world is not a matter for belief because you perceive it. Therefore the Lord is also not something to be believed, it is a challenge to understand Him. If the Lord is in heaven, not within the range of your perception or inference, then He becomes a matter for belief. In that case, you simply accept what you are told without asking questions. But the Lord of the Hindus is not a matter for belief. Hindus do not simply believe in God, they understand God.

That is the reason why Hindus even worship space. There is a temple dedicated to Lord Nataraja in Chidambaram, in south India. There is in that temple, what they call *ciambara-rahasyam*, meaning the secret of *Citambaram*. Cit means the all-knowing God and *ambara* means space and so, in this temple they worship the Lord as space. When as a young boy, I first went to this temple, I was eager to know about this *rahasyam*. When the priest removed the curtain at the time of showing the *arati*, I found there was no form. All there was, was a garland of golden *bilva* leaves hanging in space. So the secret, *rahasyam* is that space itself is the Lord. Similarly, there is a temple where air is worshipped as the Lord and another where fire is the Lord and so on. Only a *vaidika* can worship the elements, namely, space, air, fire, water and earth as the Lord. That is the vision of the *Vedas*.

You do not require a particular altar to invoke the Lord. You can invoke Him anywhere because what is it that is not the Lord? The whole order is the Lord, all the laws are the Lord. That is the appreciation of the Lord on the part of a mature person.

Maturity is nothing but the appreciation of what is. To be objective, to be alive to the reality, is maturity. These are all simple facts. We are not believing in anything. We just appreciate the facts, do not take things for granted. We are talking about what is and so there is no question of belief. We can see that gold is different from copper and that is different from lead because each metal has its own atomic weight, its own physical and other properties. But a physicist knows that all of them are nothing but energy, quanta of energy.

That is not a belief. If someone says, 'I don't see that,' then that person may have to believe but that is not a belief that one has to live with and die with, like the belief of a God in heaven. What we have here is *sraddha*, belief pending discovery. There is something to be understood. We understand the difference and at the same time, understand the non-difference, something more than what meets the eye. That is the vision of the *Vedas*, that the whole creation is non-separate from *isvara* because He is the efficient as well as the material cause.

The Lord is called 'He' from the standpoint of the maker and called 'She' from the standpoint of the material. In fact, we use He and She interchangeably and use 'It' to indicate the Truth of them both.

Since the Lord is everything, He is all the names, all the forms and therefore we can invoke Him in any name, in any form. This is the mature way of looking at the worship of God. We can pray to Him in any language because He is omniscient and therefore should know all the languages. In fact, He should respond even before we call Him. This is not tolerance or anything, this is only understanding. No doubt is raised, but in this particular case, we are not just tolerant. We have total acceptance as far as worship is concerned, prayer is concerned.

That is why very often we find many *devatas*, deities in a typical *puja* room. Every aspect of the Lord is represented there. We look upon the Sun as God, so we have *Suryadevata*; we look upon air as God, so we have *Vayudevata*; we look upon earth as God, so we have *Prthvidevata*; and so on. We worship the *nimitta-karana*, the intelligent cause, and the *upadana karana*, the material becomes the symbol for that. We worship the omniscient, omnipotent Lord through the symbol of *upadana*. The sun, the moon, the air, etc., become the symbols through which we worship the Lord. We have varieties of *devatas* through whom we worship one God.

The Only God

We do not even say, 'one God.' We say, 'only God.' When you say there is one God, that means you are different from Him and He is situated somewhere in the heavens. If God is different from you, He does not include you, which means His power does not include your power. If He is different from you, then He is different from me and different from all the living beings. That means God's power does not include the power that you have, that I have, that other gods and demigods have, that the mosquitoes and the bugs have. Then He can only be mighty but not almighty. Then He is like my uncle who is also a very powerful man. But even a mighty person is subject to limitations. Even the president of the USA, a mighty person, is subject to mosquito bites and attacks from viruses! Similarly, the mighty God will also be subject to such limitations.

So, understand, it is not that there is one God. There is *only* God and so if someone invokes Him as Allah, that is fine; if someone invokes Him as Jesus, that is also fine. We have no problem at all. If someone cannot accept the fact of people invoking God in different names and forms, it is his/her problem. We have no problem because we do not have many gods, we do not even have one God, we have *only* God.

There are people who think that God should only be invoked in a particular name and form. Once I was travelling by train. I was sitting by the window and another man was sitting on the opposite berth, by another window. He was reading a book. A third passenger in the compartment was watching this man reading the book. After a while, he asked this man:

'What are you reading?'

'I am reading the Gita the other one replied.'

'What is the Gita?'

'It is a Hindu scripture?' 'Who is the hero?'

'Lord Krishna.'

'Oh! Is Krishna God?'

'Yes, Krishna is God.'

"Then how about Rama?'

'Rama is also God.'

'How about Narayana?'

'He is also God.' 'How about Ganesa?'

'He is also God.'

'How many gods do you have? Are you not getting confused?

'I go to my puja room and I show arati before all of them, so they are all happy. I have no confusion.'

'How can you not be confused? You must be confused with so many gods,' insisted the other man and to prove his point, he started telling a story. While telling the story, he was also occasionally looking at me to make sure that I also listened to him. The story was like this.

'Once upon a time, two men were travelling together. They happened to come across a river. Neither of them knew swimming but since there was not much water in the river, there decided to walk through it. As they reached the middle of the river, there was a flash flood and they found themselves drowning even before they could realise what was happening. There was no way they could be saved and they started calling out for the Lord.'

'One of them happened to be a Hindu and he started crying out, "O, Narayana, please come, please come, please save me." Lord Narayana heard his cries and came to his rescue but before the Lord could rescue the man, he started crying out, "O Sadasiva, please come, please save me." Lord Narayana thought that the man was not calling Him but rather calling Lord Sadasiva and so He went back'.

'Now, Lord Sadasiva heard the prayers and started towards the drowning man but before He could reach him, the man changed his mind and started calling on Lord Ganesa for help. So Lord Sadasiva also returned and the man got drowned before Lord Ganesa could rescue him.'

'The other person was a Christian and he cried out, "O Jesus, please save me. O Jesus, please save me." And see what happened? A log of wood came floating in the water, this man got hold of it, and safely crossed the river.'

Do you see what happens when you have so many Gods?' the narrator concluded the story and having proved his point, triumphantly looked at me.

I thought for a moment and then asked him, 'When did this happen?' He could not reply, and so I said, 'Let us suppose this incident happened on a Friday afternoon at 4 o'clock, okay?'

'Okay,' the man said. Then I said, 'Now at the same time that this drowning man was calling out for Jesus in India, a woman in London met with a car accident and was crying out, 'O Jesus, please save me.'

At that very moment, a man in Johannesburg was attacked with a knife and was crying out, 'O Jesus, please help me.' At the same time a woman in New York, suffering from labour pain, was saying, 'O Jesus please help me.'

'Please tell me, where will Jesus go? All these people are faithful Christians and if Jesus goes to any one of them, who will take care of the rest? See, we Hindus have no such problem. Our Gods will share the jobs—Narayana you go there. Ganesa you go there!'

I must admit that my logic was no better than the logic of the other man, but it was adequate to silence him. He was lucky that the train happened to stop at a station at the very moment, and the man quickly got up and left.

This is silly. We do not worship many gods, we do not even worship one God; we worship the only God. We only invoke Him in various names and forms. Every aspect becomes a *devata*. This is the vision of *isvara* of a mature person.

The Culture Reflects the Vision

If this is understood, then we can see how Indian religious culture is based on this vision. For example, when we greet each other, we say: Namaste'—Salutation to you. The two hands are brought together in a folded fashion. Each hand is quite different from the other; the right is not the left and the left is not the right. But the right is I and the left hand is also I. Similarly, you are also the Lord and I am also the Lord, and therefore you remind me of the Lord and I remind you of the Lord, because both are conscious beings.

This body is looked upon as a temple. Hence, when I take a bath, it is not merely cleaning this body, but it is also bathing the Lord. This dot on the forehead is also a form of worship to the Lord; it is not just ornamentation or beautification. Application of *vibhuti* or ashes on the forehead and on the body is similarly a form of worship to the Lord who is the conscious being. The Lord is the consciousness in me, the mind in me, the *prana* in me, the sense organs in me. As Lord Krsna says in the *Bhagavad Gita*, "He is the food that we eat. He is also the digestive power in the stomach and He is the eater too." Our knowledge, memory, everything is due to Him. And therefore, as a part of worship to Him, we, use sandalwood paste, *kumkum*, etc, in the form of *tilakam* on the forehead. In the act of worship, we offer to the Lord whatever is fragrant, whatever is colourful. Women put flowers on the hair. Again, that is not for beautification or ornamentation. It is an offering to the Lord. Flowers are fragrant and beautiful and therefore they are offered to the Lord. This is our religious culture.

And so, when you come out with a *tilakam* on your forehead, you remind me of the Lord and when you see me with a *tilakam* on my forehead, I remind you of the Lord and that is why we greet each other with a *namaskara*, salutation. As *isvara*, every one of us deserves salutation.

Indian culture is a religious culture, and the religion is based upon this vision of the scriptures that the Lord is everything. We find that vision manifest in our day-to-day life. Understanding of that requires a certain maturity on our part.

Emotional Intelligence and Leadership Excellence

A Brief

A study was conducted on 358 managers across the Johnson & Johnson Consumer & Personal Care Group (JJC&PC Group) globally to assess if there are specific leadership competencies that distinguish high performers from average performers. Participants were randomly selected, then coded for performance rating, potential, gender, functional group and regional area. More than 1,400 employees took part in a 183-page question multi-rater survey that measured a variety of competencies associated with leadership performance including those commonly referred to as Emotional Intelligence. Results showed that the highest performing managers were significantly more 'emotionally competent' than other managers. There was strong inter-rater agreement among supervisors, peers and subordinates that the competencies of Self-Confidence, Achievement Orientation, Initiative, Leadership, Influence and Change Catalyst differentiate superior performers. The high-potential managers received higher scores in the emotional competencies by their peers and supervisors, but not by subordinates. Some gender difference was found, with supervisors rating females higher in Adaptability and Service Orientation, while peers rated females higher on Emotional Self-Awareness, Conscientiousness, Developing Others, Service Orientation and Communication. Direct reports ranked males higher in Change Catalyst.

History

Late in 1998, *a Harvard Business Review* article entitled 'What Makes a Leader', caught the attention of senior management at Johnson & Johnson's Consumer Companies (JJCC). The article, written by Daniel Goleman, spoke on the importance of Emotional Intelligence (EI) in leadership success, and cited several studies that demonstrated that EI is often the distinguishing factor between great leaders and average leaders. Goleman posits that the foundation of emotional competency is Self-Awareness, the knowledge of one's own abilities and limitations as well as a solid understanding of factors and situations that evoke emotion in one's self and others. Equipped with this awareness, an individual can better manage his own emotions and behaviour and better understand and relate to other individuals and systems.

Long committed to leadership education and development, JJCC leadership decided to fund a study that would assess the importance of Emotional Intelligence in leadership success across the J&J Consumer Companies. Specifically, the project, which involved more than 1,400 employees in 37 countries, set out to determine if the emotional, social and relational competencies identified by Goleman and other EI theorists did, in fact, distinguish high performing leaders at JJCC.

Study Design and Methodology

The study design was centred around a 183-question multi-rater survey that was a blend of the J&J leadership competency model, the Standards of Leadership (SOL), and the Emotional Competence Inventory (ECI) that was based on the work of Richard Boyatzis and Daniel Goleman. The Standards of Leadership contained a traditional set of managerial and leadership competencies, built around the Johnson & Johnson Credo, which embodies the company's orientation of business philosophy towards responsibility, integrity and ethical behaviour. The SOL core competencies include Drives Business Results, Promotes Innovation, Manages Complexity, Customer Focus, Develops Others, Builds Partnerships, Fosters Change and Lives the Credo Values. The Emotional Competence Inventory (ECI), contains 20 social and emotional competencies organised into four main clusters or behavioural groups, namely, Self-Awareness, Self-Management, Social Awareness and Social Skills. A total of 358 managers were randomly selected from across the J&J Consumer & Personal Care Groups. Participants were 55 per cent male, 45 per cent female and regionally distributed as follows: North America 40 per cent; Europe 25 per cent; Asia, Africa-Middle East, 20 per cent; and Latin America, 15 per cent. Participants were required to have a minimum of two years in a management position within J&J and fluency in English.

After selection, regional human resource representatives provided additional participant information including functional area of responsibility, and performance ratings and potential ratings for the previous two performance years. Participants were coded by broad functional area, Administration, Marketing, Operations, or Research and Development. They were also identified as high-performing (HiPR) if their rating numbers were in the 'exceeds expectations' range, or greater than 4.0 on a five-point scale for performance. Performance ratings are determined by a combination of achievement against business objectives, the 'what' of performance, as well as behaviour on the job, the 'how' as measured by the J&J Credo and the Standards of Leadership. Individuals were also coded for potential on a five-point scale, and rated as high-potential (HiPO), if their rating was at least 4.0, indicating 'promotable to the next level or above'.

Potential ratings are determined by a combination of an individual's performance rating and potential for taking on added responsibility in the organisation. An individual considered to be of a 'high potential' will typically have a track record of accomplishment over several performance periods and be perceived as ready to move up at least one level in the organisation or assume a wider span of control and responsibility at the current job level. Both the performance rating and potential code are success indicators within the organisation and determine promotion, compensation and position in succession planning schemes. Participants were instructed to select a minimum of one supervisor and four additional raters, to complete the web-based survey. Raters were asked to rate the leader based on behavioural statements and whether the statements were true for the leader. Scores were based on a seven-point Likert scale, with one being the lowest rating 'slightly agree' to seven being the highest, 'strongly agree.' A total of 1415 employees completed the survey and data were captured into a database in accordance with coded variables.

Statistical Analysis

The data were analysed to compare the ratings of groups defined by region, gender, function and performance and potential. Gender, potential and performance, each consisted of only two categories, male and female, average and high potential (HiPO) for 4.0 or under, and over 4.0 for the high potentials (HiPR). The mean ratings for these groups were compared using an independent sample T test. For region and function, each of which consisted of four categories, multiple regression procedures were used. For these analyses a set of 'dummy' variables was created to represent the four different categories. The dummy variables were then used in the regression analysis to predict the ratings. If the regression results showed a significant regression weight for one or more of the variables, the conclusion would be that the mean ratings for that variable were higher or lower than that of the remaining variables.

Results

EI and High Performing Leaders (HiPR)

The study revealed a strong relationship between superior performing (HiPR) leaders and emotional competence, supporting theorists' suggestions that the social, emotional and relational competency set, commonly referred to as Emotional Intelligence, is a distinguishing factor in leadership performance. Leaders who received performance ratings of 4.1 or greater on a 5-point scale were rated significantly higher than other participants in all four of the Emotional Intelligence dimensions of Self-Awareness, Self-Management, Social Awareness and Social Skills by Supervisors and Subordinates. Peers found HiPR leaders to be stronger in the Self-Awareness and Self-Management clusters. Six competencies were found to distinguish HiPRs across all three rater groups, specifically, Self-Confidence, Achievement Orientation, Initiative, Leadership, Influence and Change Catalyst.

This finding is consistent with conclusions reached by McClelland (1998), in a study of leaders in 30 different organisations, that found the most powerful leadership differentiators were Self-Confidence, Achievement Drive, Developing Others, Adaptability, Influence and Leadership.

In the study of the 20 emotional competencies measured, subordinates and supervisors rated HiPR leaders stronger in 17, and 14 EI competencies, respectively. Peers found HiPR leaders to be stronger in nine of the 20 emotional competencies.

EI and High Potential Leaders (HiPO)

Supervisors rated high-potential leaders significantly higher on 13 of the 20 emotional competencies measured, as well as in the Self-Awareness, Self-Management and Social Skills clusters. Peers were less able to distinguish the HiPO leaders, rating them differently in six of the 20 competencies measured. With the exception of a slight difference in the area of Conscientiousness, subordinates did not rate HiPO leaders differently than other participants.

Supervisors' enhanced ability to recognise high potentials in this study may be understandable given a few factors. Supervisors are aware of employee potential status since they are instrumental in determining potential ratings for their direct reports. Knowing potential status of the participants while assessing them may have biased survey scores.

Table 4.1

Mean Ratings on ECI by Performance Rating

Cluster Competency	*Supervisor*		*Peer*		*Direct Report*	
	High Potential	*Average Potential*	*High Potential*	*Average Potential*	*High Potential*	*Average Potential*
Self-Awareness	92.6**	83.7**	91.0*	85.6*	91.5*	85.0
Emotional Self-Awareness	16.1	15.2	16.0	15.7	15.2	15.2
Accumulated Self-Assessment	34.7*	31.6*	33.4	32.0	33.7	31.9
Self-Confidence	40.6*	37.1*	41.8***	37.9***	41.7***	37.8***
Self-Management	175.2**	159.4**	171.6**	161.5**	173.8**	160.6**
Self-Control	20.8	20.4	21.4	20.7	21.8*	20.1*
Trustworthiness	24.1*	22.5*	22.3	21.9	22.8*	21.3*
Conscientiousness	30.7	28.9	30.0	28.7	30.2	29.0
Adaptability	28.5**	26.3**	27.1	25.8	27.7**	25.8**
Achievement Orientation	35.6**	31.4**	34.7**	32.3**	34.8**	32.3**
Initiative	34.8**	31.2**	34.7**	31.4**	34.3**	31.4**
Social Awareness	63.0*	57.8*	61.5	59.6	62.8*	57.9*
Empathy	40.2*	36.8*	38.0	37.7	38.9*	35.6*
Organisational Awareness	22.6	20.8	23.8***	21.7***	24.9**	22.3**
Social Skills	306.3**	273.0**	297.3	284.4	300.4**	272.9**
Developing Others	28.4	26.1	28.4*	26.7*	28.4*	26.3*
Service Orientation	41.1*	37.3*	39.5	37.6	40.4*	37.6*
Leadership	23.4**	19.6**	22.1**	20.5**	22.0***	19.7***
Influence	39.4**	34.8**	39.2**	36.3**	39.5**	36.0**
Communication	32.0	29.7	33.1*	30.9*	33.4*	31.3*
Change Catalyst	40.4***	35.3***	39.4**	35.0**	39.7***	36.6**
Conflict Management	27.8*	25.5*	27.4	26.0	27.3*	25.1*
Building Bonds	23.5*	21.0*	22.9	21.7	23.5***	21.2***
Teamwork	47.2*	43.0*	45.4	43.8	46.1*	42.5*

* $p = .05$

** $p = .01$

*** $p < .001$

Table 4.2

Mean Ratings on ECI by Potential

Cluster or Competency	*Supervisor*		*Peer*		*Direct Report*	
	High Potential	*Average Potential*	*High Potential*	*Average Potential*	*High Potential*	*Average Potential*
Self-Awareness	87.6***	80.7***	86.9	84.6	86.5	86.1
Emotional Self-Awareness	15.8	15.1	15.6	15.8	15.6	15.6
Accumulated Self-Assessment	32.6**	30.7**	32.4	31.6	32.3	32.3
Self-Confidence	38.9***	35.0***	39.1**	37.1**	38.7	38.0
Self-Management	164.4***	154.9***	162.8*	157.2*	161.6	163.2
Self-Control	20.8	20.1	20.4	20.7	20.7	20.2
Trustworthiness	22.4	22.0	21.5	21.6	21.5	21.0
Conscientiousness	29.4	28.4	29.1	28.5	29.6	28.5
Adaptability	26.3**	24.6**	26.1	25.6	26.1	26.1
Achievement Orientation	32.7***	30.0***	33.1***	31.3***	33.0	32.0
Initiative	32.4***	29.8***	32.2**	30.7*	31.8	31.4
Social Awareness	58.5	57.1	59.0	59.2	59.8	58.7
Empathy	37.1	36.7	37.0	37.4	37.0	36.5
Organisational Awareness	21.3	20.3	22.1	21.7	22.8	22.2
Social Skills	280.7*	264.6*	284.1	278.5	280.7	279.0
Developing Others	26.8*	25.2*	26.6	26.3	27.0	26.6
Service Orientation	38.1*	36.0*	37.7	37.5	38.7	37.8
Leadership	20.9**	19.3**	21.1**	20.0**	20.5	20.0
Influence	35.9	33.9	36.6	36.0	37.2	36.4
Communication	30.6*	28.9*	31.4	30.7	32.1	31.2
Change Catalyst	36.8**	34.1**	37.1*	35.5*	37.4	36.7
Conflict	26.2*	25.0*	26.2*	25.4	25.9	25.3
Building Bonds	21.9***	20.2***	21.7	21.5	22.0	21.5
Teamwork	44.0	42.2	43.7	43.2	43.5	43.2

* p = .05

** p = .01 ***p<.001

Another possibility is that supervisors, being charged with succession planning responsibility, may look for the demonstration of the competencies they know are predictive of success at higher levels in the organisation, while subordinates, in particular, may focus on competencies needed for success in the current role, which may in fact be different.

It is also likely that high potential individuals make an effort to demonstrate reach capabilities to their supervisors in an attempt to influence their opinion regarding their promotability and future potential.

EI and Gender

Relative to the many differences found for performance and potential, there were fewer differences relating to gender, however a few are noteworthy. Peer ratings show differences in five emotional competencies, Emotional Self-Awareness, Conscientiousness, Developing Others, Service Orientation and

Communication. In all of these areas, women received higher ratings. Supervisor ratings showed significant differences on two emotional competencies, specifically women were rated higher on both Adaptability and Service Orientation. Direct Report ratings showed only one significant difference, men were rated higher on the competency, Change-Catalyst.

Research concerning gender difference in leadership performance has found little evidence to suggest that males and females differ in their leadership effectiveness

1. Ragins, 1991
2. Eagly, Karau and Makhijani
3. 1992, 1995
4. Landau, 1996

In particular, several studies have demonstrated that there is little to no difference in satisfaction levels of subordinates of either male or female leaders

1. Osborn and Vicars, 1976

2. Ragins, 1991
3. Carless, 1998

The findings of the current study support this research. However, some studies suggest that the style by which males and females lead has consistently been found to be different. A meta-analysis conducted by Eagly and Johnson (1990) found females to have better social skills and described as 'interested in other people'. Women leaders as a group, when compared to male leaders as a group, tend to be described as more friendly, pleasant and socially sensitive (as cited in Eagly and Johnson, 1990). This finding is consistent with the current study, showing higher scores for females in several of the interpersonal and social competencies measured.

Prior research on gender difference in Emotional Intelligence have shown that in terms of total EI, men and women do not seem to differ; however there is evidence that women and men may differ on specific competencies. Bar-On (2000) analysed the scores on over 7,700 administrations of the Emotion Quotient Inventory (EQ-i) and found that while men and women did not differ on the total EI, women did score significantly higher on Empathy, Interpersonal Relationships and Social Responsibility, while men scored higher on Self-Actualisation, Assertiveness, Stress Tolerance, Impulse Control and Adaptability.

Where Bar-On found that men where more adaptable, the current study found that supervisors found women to be more adaptable.

However, consistent with Bar-On's findings, that females show more empathy and are more skilled in interpersonal relationships, our findings suggest peers find females to have higher levels of Self-Awareness, are more Service Oriented, have better Communication Skills and are more adept in Developing Others. However, it must be noted that the research by Bar-On is based on a self-report measure and does not employ a 360-degree methodology as in the current study. The significant difference between self-ratings and the ratings of others is a consistent finding in the literature, and thus generalisations may or may not be appropriate.

Table 4.3

Mean Ratings on ECI by Gender

Cluster or Competency	*Supervisor*		*Peer*		*Direct Report*	
	Male	*Female*	*Male*	*Female*	*Male*	*Female*
Self-Awareness	82.8	85.0	84.5*	87.4*	86.5	86.0
Emotional Self-Awareness	15.2	15.6	15.3***	16.4***	15.5	15.7
Accumulated Self-Assessment	31.5	31.7	31.8	32.3	32.6	31.9
Self-Confidence	36.1	37.6	37.5	38.7	38.4	38.4
Self-Management	157.4	161.7	159.5	160.5	162.2	162.6
Self-Control	20.3	20.6	20.5	20.5	20.7	20.2
Trustworthiness	22.3	22.0	21.6	21.5	21.7	21.7
Conscientiousness	28.5	29.4	28.3***	29.5***	29.0	29.1
Adaptability	24.9*	26.1*	25.6	26.1	26.2	25.9
Achievement Orientation	31.0	31.6	31.9	32.5	32.8	32.1
Initiative	30.7	31.3	31.1	31.9	31.8	31.2
Social Awareness	57.5	58.0	58.6	59.9	59.7	58.5
Empathy	36.5	37.3	36.7	38.0	37.0	36.4
Organisational Awareness	20.8	20.7	21.7	22.2	22.8	22.1
Social Skills	266.8	279.6	278.0	286.2	281.6	277.1
Developing Others	25.5	26.6	26.0*	27.0*	27.0	26.6
Service Orientation	36.2*	38.0*	36.9*	38.4*	38.4	38.1
Leadership	19.8	20.4	20.3	20.9	20.5	19.8
Influence	34.4	35.4	35.9	36.9	37.1	36.3
Communication	29.8	29.6	30.6*	31.7*	31.9	31.2
Change Catalyst	34.6	36.3	36.0	36.5	37.6*	36.2*
Conflict	25.5	25.8	25.5	26.2	25.9	25.3
Building Bonds	20.8	21.2	21.4	21.8	21.8	
Teamwork	42.4	43.8	43.1	44.0	43.6	43.0

* p = .05

** p = .01

*** p<.001

While the current research does not provide a consistent pattern of gender effects across all rater groups, the pattern of females being rated significantly higher on several competencies, in particular by peer raters, is interesting. Several hypothesis have been put forward to account for gender differences including biological differences, differences in early childhood socialisation in same sex play groups, and the fulfillment of culturally prescribed gender-role expectations. The differences in interpersonal processes and motives of males and females may also be related to types of self-schemes (for example, independent vs. interdependent) that tend to be held by males and females as a group (Cross and Madson, 1997).

One explanation may be that women are more likely to play out their preference for interdependence with a peer group given that peer relationships do not have the power differential and, subsequently, the role demands that the subordinate or supervisory roles have. Women may openly express feelings, demonstrate vulnerability, compromise and collaborate with peers, while doing so in their supervisory role may seem inappropriate, and in their subordinate role, it may be perceived by the woman as too risky.

EI and Regional Differences

Some scattered differences in ratings by region were observed. For example, leaders from Asia received lower scores from supervisors compared to other participants, while peers rated the North American leaders significantly higher than other participants. Direct reports gave higher ratings to leaders from Europe and North America than they did to leaders from the other two regions. The variations found probably reflect cultural differences in rating standards as opposed to a true reflection of performance difference.

EI and Functional Differences

Although some significant differences were observed across functional areas, the number of participants in each functional category was not sufficient to draw any conclusions.

Organisational Response to the Study

As a result of the study, the BCC enhanced their selection and performance management practices in several ways:

The company's leadership model, the Standards of Leadership, was modified to include the distinguishing emotional competencies found to be missing from the model. This is a particularly important step given the fact that the Standards of Leadership along with the Credo form the foundations for selection, assessment and development activities. The enhanced model has been integrated into performance review and succession planning processes, and protocols for selection have been modified to include the appropriate emotional competencies.

A new on-line 360-degree feedback survey has been developed based on the newly enhanced model. The Development Advantage, Standards of Leadership 360-degree Feedback Survey with Emotional Intelligence is available to all employees and helps individuals and groups assess their current level of performance and receive development suggestions for enhancing performance.

Educational and developmental programmes have been developed and launched across the Consumer and Personal Care Groups globally, to familiarise employees with the concepts of emotional, social and relational competency, and to share results of the leadership study. These sessions also served as the launch for the newly enhanced leadership model and survey.

Efforts to build skill in EI throughout the organisation are ongoing. Board members and their teams have begun assessment and skill-building activities around EI and individuals and groups throughout the organisation have initiated programmes and processes to enhance the emotional competency of the organisation and its members.

Conclusions and Further Steps

This study supports the position that emotional competence differentiates successful leaders. High performing managers at the Johnson & Johnson Consumer and Personal Care Group were seen to possess significantly higher levels of Self-Awareness, Self-Management Capability, Social Skills and Organisational Savvy, all considered part of the Emotional Intelligence domain.

Research has shown that Emotional Intelligence, like technical skill, can be developed through a systematic and consistent approach to building competence in personal and social awareness, self-management, and social skill. However, unlike technical skills, the pathways in the brain associated with social and emotional competencies are different than those engaged by more cognitive learning. Because the foundations of social and emotional competencies are often laid down early in life and reinforced over several years, they tend to become synonymous with our self-image and thus need focused attention over time to bring about change (Cherniss et. al., 1998).

The commitment and systematic approach taken at the JJCC is consistent with the focused approach necessary to build emotionally competent organisations. A strategic cycle of assessment > learning > practice > feedback over time will enable organisational members to build the competencies that can drive personal success and develop high performing leaders for the organisation.

5

Sameness of Mind

One Has to Pay Attention

Life is meant to discover fullness. All pursuits in our life are for freedom, freedom from being small. All the time, I struggle to prove myself to be someone desirable, important, credible in your eyes. I want to see, through your eyes, that I am somebody. A hundred people have to tell me that I am wonderful.

Everyone is struggling to be free from being small, limited, bound, mortal and so on. The vision of our *sastras* is that you are already free. If you think you are bound, that is purely a sense feeling. That the self is free is to be discovered. Freedom is your nature and you have to discover that freedom. You have to know that you are already free.

Knowledge calls for a certain preparedness and that is what I call emotional maturity. You require to be prepared for any knowledge. Here is a man who wants to learn calculus and does not know whether five plus four is eight or ten!

It is not that he cannot learn calculus. He has a desire to learn, a capacity to learn, but he must start from the beginning and the study of calculus can begin only when he is ready for it.

Everyone is ready for *Vedanta* when there is a certain emotional maturity, because all we are doing is analysing our own experiences. All of you have experiences and so, all of you are ready to learn *Vedanta*, but a certain emotional maturity is called fora, that is the same as *adhikaritvam*, fitness, preparedness. This preparedness itself is a great blessing, but it does not come naturally. You have to usher in this preparedness. You have to pay attention. You remain the same unless you pay attention.

I recently met a man in his seventies. He said: 'Swamiji, everything is all right with me'—meaning thereby that his sons and daughters are all married and well settled, and he himself has a house of his own and a car and servants and so on, 'but there is no peace of mind'. I asked him: 'Why?' 'Because my sons do not care for me,' he replied. 'How do you say they do not care for you?' 'Because they don't write to me.' In fact, his sons do care for him but they are not regular in writing letters because either they are very busy or they have their own problems, or they postpone writing and then it gets too late to reply to his letter. And even if they do not write, it is good. As a true Hindu, this man must be a *sannyasi* by now. *Sannyasa* is the best retirement plan because one does not need anything. One need not actually become a sannyasi but there should be that maturity. The problem is this man, even when he is in his seventies, is insecure.

You were insecure as a child when you wanted your mother and father to take care of you. You felt lonely and insecure if they left you behind. And now, after all these years, when you are a grandfather, you are still insecure. What have you achieved? A person does not grow unless inner growth takes place. And that does not happen unless one pays attention.

Be a *Karmayogi*

As I said earlier, everyone is a bundle of likes and dislikes. Desire to fulfil them is natural and so you undertake an action to fulfil either a like or a dislike. Any one of the following can be the result of an action:

(i) the result is in keeping with your expectation;
(ii) you get more than your expectation;
(iii) you get less than what you expected;
(iv) you get just the opposite result.

Let us say you have a stomach problem and you take some medicine. The result can be:

(i) the stomach problem goes away; or
(ii) the medicine cured not only the stomach problem but even your knee pain is also gone; or
(iii) the pain is somewhat reduced, but not gone completely; or

(iv) you discover that you are allergic to the particular medicine taken by you and now your whole stomach is ulcerated.

Thus, for any undertaking, these four kinds of results are possible. Now, when you undertake something, should you not be prepared for any one of these four results? You had better be. It is immature not to be prepared for them.

Even a simple action such as crossing a road entails any of the four results; you cross the road as desired; not only do you cross the road but meet a person whom you had wanted to meet for a long time; or you get caught in the middle of the traffic and escape with great difficulty; or a car suddenly comes from somewhere and hits you and you wind up in a hospital!

We are neither omniscient nor omnipotent. Both our knowledge and our power are limited. If we knew everything, we could avoid all accidents and could accomplish everything we wanted. We cannot accomplish everything we want for want of knowledge. Sometimes, in spite of having knowledge, we cannot accomplish what we want because we do not have the required power at our command. Suppose a man is falling from a tree. He knows that he is going to get injured, but he cannot avoid it. Thus, we do not call all the shots for want of knowledge and for want of power. But still we do not undertake various actions because we have these likes and dislikes which we wish to fulfil. And these undertakings will produce any of these four kinds of results. How are we going to take it? Lord Krishna says: Be a *karmayogi*.

Lord Krishna gives two definitions of *karmayoga* in the *Bhagavad Gita:*

Samatvam, yoga update
[Sameness is called yoga]
(*Bhagavad Gita* II 48)
Yogah karmasu kausalam
[With respect to action,yoga is the kausalam]
(*Bhagavad Gita* II 50)

We have to understand both these definitions.

Sameness Towards Results

Let us first take *samatvam* which means sameness. Sameness is *yoga*. Now, what does this sameness mean? Can there be sameness with reference to action? It cannot be because every action is different from another: sitting is different from standing and that is different from running. Even for the Lord, creation is one action; maintenance is another and destruction, yet another. There cannot be sameness of desires because an action is performed to achieve a certain end. I perform different actions because I want to achieve different ends. Can there be sameness in the result? Since actions are different, the results are going to be different, and even for the same action the result can be different at different times. Then where can there be *samatvam*? It can only be with reference to our attitude towards the result of an action.

Nityam ca samacittatvam istanistopapattisu

[Always maintaining sameness of the mind in the wake of the desirable and the undesirable]

(*Bhagavad Gita* XIII 9)

The result is called *istam* or desirable when it is in keeping with my expectation or better than what I expected. It is *anistam* or undesirable when it is less than what I expected or is contrary to my expectation. Sameness towards desirable and undesirable results is called *yoga*. This is what I would call emotional maturity. So, *yoga* with reference to action is nothing but simple emotional maturity. Hence, there is nothing special in being a *karmayogi*. It is expected of everyone. When one is born, one has to grow not only physically but emotionally too. That is a part of the programme of living. Hence *samacittatvam*. Sameness of the mind towards the result is yoga.

Lord Krishna talks about the attitude one should have towards life, in this famous verse:

karmanyevadhikaraste ma phalesu kadacana
Ma karmaphalaheturbhurmatesango 'stvakarmani

[You have choice only with reference to the action but definitely not with reference to the results. Do not become the author of the result of the action nor may you have attachment towards inaction]

(*Bhagavad Gita* II 47)

You have choice with respect to performing an action, but definitely not in determining the result of the action. Understand this well. Understand this intimately because it concerns your day-to-day life. You cannot interpret a *sastra*, scripture, like the *Bhagavad Gita*, which is the scripture of a living religious culture without looking into the attitudes, rituals, art, etc., of the people who have their roots in the *sastra*.

The Lord says: You have a choice over action. Why? Because you have *kartrtva*, the sense of doership. A donkey does not have *kartrtva* in the sense that it does not deliberate or premeditate upon an action. If it feels like kicking, it kicks even if the person it kicks happens to be its owner! A donkey cannot be taken to a court of law because it is not deliberate in its action. It does not have *kartrtva*, doership, even though it performs actions because it has no choice over its action. But as a human being, you have free will and therefore you have a choice over your action.

Karmani is the seventh case of the word *karman* not in the sense of location, but in the sense of object. So the meaning of the word *karmani* is not, 'in action' but, it is, 'with reference to an action.' And the Lord says: *Karmani eve to adhikarah*—you have choice only with reference to action. The meaning of the word 'only' is clarified by the Lord Himself: *ma phalesu kadacana*—but definitely not with respect to the results.

This verse is very often misunderstood and we find *karmayoga* being defined as: Perform action without expecting a result. Even the person who writes a book on *karmayoga* prints only a certain number of copies of the book. Why? Because he does not expect to sell more copies than that. The author performs the action of printing the book with the expectation of a certain sale, but advises people to perform action without expecting any result!

People do not understand how much this kind of an interpretation affects the psyche of the people. There are any number of people who think that *karmayoga* means performing action without expecting any result, and they develop a spiritual complex because they find they cannot fulfil this requirement.

Nobody can perform an action without expecting a result. Even a fool will not undertake something without a certain end in mind. Lord Krishna simply makes a statement of fact; You have a choice with respect to performing an action but not with reference to its result. This is not advice, it is a simple statement of fact. You can perform an action you feel proper, but having performed an action, you have no choice with reference to the result. It takes a lot of maturity to understand this.

Isvara is Karmaphaladata

When I clap with my hands, there is sound. I have no choice in not producing this sound. I should not expect a result that is not inherent in the action. If I do, my expectation will not be fulfilled. Then I should learn from the result and become wiser. But having performed the action of clapping, I cannot insist that sound should not be produced. I can learn from the result and become wiser than I was a minute ago. An action produces a result that is inherent in action itself and hence, I have a choice or freedom in performing an action but not in determining its result. This has to be understood very well, very intimately.

Then the Lord says: *Ma karmaphalahetuh bhuh*-Do not become *hetu* or cause of *karmaphala*, the result of action. You are *karma-hetu* (cause for an action) but not *karmaphala-hetu* (cause for the result of the action).

When I drop this flower, it falls downward. Dropping a flower is an action, and I am the cause or the author of that action. But I am not the author of its coming down. Falling of the flower is a result of certain conditions which I have not created. I may release the flower but it may not fall down if these conditions are not fulfilled. In a spaceship, in the zone of zero gravity, the flower will not fall down when released, but will perhaps go sideways.

Thus the law governing the result is the *hetu* for the result and not the one performing the action. Even performance of action is governed by laws. I can raise my hand only in accordance with the laws, but I still call myself the *karta* or performer of the action of raising my hand because I can choose not to raise it. I have a choice in dropping the flower or not dropping it, but having dropped it, its destiny will be governed by laws which are universal.

Who created these laws? Not you and I. Laws are a part of the world and the world is not created by you. It is created by *isvara* and it is not separate from Him. Therefore, when the flower falls down, who brings it down? *Isvara* brings it down. Thus, *isvara* is the *karmaphala-hetu* while you are *karma-hetu*. Therefore, the result that an action produces, whether it is more or less, or equal or opposite, comes from *isvara*. This is the appreciation of *isvara* as *karmaphala-data*, and that is maturity.

***Prasada* (Grace)**

Once it is established that *isvara* is the *karmaphaladata*, we can see how this fact is translated in our day-to-day life, when we look at our religious culture. Let us say you are invited by your friend to his house and he offers you a flower, as a sign of welcome, when you reach his house. You accept the flower and you smell it to enjoy its fragrance. Now suppose this friend has an altar of Lord Ganesa in his house, and he first offers it to Lord Ganesa and then gives it to you. How will you take it now? Remember, you are born in India and have been brought up in the Hindu culture.

Tell me, how will you receive the flower? Will you smell it? No. You will touch your eyes with it. The flower is the same; the person who offered it to you is the same: the recipient is also the same, but the flower has undergone a change. Now it comes from the altar of the Lord. The eyes see the same flower but the mind sees it differently and therefore, you place the flower on your eyes because it is as sacred as the eyes. There is a *bhavana*, an attitude involved in it.

That is why we say that Hindu religion is based on *bhavana*, attitude, born of the vision of *isvara*. You see here something more than a flower. The flower comes from the altar of the Lord and therefore, it is called *prasad*. And *prasada* brings *prasannata*, a glad acceptance on your part. When you appreciate the fact that the flower comes from the altar of the Lord, the flower gets transformed into *prasada*. There is no equivalent word in English for *prasada*.

Prasada can be anything. A tulsi leaf can be *prasada*, a flower petal can be *prasada*, a sugar crystal can be *prasada*, a *laddu* can be *prasada*, or even ash can be *prasada*. Every child is a *prasada* because it is given, and what is given is *prasada*. Every day, the food that is cooked is first offered to the Lord and so that is also *prasada*. *Prasada* is not an object. It is born purely of understanding. The understanding of the reality is the basis for *prasada*.

A man was once offered a *laddu* and he politely declined to accept it because he had a high blood sugar condition. He was quite well known for his love for the *laddu* but the doctor had advised him to stay away from eating sweets, and so he could not accept the *laddu*. Then he was told that the particular *laddu* came from the temple of Tirupati. 'Oh, really' Then it is a different matter. The man accepted the *laddu*! Why? Because it is no more a mere *laddu*, it is *prasada*. The moment it is known that a given object comes from the altar of the Lord, it gets transformed into *prasada*. That is education.

Lord Krsna says, 'You do not become the author of *karmaphala*, because I am its author'. And therefore, whether *karmaphala* is more, less, equal or opposite, it is *prasada* because it comes from the Lord. Thus every *karamaphala* is looked upon as *prasada* from the Lord. This is *samacittatvam*, sameness of the mind with reference to *karmaphala*. Thus sameness is born of understanding, it cannot be forced upon anybody. It is always born in the wake of some knowledge of reality. That is why I said that we should be alive to the reality of our being the *karta* or the agent of action and the Lord as the giver of the result. Therefore, even if I do not get what I expected, I still accept the result and having become wiser, I work harder. There is no regret.

People often ask this question: 'Swamiji, if I accept everything as *prasada*, will I not become a passive, submissive person?' Here we have to ask you that if you do not accept the result of *prasada*, then how will you accept it? If the result is not accepted cheerfully, it will be accepted with regret and disappointment, dejection and despair. How is that going to make you dynamic? It is wrong to think that one becomes submissive by accepting the situation as *prasada*. In fact, you will become dynamic only if you accept the result of *prasada*, because in that case you will be able to accept the result as it is and proceed with your life. 'Sir, the ship got sunk,' 'So what?'—that is *prasada*. A person becomes wiser by his attitude of *prasada*.

Let us say your friend is getting married and you have been given the assignment of welcoming people at his wedding reception. You stand there at the entrance and welcome people as they come into the reception hall. You receive all the guests with a smile whether you are acquainted with them or not. Even if a friend of yours walks in as a guest, you receive him as well and ask him to proceed. There is no time to talk to him because other guests are also coming and you have to receive them too. Now comes along a man who is your avowed enemy. How will you treat him? You must remember that you are at present representing your friend, and therefore your personal likes and dislikes should not come into play. So, you somehow work out a smile and receive this man also as you would receive a friend. This is *samatvam*, sameness of the mind. You welcome whatever comes to you. Your whole life becomes a learning experience.

There is No Failure

Everyone is *alpajna*, limited in knowledge, and *alpasaktiman*, limited in power and skill, and therefore everyone is a born failure. You cannot even be sure that you will be able to cross the road and reach the other side safely. In the process of crossing, you can be run over by a truck or struck by an auto rickshaw! We think that accidents always happen to others, but they can happen to us also. This uncertainty, born of the limitations of knowledge and power, applies to all the endeavours in life. There is every possibility that you may not get what you want in a given endeavour because your knowledge is limited, your abilities are limited.

Any futuristic projection is based on your present knowledge, and however pragmatic you may be in making a projection for a future event, you can never be sure that it will come true, because any number of unforeseen things can happen. A futuristic projection is only a hope, nothing more, and you can add prayer to it and make it a prayerful hope. There is nothing to be sure of, nothing to be proud of. Even as I am talking, where is the guarantee that I will be able to complete what I am saying? Anything can happen to anybody at any time, and therefore we better understand that no projection is valid; it is just a hope based on certain data available at the time of projection, and that data can never be complete. Only the one who is omniscient would really know what exactly is going to happen. Hence, what is up in the sleeve of the future is always a conjecture, a hope.

Thus, everyone is a born loser. But at the same time, look at yourself. You are a successful person. You seem to enjoy a lot of grace because you were able to open your mouth whenever you wanted. We eat all kinds of things and are still surviving, which shows that God is very much with us. All these years, I have been walking, talking, eating, digesting. Looking at the hygienic conditions in India, it is a wonder that we continue to survive! Every day is grace for us. I must clap when I wake up in the morning—one more day! Every day is a graceful day because there is no reason why I should wake up in the morning. That clap is maturity. I live day by day and there is an appreciation in that clap that there is something that makes the difference between success and failure. I find myself successful all the time. Nobody is a failure. When you breathe out, where is the guarantee that you will breathe in? The heart is beating; lub, dub, lub, dub.... There is a gap between lub and dub and all the grace has been flowing in this gap. I see grace all the time. This is where we branch out from the orbit of psychology. I am a mature person when I recognise that with all my limitations of power and knowledge, I have been gracefully successful, that there is a factor that makes a difference between success and failure. I am a mature person if I recognise that. If a person recognises this factor, we call him or her a religious person and for the one for whom this has become a reality, we can call that one a spiritually enlightened person. Both of them are mature—there are stages in maturity. There is nothing beyond maturity.

If one's marriage does not work or if one's business is unsuccessful, one looks upon oneself as a failure. I would say that is an immature conclusion. If you look at yourself, you are a successful person every way. You open your eyes and you are able to see. Well, why should that happen? There can be a retinal detachment at any moment.

You were able to lift your hand whenever you wanted. That need not necessarily happen. There can be thrombosis.

This is not an emotional logic. I want you to see that there is something that governs your life. There is some force, some order that keeps you going, alive, active. A devotee would call it grace. You may say it is *karmaphala*, the result of what you have done in the past, and that you have earned it. But we do not know which action resulted in this particular result. When we cannot track a particular action as responsible for a given situation, we call it grace.

For example, when we do not know the cause for the occurrence of an incident, we call it an accident. When the causes become known, the accident reduces to an incident. Similarly, when I have earned the grace, I have definitely worked for it, either now or in the past, but I cannot say in what manner, and therefore we call it grace. It is a graceful way of acknowledging a *karmaphala* in as much as we do not know which action has brought this particular result.

This discovery, this understanding—that you are a winner all the time in spite of the fact that you should always have been a loser on account of your limitations in knowledge and ability—is very important. It brings about a certain attitude towards situations that are pleasant and unpleasant. In your maturity, you are able to accept the unpleasant also. The capacity to stomach, to accommodate, to accept a fact is possible only when there is an awareness. An unpleasant situation is as legitimate as a pleasant situation.

According to Lord Krishna, there is no failure at all. Every action produces a result and therefore *karmaphala*, the result of action is called *rtam*, that which is bound to happen. You have asked for it and so you get it. There is no way of avoiding phala, the result, when once karma is performed. You can perform another action and thereby, neutralise the result of a previous action. That is called *prayascitta*, expiation. A reaction is inherent in the very action. One can do something else to alter a situation, but it is doing that produces a result, non-doing does not.

Failure can be there only when success is in your hands, when you call all the shots. When that is not the case, there is no failure. No one is a failure. Everyone is learning. We learn from experiences and so, there is no regret. Our culture is a learning culture, not a regretting culture. We keep learning from our experiences. If we find we have done something wrong, we do *prayascitta-karma* to neutralise it. That is a positive step. We do not have confession, etc. If I have done something wrong to somebody, I do something good to that person. That is *pratipaksa-bhavana*, doing the opposite. Thus, there is learning all along life, and that is a mature way of responding to success and failure. There is *nityam samacittatvam*, sameness of the mind with respect to the result of the action, because it is *prasada* from the Lord.

Everything is Sacred

There is *yoga*, if there is *samatvam*,sameness of the mind, which is the capacity to accept unfavourable situations without reaction on our part. *Samatvam* is something more than pragmatism. A pragmatic person is also one who takes things as they come—but that is easier said than done. Therefore, mere secular pragmatism is not *karmayoga*. *Karmayoga* is to appreciate *isvara*.

There is no such thing as secular *karmayoga*. Religion is always involved in the life of a Hindu. In fact, we do not have a word equivalent to secularism because we do not compartmentalise life as secular or sacred. Everything is sacred for us because everything is *isvara*. Even disciplines of knowledge cannot be divided into secular and sacred.

It is said in the Vedas: *Dye vidye veditavye....para caivapara ca*. One should pursue two disciplines of knowledge; *para* and *apara*. *Para-vidya* is that by which the Truth is known. So, the knowledge which has *brahmana* or *atma* as the subject is *para-vidya* and all other disciplines of knowledge, concerning non-self, are *apara-vidya*. So, knowledge is classified according to the subject it deals with, namely, *atma* and *anatma*, that is the Self and the Non-self. Thus, *para-vidya* involves an enquiry into the nature of the Lord, the Self, the Truth, all of them being the same. *Apara-vidya* is everything else. Even the *Karmakanda*, ritual section of the *Vedas*, is *apara-vidya* and the *Vedangas*, the limbs of the *Vedas*, namely, Phonetics, Grammar, Astronomy, Prosody, etc., are also *apara-vidya*. Physics, Chemistry, History, Economics, all of these are also classified as *apara-vidya*.

Hence, knowledge, in our culture, is classified according to the subject it deals with but not as secular or sacred, because all knowledge is sacred for us.

Goddess Sarasvati is the presiding deity of knowledge and therefore, on the day of the worship of Sarasvati, we place all our books—*Gita, Ramayana*, Grammar, History and all the rest—to make an altar for the Goddess of Knowledge, and offer prayers. A book is a symbol of knowledge, a symbol of Goddess Sarasvati and therefore, no Hindu will consciously step on a book. If I step on a book by chance, I seek pardon—it does not matter what the book is about. Any book is a symbol of knowledge and therefore sacred.

Money is also sacred in our culture because it is a symbol of Goddess Laksmi, and so we never deliberately step on a currency note. Laksmi stands not only for wealth, but also for all resources. Money, skill, time, manpower—all of these are resources. They are all Laksmi and we look upon them as sacred.

There is no secular aspect in Hinduism. There is no *karmayoga* unless we recognise *isvara*. There is no secular *karmayoga* because there is no secular Hinduism. There is nothing secular in the world because, according to our vision, everything is *isvara*. Recognition of *isvara* as *karmaphaladata*, giver of result of action, is *karmayoga*. Every result is born of *isvara* whose laws produce the result and therefore, I accept every result as *prasada*.

Cessation of Sorrow

Prasada, the cheerful acceptance of the situation as it comes to me—because every situation is the result of some action or the other—enables me to neutralise my ragas and *devas*. A man's life is like a see-saw because of likes and dislikes. There is a problem when what I do not like happens. There is again a problem when what I like does not happen. It is very common in life that what I want, does not happen, and what I do not want keeps happening. That is because our likes and dislikes are countless while our knowledge and power are limited. There is no way of fulfilling all the likes and dislikes with the knowledge and power we have at hand. Therefore, we often do not get what we want and there is constantly a reaction on our part in terms of anger, frustration, etc. In time, the person becomes a personality.

Everyone is born a person, *purusa*, but in time, the person turns into a personality. One is a person as a child, but slowly, various angularities are acquired because of failures and disappointments one meets in life. They transform a person into a personality. That is why everyone has those buttons, vulnerable areas, which throw one out of gear. This personality is nothing but likes and dislikes. It is best that they are allowed to express themselves in terms of desirable legitimate activities, and when the results come, accept them as *prasada*. We cheerfully welcome the results as they come because they come from the Lord. When we accept the situations happily, likes and dislikes no more govern our responses, they no more remain a source of disturbance. I am happy if they are fulfilled, I am happy even if they are not fulfilled. In that case, I can afford to have likes and dislikes because they do not disturb me.

The capacity of likes and dislikes to strike me down in terms of anger, frustration, despair, etc., is neutralised by *prasada-buddhi*, the attitude of glad acceptance. Lord Krishna says in the Gita:

Prasade sarvaduhkhanam hanirasyopajayate.

[There is cessation of sorrow for this one (*karmayogi*) when there is *prasada*, cheerfulness of the mind]

(*Bhagavad Gita* II 65)

There is no sorrow for the *karmayogi* because he enjoys a cheerful mind that is brought about by the attitude of *prasada* which is the same as *samatvam*, sameness of the mind, born of the recognition of *isvara* as *karmaphaladata*.

6

Emotional Intelligence

A Critical Analysis

'Emotional intelligence' has raised the question of whether it is possible to improve the social and emotional competence of adult workers. Research in training and development, sports psychology and behaviour change suggest that it is possible, but the typical approach used in corporate training programmes usually is flawed. Social and emotional learning is different from cognitive and technical learning, and it requires a different approach to training and development.

This report presents 22 guidelines for developing emotional intelligence in organisations, based on the best knowledge available on how to promote social and emotional learning. It has been estimated that American business each year loses between 5.6 and 16.8 billion dollars by not consistently following these guidelines. The basis for this estimate can be found in the last section of the report.

Research for this report was conducted under the auspices of the Consortium for Research on Emotional Intelligence in Organisations (CREIO). The Consortium is made up of nine individuals from academia, government, and the corporate sector. All of the individuals are recognised experts with considerable experience in both research and consulting. The Consortium has been funded by the Fetzer Institute, a private foundation located in Kalamazoo, Michigan.

Bringing Emotional Intelligence to the Workplace

When the book, Emotional Intelligence, appeared in 1995, many business leaders agreed with the basic message that success is strongly influenced by personal qualities such as perseverance, self-control and skill in getting along with others.[1]' They could point to 'super sales persons' who had an uncanny ability to sense what was most important to the customers and to develop a trustful relationship with them. They could point to customer-service employees who excelled when it came to helping angry customers to calm down and be more reasonable about their problems with the product or service. And they also could point to brilliant executives who did everything well except get along with people, or to managers who were technically brilliant but could not handle stress, and whose careers stalled because of these deficiencies. Business leaders well understood how valuable these 'emotionally intelligent' employees are to an enterprise.[2]

But what about the many workers who lack these important emotional competencies? Is it possible for adults to become more socially and emotionally competent? Many business leaders are less certain about this question. For instance, the dean of a major business school, when asked about the importance of emotional intelligence at work, enthusiastically agreed that it was crucial. But when we asked him, how his school attempted to improve the emotional intelligence of MBA students, he said, 'We don't do anything. I don't think that our students' emotional intelligence can be improved. By the time they come here, they're already adults, and these qualities are developed early in life.'

---

1. 'Emotional intelligence', as we use the term here, refers to about two dozen social and emotional abilities that previous research has shown to be linked to successful performance in the workplace. These abilities can be grouped into five core areas: self-awareness, self-regulation, self-motivation, social awareness and social skills. For research on the link between these abilities and performance, see, Spencer Jr., L.M., D.C. McClelland and S. Kelner (1997). *Competency Assessment Methods History and State of the Art*. Paper presented at a meeting of The Consortium for Social and Emotional Competence in the Workplace.

2. Many studies have confirmed that the so-called 'soft skills' are critical for a vital economy. For instance, see Secretary's Commission on Achieving Necessary Skills (SCANS) (1991). *What Work Requires of Schools*. U.S. Department of Labor; Carnevale, A.P., L.J. Gainer and A.S. Meltzer (1998). "Workplace Basics: The Skills Employers Want", *Training eT Development Journal* 42: 22-25; Spencer et al. *op. cit.* no. 1; Boyatzis, R.E. (1982). *The Competent Manager: A Model for Effective Performance.* New York, USA: John Wiley & Sons. See also the work of Hall, who has argued that executive development increasingly involves 'personal development', i.e., how the individual deals with work/life issues, stress, and health. See Hall, D.T. (1995). "Executive Careers and Learning: Aligning Selection, Strategy, and Development", *Human Resource Planning* 18: 14-23.

On the other hand, there are those who seem to claim that they can raise the emotional intelligence of a whole group of employees in a day or less. Scores of consultants now are selling workshops and seminars designed to help people become more emotionally competent and socially skilled. Some of these programmes are quite good, but others make unrealistic claims. The worst ones are those that involve a heavy reliance on inspirational lectures or intense, short-lived experiences—and little else.

So who is right—the sceptics who believe that nothing can be done to improve emotional competence after the age of 15, or the hucksters who claim that they can turn emotional dunces into emotional Einsteins in an afternoon? As usual, the answer lies somewhere in between.

A growing body of research on emotional learning and behaviour change suggests that it is possible to help people of any age to become more emotionally intelligent at work. However, many programmes designed to do so fail to recognise the difference between two types of learning.

Two Types of Learning

Training and development efforts in industry have not always distinguished between cognitive learning and emotional learning, but such a distinction is important for effective practice[3]. For instance, consider the example of the engineer whose career was at a standstill because he was shy, introverted and totally absorbed in the technical aspects of his job. Through cognitive learning, he might come to understand that it would be better for him to consult other people more, make connections and build relationships. But just knowing he should do these things would not enable him to do them. The ability to do these things depends on emotional competence, which requires emotional learning as well as cognitive learning.

Emotional incompetence often results from habits deeply learned early in life. These automatic habits are set in place as a normal part of living, as experience shapes the brain. As people

3. Goleman, D. (1998). *Working with Emotional Intelligence*. New York, USA: Bantam.

acquire their habitual repertoire of thought, feeling and action, the neural connections that support them are strengthened, becoming dominant pathways for nerve impulses. Connections that are unused become weakened, while those that people use over and over grow increasingly strong.[4] When these habits have been so heavily learned, the underlying neural circuitry becomes the brain's default option at any moment—what a person does automatically and spontaneously, often with little awareness of choosing to do so. Thus, for the shy engineer, diffidence is a habit that must be overcome and replaced with a new habit, self-confidence.

Emotional capacities like empathy or flexibility differ from cognitive abilities because they draw on different brain areas. Purely cognitive abilities are based in the neocortex. But with social and emotional competencies, additional brain areas are involved, mainly the circuitry that runs from the emotional centres—particularly the amygdale—deep in the centre of the brain up to the prefrontal lobes, the brain's executive centre. Effective learning for emotional competence has to re-tune these circuits.

Cognitive learning involves fitting new data and insights into existing frameworks of association and understanding, extending and enriching the corresponding neural circuitry. But emotional learning involves that and more—it requires that we also engage the neural circuitry where our social and emotional habit repertoire is stored. Changing habits such as learning to approach people positively instead of avoiding them, to listen better, or to give feedback skilfully, is a more challenging task than simply adding new information to old.

Motivational factors also make social and emotional learning more difficult and complex than purely cognitive learning. Emotional learning often involves ways of thinking and acting that are more central to a person's identity. A person who is told, for instance, that he should learn a new word processing programme usually will become less upset and defensive than if he is told that he should learn how to better control his temper or become a better listener. The prospect of needing to develop greater emotional competence is

4. Edelman, G. (1987). *Neural Darwinism: The Theory of Neuronal Group Selection*. New York, USA: Basic Books.

a bitter pill for many of us to swallow. It is thus much more likely to generate resistance to change.

What this means for social and emotional learning is that one must first unlearn old habits and then develop new ones. For the learner, this usually means a long and sometimes difficult process involving much practice. One-day seminars just won't do it.[5]

Those who study training 'have tended to consider all training the same, without regard to the purpose of the training or the type of learning involved.'[6] Some of the previous thinking about training, based largely on cognitive learning, is valid for social and emotional learning as well. However, the principles for social and emotional learning differ greatly from those that apply to purely cognitive abilities. A better source of guidance comes from research that examines social and emotional change processes more directly. Such research comes from many different fields, including sports psychology, psychotherapy and behaviour change, and personal development. This research suggests a set of guidelines for the design of effective social and emotional learning.[7] These guidelines point to components that are additive and synergistic; to be effective, social and emotional learning experiences need not adhere to all of these

5. The distinction between cognitive and emotional learning is similar to the one that Hall makes in discussing executive learning. He suggests that executive learning can be either short-term or long-term, with either a task focus or a personal focus. Using this typology, social and emotional learning involves a personal focus requiring a long-term perspective. See Hall, D.T. and P.H. Mirvis (1996). "The New Protean Career: Psychological Success and the Path with a Heart", in D.T. Hall (ed.), *The Career Is Dead: Long Live the Career.* San Francisco, USA: Jossey-Bass.

6. Tannenbaum, S.I. and G. Yuki (1992). "Training and Development in Work Organizations", *Annual Review of Psychology* 43: 399-441.

7. These guidelines emerged from a review of research conducted under the auspices of the 'Consortium for Research on Emotional Intelligence in Organizations,' originally funded by the Fetzer Institute of Kalamazoo, Michigan. Consortium members were: Richard Boyatzis, Ph.D., Prof. of Management and Associate Dean, Weatherhead School of Management, Case Western Reserve University; Robert Caplan, Ph.D., Prof. and Director of the Organizational Psychology Program, George Washington University; Cary Cherniss, Ph.D., Prof. of Applied Psychology, Rutgers University; Daniel Goleman, Ph.D., author and CEO of Emotional Intelligence Services; Marilyn Growing, Ph.D., Director of Resources and Development, U.S. Office of Personnel Management, Washington, DC; Kathy Kram, Ph.D., Associate Prof. of Management, Boston University; Richard Price, Ph.D., Prof. of Psychology, University of Michigan; Mary Ann Re, Ph.D., Manager of AT&T Corporate Employee Research, AT&T; and Lyle Spencer, Jr., Ph.D., Hay Group Research Fellow, Author (Competence at Work,) and Consultant.

guidelines, but the chances for success increase with each one that is followed.

Guidelines for Effective Social and Emotional Learning: An Overview

There are four basic phases to the training process. The first occurs even before the individual begins formal training. This initial phase, which is crucial for effective social and emotional learning, involves preparation for change. The second phase, training, covers the change process itself. It includes the processes that help people change the way in which they view the world and deal with its social and emotional demands. The third phase, transfer and maintenance, addresses what happens following the formal training experience. The final phase involves evaluation. Given the current state of knowledge about social and emotional learning and the complexity of programmes designed to promote such learning, evaluation always should be part of the process.

Phase One: Preparation for Change

Motivation is especially important in social and emotional learning.[8] Such learning can be challenging for adults who already have established a way of relating to themselves and others, and people need to be strongly committed to the change process for an extended period of time. So what can managers and trainers do to

8. Several studies have found a relationship between motivation to learn and learning performance. For instance, Hicks, W.D. (1984). "The Process of Entering Training Programs and its Effects on Training Outcomes", *Dissertation Abstracts International* 44(11-B): 3564 and Ryman, D.H. and R.J. Biersner (1975). "Attitudes Predictive of Divining Training Success", *Personnel Psychology* 28: 181-88, found a relationship between motivation to learn and dropout rates. See also Noe, R.A. and N. Schmitt (1986). "The Influence of Trainee Attitudes on Training Effectiveness: Test of a Model", *Personnel Psychology* 39: 497-523, Hicks, W.D. and R.J. Klimoski (1987). "Entry into Training Programs and its Effects on Training Outcomes: A Field Experiment", *Academy of Management Journal* 30: 542-52, Mathieu, J.E., S.I. Tannenbaum and E. Salas (1990). "The Influence of Individual and Situational Characteristics on Training Effectiveness Measures", *Academy of Management Journal* 35: 828-47. Numerous studies on social and emotional change in psychotherapy also have found a strong link between motivation and success. See for instance Burns, D.D. and S. Nolen-Hoeksema (1991). "Coping Styles, Homework Compliance, and the Effectiveness of Cognitive-Behavioral Therapy", *Journal of Consulting and Clinical Psychology* 59: 305-11, Marmar, C.R. et al. (1989). "Alliance and Outcome in Late-Life Depression", *Journal of Nervous and Mental Disease* 177: 464-72.

increase learners' motivation prior to the start of the change process? The first set of guidelines addresses this question.

1. Assess the Organisation's Needs

Good training begins with a needs assessment.[9] For social and emotional training, there are two particular challenges that must be addressed at this point in the process. First, many people in the organisation will be sceptical about the link between emotional intelligence and the bottom line. A systematic and rigorous study can help show that such a link exists. For instance, in one large financial services company, there was considerable scepticism about the value of training in 'emotional competence' until top executives saw the results of a study showing that financial advisors who coped better with the emotional aspects of work with clients sold more life insurance policies. Once they saw the connection between this particular type of emotional competence and the bottom line, the executives encouraged advisors to participate in an emotional competence training programme.

The second challenge in applying this guideline to social and emotional training efforts is to identify all of the particular competencies that are important for success. Sometimes it is easy to miss crucial ones. For instance, an initial needs assessment in one airline began with a consideration of the airline's business strategy. Because airlines are similar in price structure, a competitive advantage depends particularly on how well passengers are treated by airline personnel. As a result, the way in which flight attendants handled passengers became the focus for training efforts. Research then indicated that superior performers had two types of competencies: self-management (resilience, efficiency, adaptability) and interpersonal (caring for and managing customers well, and teamwork).

However, two other competencies, self-awareness and empathy, help support the self-management and interpersonal competencies. So the training programme also needed to include these. Only a careful assessment of the work situation, informed by an understanding

9. Goldstein, Irwin L. (1993). *Training in Organizations* (Third edition). Pacific Grove, California, USA: Brooks/Cole.

of the nature of emotional competence, enabled the consultant to identify both the surface-level and deeper competencies that affected performance.

2. Assess Personal Strengths and Limits

Two challenges confront those who wish to assess the social and emotional competence of individuals. First, people usually are less aware of skill weaknesses in the social and emotional domains.[10] They may realise, for example, that the interpersonal aspects of leading a work group are difficult and frustrating. But they may not be able to pinpoint the emotional skills they need to improve their functioning in this area.

They are probably even less aware of the underlying attitudes and ways of thinking that get them into trouble, or how those ways of thinking trigger complex emotional response patterns that impede their effectiveness in dealing with difficult employees, customers or co-workers.

Second, these competencies are manifested primarily in social interaction. Therefore, the best approach usually involves ratings by those who interact with the person. However, the beliefs, motives and feelings of the rater influence ratings of social and emotional competence. The boss's view of a manager's self-awareness or ability to empathise may be very different from the perspective of the manager's peers and subordinates. The best assessment approach for initiating social and emotional learning thus, is usually based on multiple ratings conducted from multiple perspectives, such as 360-degree assessments that include boss, peer and subordinate ratings.[11]

Three hundred sixty feedback' now is used regularly in industry for a variety of purposes, and organisations vary in how well they use this tool. When not managed well, it can create resistance rather than readiness. In the most effective development programmes, the

---

10. This point is supported by research on empathy. For example, Davis, M. and L. Kraus (1997). "Personality and Accurate empathy", in. W. Ickes (ed.), *Empathic Accuracy*. New York: Guilford Press, have found that there is no correlation between people's estimates of their empathy and their scores on objective tests of empathy.

11. Spencer et al., 1997, *op. cit*.

participants are helped to review these ratings and then use them to identify the competencies that should be the focus of training efforts. Ultimately, however, the motivating power of an assessment is affected by how credible it is to the learners. The trainees need to have faith in the assessment method.[12]

3. Provide Feedback with Care

Motivation for change can be enhanced when people are given feedback on the assessment results.[13] However, there are many pitfalls in giving people feedback on their social competence. These competencies are closely linked to a person's identity and self-esteem. It is one thing, for example, to be told that you need to work on the back-swing of your chip shot in golf, but it is quite another to be told that you need to handle stress better. If the feedback is not provided with sensitivity and skill, people often become defensive.

People are more likely to respond positively to feedback when they trust and respect the person who gives it. People are also more likely to be motivated to change when they believe that the feedback is constructive and accurate[14] and they are helped to identify the specific steps they can take to improve.[15] People also need sufficient time to think about the information and its implications. And in social and emotional development efforts, it is especially important that the feedback occurs in an atmosphere of safety.

The understood purpose of the feedback also affects its motivational and emotional impact. When, for instance, it is used for appraisal purposes, and one's supervisor gives the feedback,

12. Noe and Schmitt *op. cit.*

13. Kolb, D.A., S.K. Winter and D.E. Berlew (1968). "Self-directed Change: Two Studies", *Journal of Applied Behavioral Science* 4: 453-71.

14. Ilgen, D.R., C.D. Fisher and M.S. Taylor (1979). "Consequences of Individual Feedback on Behavior in Organizations", *Journal of Applied Psychology* 64: 349-71.

15. Korsgaard, M.A. and M. Diddams (1996). "The Effect of Process Feedback and Task Complexity on Personal Goals, Information Searching, and Performance Improvement", *Journal of Applied Social Psychology* 26: 1889-1911; French, J. R. P., H.H. Meyer and E. Kay (1966). "Participation and the Appraisal System", *Human Relations* 19: 3-20, Latham and Yukl *op. cit.*; Bassett, G.A. and H.H. Meyer (1968). "Performance Appraisal Based on Self Review", *Personnel Psychology* 21: 421-30.

the impact often is negative. On the other hand, when it is used for development purposes and the person giving the feedback is viewed as a disinterested individual whose motivation is to help, then the consequences tend to be much more positive.[16] For instance, in a large computer software company, an executive development specialist provides the individual with the results of a 360-degree assessment strictly in confidence, one-to-one: No copies of the results are kept. The feedback is used only as a development tool.

4. Maximise Learner Choice

People generally are more motivated to change when they freely choose to do so.[17] In social and emotional training, however, choice is particularly important. Because these competencies are so close to the essence of what makes us the people we are, it is better if we are free to choose whether or not to engage in such training. It is also better if the choice is real. If trainees are given a choice but not assigned to the training they initially chose, they will be less motivated to learn than those who were given no choice.[18]

5. Encourage Participation

Because social and emotional learning is viewed as 'soft' and thus somewhat suspect, employees will tend not to choose to participate in it unless they believe that the organisation's management strongly endorses it. The words and actions of supervisors are especially important. Trainees are more willing to participate in development activity if their supervisors indicate that they support it. In a large

---

16. Boyatzis, R.E. (1998). "Self-directed Change and Learning as a Necessary Meta-competency for Success and Effectiveness in the 21st Century", in R. Sims and J.G. Verese (eds.), *Keys to Employee Success in the Coming Decades*. Westport, CN, U.S.A: Greenwood Publishing.

17. Hicks, 1984 *op. cit.*; Clark, C.S., G.H. Dobbins and R.T. Ladd (1993). "Exploratory Field Study of Training Motivation", *Group and Organizational Management* 18: 292-307, Mathieu, J.E., S.I. Tannenbaum and E. Salas *op. cit.*; Quinones, M.A. (1995). "Pretraining Context: Training Assignment as Feedback", *Journal of Applied Psychology* 80: 226-38, Ryman and Biersner *op. cit.*

18. Baldwin, T.T., R.J. Magjuka and B.T Loher (1991). "The Perils of Participation: Effects of Choice of Training on Trainee Motivation and Learning", *Personnel Psychology* 44: 51-65, Magjuka, R.J., T.T Baldwin and B.T. Loher (1994). "The Combined Effects of Three Pretraining Strategies on Motivation and Performance: An Empirical Exploration", *Journal of Managerial Issues* 17: 282-96.

financial services company, a training programme in emotional competence was popular in part because several regional vice presidents encouraged their management groups to participate and then attended the programme with them.

The same has been true for 'crew resource management training,' a programme that teaches airline crews the social and emotional skills that help them to work better as a team. When senior management has demonstrated a real commitment to this programme by providing intensive and recurrent training, there has been greater acceptance of it among the crews. Acceptance also has increased when check airmen and instructors emphasise concepts from the training during other training and checking.[19]

6. Link Learning Goals to Personal Values

People will be most motivated to learn and change if they believe that doing so will help them achieve goals that they value.[20] For instance, in teaching airline crews how to work better in the cockpit as a team, it usually is more effective to teach them 'how to get a team off to a good start,' and 'how to address conflicts among members constructively,' rather than to teach them about 'behavioural styles'.[21]

Often the most salient personal values will be work-related, but they need not be. Trying to motivate learners by showing them that training will contribute to career success will be difficult if success is

---

19. Helmreich, R.L. and H.C. Fourshee (1993). "Why Crew Resource Management? Empirical and Theoretical Bases of Human Factors Training in Aviation", in E.L. Wiener, B.G. Kanki and R.L. Helmreich (eds.), *Cockpit Resource Management*. New York, USA: Academic Press. pp.3-46. See also Baldwin, T.T. and R.J. Magjuka (1991). "Organizational Training and Signals of Importance: Effects of Pre-training Perceptions on Intentions to Transfer", *Human Resources Development* 2: 25-36. Clark et al. *op. cit.*; Facteau, J.D. et al. (1995). "The Influence of General Perceptions of the Training Environment on Pretraining Motivation and Perceived Training Transfer", *Journal of Management* 21: 1-25; Maurer, T.J. and B.A. Tarulli (1994). "Investigation of Perceived Environment, Perceived Outcome, and Person Variables in Relationships to Voluntary Development Activity by Employees", *Journal of Applied Psychology* 79: 3-14; Noe, R.A. (1996). "Is Career Management Related to Employee Development and Performance", *Journal of Organizational Behavior* 17: 119-33.

20. See Peterson, D.B. (1996). "Executive Coaching at Work: The Art of One-on-One Change", *Consulting Psychology Journal* 48: 78-86.

21. J.R. Hackman, "Teams, Leaders, Aria Organizations: New Directions for Crew-oriented Flight Training', in Winer et al. *op. cit.*: 51.

unimportant to them.[22] Fortunately, other incentives for social and emotional learning are not difficult to find. In one popular emotional competence programme, many participants reported that the skills they learned were as valuable in managing relationships at home as they were at work.

7. Adjust Expectations

Expectations about performance can become self-fulfilling prophecies. People who are confident that they can succeed in a training programme will tend to be more motivated and, not surprisingly, more successful.[23] Unfortunately, in the case of social and emotional learning, many people are sceptical that emotional intelligence can be improved. And people who find social and emotional problems challenging will be, particularly dubious about their ability to improve. To maximise motivation, learners need to believe not only that greater emotional competence will lead to valued outcomes, but also that it can be improved. Furthermore, they need to have a realistic expectation of what the training process will involve.[24]

---

22. Noe and Schmitt *op. cit.*

23. Ryman and Biersner *op. cit.*; Gist, M.E., C. Schwoerer and B. Rosen (1989). "Effects of Alternative Training Methods on Self-efficacy and Performance in Computer Training", *Journal of Applied Psychology* 74: 884-891; Froman, L. (1977). "Some Motivational Determinants of Trainee Effort and Performance: An Investigation of Expectancy Theory", *Dissertation Abstracts International* 38(5-B): 2411; Moitra, S. (1977). "A Pre-program Evaluation Model Determining Training Effectiveness, based on the Expectancy Theory of Work-motivation", *Dissertation Abstracts International* 38(3-B): 1455. Research on change processes in psychotherapy also suggests that efficacy expectations play a crucial role in motivation for change. For instance, Grencavage, L.M. and J.C. Norcross (1990). "Where are the Commonalities among the Therapeutic Common Factors?", *Professional Psychology: Research and Practice* 21: 372-78, reviewed 50 publications on diverse forms of psychotherapy in order to distil common change factors. They found that the most frequent client characteristic mentioned was 'positive expectancies and hope for improvement.' See also Bandura, A., N. Adams and J. Beyer (1977). "Cognitive Processes Mediating Behavioral Change", *Journal of Personality and Social Psychology* 35: 125-39; Marmar, C. R. et al. (1989). "Alliances and Outcome in Late-life Depression", *Journal of Nervous and Mental Disease* 177: 464-72.

24. The trainer's expectations also are important. In several studies, the trainees learned more when their trainers were told they had trainees with very high success potential. See Eden, D. R. and G. Ravid (1982). "Pygmalion versus Self-expectancy: Effects of Instructor- and Self-expectancy on Trainee Performance", *Organizational Behavior and Human Decision Processes* 3: 351-64; and Eden, D. R. and A.B. Shami (1982), "Pygmalion Goes to Boot Camp: Expectancy, Leadership, and Trainee Performance", *Journal of Applied Psychology* 67: 194-99.

Trainers can help enhance learners' self-efficacy in various ways. For instance, in the JOBS programme, an award-winning programme designed to help unemployed workers to overcome discouragement and find new jobs, the participants observe the trainers engaged in a role-play of a job interview. The trainers intentionally make several mistakes during the role-play. The participants then provide suggestions for improving performance, and the trainers do the role-play again, incorporating the participants' suggestions. The participants see how useful the suggestions are, and the trainers point out that the participants have demonstrated that they already know most of what the experts know about how to do a job interview well.[25]

8. Gauge Readiness

Research on a wide variety of behaviour change programmes suggests that people go through several stages of readiness for change before they are ready to make a true commitment.[26] In the first stage, they deny that they have any need for change. In the next stage, people begin to see that they need to improve, but they are not sure that anything can be done about their problems and they put off making a decision. In the third stage, the individual recognises that there is a problem and also that there are ways of dealing with it, but the person has not made a concrete plan to act. It is not until the fourth stage that the person is ready to act. People at this stage have a concrete plan, and they put it into action. Before training begins (or towards the beginning), the training staff should, ideally, assess the readiness stage of each potential participant. They then would design an appropriate intervention based on that assessment, which will differ for people at each stage of readiness.

25. Caplan, R.D., A.D. Vinokur and R.H. Price (1997). "From Job Loss to Re-employment: Field Experiments in Prevention-focused Coping", in G.W. Albee and T.P. Gullotta (eds.), *Primary Prevention Works: Issues in Children's and Families' Lives*. Vol. 6. Thousand Oaks, California, USA: Sage. pp.341-79.

26. Prochaska, J.O., J.C. Norcross and C.C. DiClemente (1994). *Changing For Good: The Revolutionary Program that Explains the Six Stages of Change and Teaches You How to Free Yourself From Bad Habits*. New York, USA: W. Morrow.

Phase Two: Training

In social and emotional learning, motivation continues to be an important issue during the training phase. The amount of time, effort, and potential threats to one's self-esteem that occur during social and emotional learning suggest that trainers continue to monitor the individual's motivation and intervene to bolster it. One of the most important factors influencing motivation during the training phase is the relationship between the trainer and the learner.

9. Foster a Positive Relationship Between the Trainer and Learner

In social and emotional learning, the relationship between the trainer and learner is critically important.[27] For instance, in a programme designed to teach people to be more assertive, the participants were less likely to drop out and showed more positive change at the end of the programme if they had a positive relationship with the trainer.[28]

Several studies have suggested that trainers who are empathic, warm, and genuine—which are, of course, attributes of emotional intelligence—develop more positive relationships with participants in behaviour change programmes, and they are more likely to be

27. In a study of 50 articles on factors associated with change in psychotherapy, the researchers found that 'development of a therapeutic relationship or working alliance' was the most frequently cited (Grencavage and Norcross *op. cit.*). A meta-analysis of 24 studies found an average effect size of r=.26 for the link between the quality of the therapeutic alliance and outcome (Horvath, A.O. and B.D. Symonds (1991). "Relation between Working Alliance and Outcome in Psychotherapy: A Meta-analysis", *Journal of Counseling Psychology:* 139-49.

28. Ford, J.D. (1978). "Therapeutic Relationship in Behavior Therapy: An Empirical Analysis", *Journal of Consulting and Clinical Psychology* 46: 1302-14.

successful.[29] Trainers who use a directive-confrontational style only succeed in making participants more resistant.[30]

In the JOBS programme, the trainers work to develop a trusting relationship with the participants by engaging in a moderate degree of self-disclosure. For instance, the trainers talk about their own experiences in coping with job loss, emphasising the normal experiences of self-doubt, encounters with barriers and setbacks, persistence in the face of these barriers, and ultimate success. This self-disclosure encourages the participants to identify with and admire the trainers, which facilitates social and emotional learning.[31]

10. Maximise Self-Directed Change

People are more likely to develop emotional competence when they decide which competencies to work on and set their own goals. Training for emotional competence also benefits when the trainer adapts the training to match the person's needs, goals and learning style

---

29. There has not been much research on the link between trainer qualities and training outcomes in the context of work organizations. What little research there is has examined academic classroom learning, and it has identified ideal trainer qualities such as, 'Is well organized' and 'Answers questions clearly and thoroughly' (Goldstein *op. cit.*). On the other hand, research on behaviour change in other contexts has amply documented the link. See, for example, Blatt, S.J. et al. (1996). "Interpersonal Factors in Brief Treatment of Depression: Further Analyses of the National Institute of Mental Health Treatment of Depression Collaborative Research Program", *Journal of Consulting and Clinical Psychology* 64: 162-71; Burns, D.D. and S. Nolen-Hoeksema (1992). "Therapeutic Empathy and Recovery from Depression in Cognitive-behavioral Therapy: A Structural Equation Model", *Journal of Consulting and Clinical Psychology* 60: 441-9; Henry, W.P., T.E. Schacht and H.H. Strupp (1986). "Structural Analysis of Social Behavior: Application to a Study of Interpersonal Process in Differential Psychotherapeutic Outcome", *Journal of Consulting and Clinical Psychology (Special Issue: Psychotherapy Research)* 54: 27-31; Kolden, G.G. (1996). "Change in Early Sessions of Dynamic Therapy: Universal Processes and the Generic Model of psychotherapy", *Journal of Consulting and Clinical Psychology* 64: 489-96; Valle, S.K. (1981). "Interpersonal Functioning of Alcoholism Counselors and Treatment Outcome", *Journal of Studies on Alcohol* 42: 783-90.

30. Miller, W.R., R.G. Benefield and J.S. Tonigan (1993). "Enhancing Motivation for Change in Problem Drinking: A Controlled Comparison of Two Therapist Styles", *Journal of Consultingland Clinical Psychology* 61: 455-61. Other researchers have found negative associations between outcome and behaviors such as 'blaming and belittling' (Henry, Schacht and Strupp *op. cit.*) and 'attacking' (Najavits, L.M. and H.H. Strupp (1994). "Differences in the Effectiveness of Psychodynamic Therapists: A Process-outcome Study", *Psychotherapy* 31: 114-23).

31. Caplan et al., *op. cit.*

preferences.[32] For instance, in one stress management programme, the participants were taught a variety of approaches to relaxation. Then they were encouraged to try each one and select the best one for them. And if none worked well, they were encouraged to try other approaches to managing stress, such as improving their time management skills. The basic message of the programme was that people differ, and no one approach to managing stress will work well for everyone.

11. Set Clear Goals

Social and emotional learning benefits from specific clear goals. A goal such as 'learn how to listen better to subordinates' is less effective than 'use active listening with subordinates at least three times each day for three weeks.' Specific and challenging goals help support social and emotional learning because they maximise self-efficacy, mastery and motivation. The most effective trainers are able to help the learners set clear and challenging goals without infringing on the learners' sense of ownership for the goals.[33]

---

32. Although there is some research support for self-directed change in the training and development literature (e.g., Frayne, C.A. and G.P. Latham (1987). "Application of Social Learning Theory to Employee Self-management of Attendance", *Journal of Applied Psychology* 72: 387-92; Gist, M.E., C.K. Stevens and A.G. Bavetta (1991). "Effects of Self-efficacy and Post-training Intervention on the Acquisition and Maintenance of Complex Interpersonal Skills", *Personal Psychology* 44: 837-61; Kolb, D.A. and R.E. Boyatzis (1970). "Goal Setting and Self-directed Behavior Change", *Human Relations* 23: 439-57; Spencer, L.M. and S.M. Spencer (1993). *Competence at Work: Models for Superior Performance*, New York, USA: John Wiley & Sons Inc.; Tannenbaum and Yukl *op. cit.* The strongest support for this approach comes from research on behavior change. See, for instance, Sonne, J.L. and D. Janoff (1982). "The Effect of Treatment Attributions on the Maintenance of Weight Reduction: A Replication and Extension", *Cognitive Therapy and Research* 3: 389-97. Research on the processes that people use to change on their own also supports the notion that change is facilitated by self-control. Stories of successful life change attempts, compared to unsuccessful ones, were more likely to involve self-reward and self-reinforcement. And the successful changers were more likely to feel they had control over their behaviour, and greater self-control in general (Heatherton, T. F. and P.A. Nichols (1994). "Personal Accounts of Successful versus Failed Attempts at Life Change", *Personality and Social Psychology Bulletin* 20: 664-75.

33. One early study of the use of goals in training (Kolb, D.A., S.K. Winter and D.E. Berlew (1968). "Self Directed Change: Two Studies", *Journal of Applied Behavioral Science* 4: 453-71), found that self-directed change was enhanced when the method was modified to emphasise conscious goal-setting. In the organisational behaviour literature, goal-setting has been shown to improve performance across a wide range of domains (Locke, E.A. and G.P. Latham (1990). *A Theory of Goal Setting and Task Performance.* Englewood Cliffs, New Jersey, USA: Prentice-Hall; Wexley, K.N. and T.T. Baldwin (1986). "Post-training Strategies for Facilitation of Positive Transfer: An Empirical Exploration", *Academy of Management Review* 29: 503-20).

12. Break Goals into Manageable Steps

For many people, trying to bring about even modest improvements in emotional competence can be frustrating. Although challenging goals are more motivating than simple ones, it also helps if the goals are attainable. When people reach a goal, their self-efficacy increases, which leads to the setting of new, more challenging goals.[34] For instance, one MBA student lacked the self-confidence necessary to approach people about part-time jobs. The larger goal of developing self-confidence was overwhelming (and also vague), but he was helped to break it into smaller, more realistic action steps. The first was to update his resume; which was easy; there was no need to approach anyone. The next steps, which were increasingly difficult, were to call the chairman of the finance department by the next month to request a meeting, then meet with the chairman to discuss opportunities, then do the same with his mentor, a local executive. Finally, he would search the local want ads and call to apply for promising jobs. In this way, the goal of increasing self-confidence became attainable, and steady progress and success rather than frustration and failure characterised the process.

13. Maximise Opportunities to Practice

The relationship between practice and learning is one of the oldest and best-established principles in psychology. In social and emotional learning, there often must be more practice than in other types of learning because old, ineffective neural connections need to be weakened and new, more effective ones established. Such a process requires repetition over a prolonged period of time. And learners need to practice on the job, not just in the training situation, for transfer to occur.

Relying on a single seminar or workshop is one of the most common errors made in social and emotional learning programmes. Even an intense workshop lasting several days usually is not

---

34. Snyder, C.R. (1993).*The Psychology of Hope*. New York, USA: Free Press; Bandura, A. and D. Cervone (1983). "Self-evaluative and Self-efficacy Mechanisms Governing the Motivational Effects of Goal Systems", *Journal of Personality and Social Psychology* 45: 1017-28; Hall, Douglas T. (1976). *Careers in Organizations*. Santa Monica, California, USA: Goodyear.

sufficient to help people unlearn old, entrenched habits and develop new ones that will persist. The most effective training programmes include repeated sessions of practice and feedback.[35]

14. Provide Frequent Feedback on Practice

Feedback is important during the change process as a way of indicating whether the learner is on track. It also can help sustain motivation, for feedback can be highly reinforcing.[36] Feedback is especially useful in social and emotional learning because the learners often have trouble recognising how their social and emotional behaviour manifests itself. In fact, because self-awareness is a core competence, those who need the most help in emotional competence programmes may be particularly weak in this area. Thus, they need even more focused and sustained feedback as they practise new behaviours.[37]

15. Rely on Experiential Methods

More active, concrete and experiential methods, such as role plays, group discussions and simulations, usually work better than lecturing or assigned reading for social and emotional learning. In

---

35. The principles of distributed rather than massed practice, and overlearning, are well established in the experimental research on learning. Baldwin, T.T. and J.K. Ford (1988). "Transfer of Training: A Review and Directions for Future Research", *Personal Psychology* 41: 63-105; Dempster, F.N. (1988). "The Spacing Effect: A Case Study in the Failure to Apply the Results of Psychological Research", *American Psychologist* 43: 627-34. Research on the 'dose-response effect' in psychotherapy also shows that the longer people work at changing, the more durable the change will be. Most people do not show stable changes until they have completed at least a dozen or more sessions (Howard, K. et al. (1968). 'The Dose-effect Relationship in Psychotherapy", *American Psychologist* 41: 159-64).

36. Goldstein *op. cit.* In a study of self-development groups conducted for students attending a business school, the amount of feedback individuals received from other group members during the last half of the group was one of two factors that predicted success. Improving the change method to enhance feedback increased the percentage of learners who successfully attained their goals from 5 to 61 per cent (Kolb, Winter and Berlew *op. cit.*). See also the study by Komaki, J.L., R.L. Collins and P. Penn (1982). "The Role of Performance Antecedents and Consequences in Work Motivation", *Journal of Applied Psychology* 67: 334-40.

37. Ilgen and his colleagues have suggested that providing too much feedback can backfire because it might reduce the learner's sense of personal control and make the learner more dependent on feedback. However, trainers are more likely to provide too little feedback rather than too much. See Ilgen, D.R., C.D. Fisher and M.S. Taylor (1979). "Consequences of Individual Feedback on Behavior in Organizations", *Journal of Applied Psychology* 64: 349-71.

order to reprogramme neural circuits connecting the amygdala and neocortex, people need to actually engage in the desired pattern of thought, feeling and action. A lecture is fine for increasing understanding of emotional intelligence, but experiential methods usually are necessary for real behaviour change.

A study of managerial and sales training programmes offered in a large corporation demonstrated the superiority of experiential methods for social and emotional learning. The programmes that used experiential methods produced twice as much improvement in performance, as rated by supervisors and peers, as did the other programmes. Furthermore, the return on investment for the experiential programmes was seven times greater.[38]

A particularly good example of experiential learning is the teaching approach used in Cockpit Resource Management. Much of 'the training involves 'flying missions' in a highly realistic flight simulator. To learn more about how they interact with one another and the effect it has on their performance, the crew is videotaped while they perform the mission, and then they view the tape with an instructor and focus on their interactions.[39]

16. Build in Support

Change is enhanced through ongoing support from individuals and small groups. Such support is especially valuable for people who are trying to improve their social and emotional competence. Coaches and mentors, as well as individuals who are going through the same

38. L. Spencer, in Bassi, L.J. and D. Russ-Eft (eds.) (1997). *What Works*. Alexandria, Virginia, USA: ASTD. Research on change processes in psychotherapy also has pointed to the superiority of experiential methods. An example was a study of the components of cognitive therapy associated with change. The results suggested that concrete methods predicted positive change in mood; but less focused, more abstract discussions did not (Robins, C.J. and A.M. Hayes (1993). "An Appraisal of Cognitive Therapy", *Journal of Consulting and Clinical Psychology* 61: 205-14). Research in neuroscience has reached similar conclusions, suggesting that emotional learning is more likely to occur when novelty, dramatic retreat settings, and powerful stimuli that engage all the senses mark the experience. (Kosslyn, S.M. and O. Koenig (1995). *Wet Mind: The New Cognitive Neuroscience*. New York, USA: Free Press).

39. Wiener et al, *op. cit.*

change process, can help sustain a person's hope and motivation.[40] Social and emotional training programmes usually are more effective when they encourage the formation of groups where people give each other support throughout the change effort.[41]

In a stress-management programme designed for a group of middle managers in a high-tech firm, the trainers assigned the participants to a 'support group' early in the first session. All small group work during the course of the programme took place in these support groups, and facilitators included activities that helped the group members to get to know one another better. The participants were encouraged to meet others in their support groups in between sessions and after the programme formally ended. The participants reported that the conversations they had in their support groups about life style and priorities were the most important factors in helping them to make positive changes in their work and personal lives.

17. Use Models

Seeing the desired behaviour modelled is particularly valuable in social and emotional learning. One cannot learn to solve quadratic equations by watching someone else do so, but one can learn a great deal about how to discuss a conflict with a co-worker by observing a

40. Kram, K.E. (1985). "Improving the Mentoring Process", *Training and Development Journal* 39: 40-43, found that mentors, in addition to helping people to get ahead, also serve as valuable role models and sources of support. In doing so, they help people to develop the social and emotional competencies that are particularly important for success. For other research on the value of mentoring, see Orpen, C. (1995). "The Effects of Mentoring on Employees' Career Success", *Journal of Social Psychology* 135: 667-68; Scandura, T. (1992). "Mentorship and Career Mobility: An Empirical Investigation", *Journal of Organizational Behavior* 13: 169-74; and Fagenson, E. (1989). "The Mentor Advantage: Perceived Career/Job Experiences of Proteges vs. Non-proteges", *Journal of Organizational Behavior* 10: 309-20.

41. There is a large research literature showing how the support provided by self-help groups can be a powerful lever for behavior change. See for instance: Levy, L.H. (1976). "Self-Help Groups: Types and Psychological Processes", *Journal of Applied Behavioral Science* 12: 310-22; Lieberman, M.A. and L. Borman (1979). *Self-Help Groups for Coping with Crises: Origins, Members, Processes, and Impact*. San Francisco, USA: Jossey-Bass; McCrady, B.S. and W.R. Miller (eds.) (1993). *Research on Alcoholics Anonymous: Opportunities and Alternatives*. New Brunswick, New Jersey, USA: Rutgers Center for Alcohol Studies; Hinrichsen, G.A., T.A. Revenson and M. Shinn (1985). "Does Self-Help Help? An Empirical Investigation of Scoliosis Peer Support Groups", *Journal of Social Issues* 41: 65-87; and Powell, T.J. (ed.) (1994). *Understanding Self Help: Frameworks and Findings*. Newbury Park, California, USA: Sage, 1994.

model do it. Learning is further enriched when trainers encourage and help learners to study, analyse and emulate the models.[42]

18. Enhance Insight

Even though experiential interventions seem to be especially productive for social and emotional learning, insight also can play a useful role.[43] Insight serves as a natural link between situations, thoughts and feelings. It enhances self-awareness, the cornerstone of emotional intelligence. And insight often paves the way for meaningful behaviour change.[44]

The most effective training combines experiential methods and the development of insight. For instance, one programme taught managers to be more aware of how their employees irritated them and to become more effective in setting limits with employees. The trainer began the lesson by showing an excerpt from a popular comedy film in which one character continually annoyed another by infringing on his personal space in various ways. After showing the film, the trainer helped the participants to shift the focus from the film to themselves and they began to see how they often allowed some of their employees to bother them in similarly annoying ways. After acquiring more insight into their own emotional reactions, the participants were ready to learn some emotional and social skills that could help them to deal with these annoying behaviours.

---

42. There is a sizable body of research on the value of models in learning. See, for example, Bandura, A. (1977). *Social Learning Theory*. Englewood Cliffs, New Jersey, USA: Prentice Hall; Tannenbaum and Yukl *op. cit.*

43. Insight was an important component in AT&T's career development program for executives. See, for instance, Bray, D.W. (1976). "The Assessment Center Method", in R.L. Craig (ed.), *Training and Development Handbook*. New York, USA: McGraw-Hill.

44. In a study of those who attempted some kind of life change, 20 per cent of those who successfully made changes 'gained new understanding of (their) situation through a sudden flash of insight into their behavior'. They also were more likely to describe themselves as having discovered `a new sense of self-knowledge and understanding'. By contrast, none of the non-changers expressed any type of insight at all (Heatherton and Nichols *op. cit.*).

19. Prevent Relapse

The essence of relapse prevention is to prepare people mentally to encounter slips, to recognise at the outset that setbacks are a normal part of the change process. Relapse prevention is especially important in social and emotional learning because participants attempting to develop these competencies are likely to encounter many setbacks as they attempt to apply new behaviours on the job. Without preparation for these setbacks, they can easily become discouraged and give up before the task of neural relearning has reached the point where the new, learned response is the automatic one.

In relapse-prevention training, people are helped to reframe slips as opportunities to learn in order to reduce the likelihood of slipping again in the future. For dealing with situations in which a mistake is likely, they are also helped to develop practical strategies such as taking a 'time out' to consult a mentor.[45] Through relapse prevention, trainees learn how to identify and overcome potential obstacles to applying new skills on the job. They also learn to monitor their progress and use methods of self-reinforcement to maintain motivation.[46]

For example, in one programme a trainer leads the participants through a discussion about a hypothetical situation in which a participant who has followed all the rules for effective and supportive feedback receives an angry response when talking with a staff member. The trainer then asks the group to describe how they would

45. Kram, 1985 *op. cit.*

46. .For instance, one study showed that adding relapse prevention to a management training program helped increase transfer of skills to the job (Tziner, A., R.R. Haccoun and A. Kadish (1991). "Personal and Situational Characteristics Influencing the Effectiveness of Transfer of Training Improvement Strategies", *Journal of Occupational Psychology* 64: 167-77). See also Burke, L. and T. Baldwin (1996). "Improving Transfer of Training: A Field Investigation of the Effects of Relapse Prevention Training and Transfer Climate on Maintenance Outcomes", *Dissertation Abstracts International, Section A: Humanities and Social Science* 57(4-A): 1725, October; Gist, M.E., A.G. Bavetta and C.K. Stevens (1990). "Transfer Training Method: Its Influence on Skill Gneralization, Skill Repetition, and Performance Level", *Personnel Psychology* 43: 501-23; Gist et al., 1991, *op. cit.*; Noe, R.A., J. Sears and A.M. Fullenkamp (1990). "Relapse Training: Does it Influence Trainees' Post Training Behavior and Cognitive Strategies?", *Journal of Business and Psychology* 4: 317-28; Vinokur, A.D. and Y. Schul (1997). "Mastery and Inoculation against Setbacks as Active Ingredients in the JOBS intervention for the Unemployed", *Journal of Clinical and Consulting Psychology* 65: 867-77.

feel in this situation and to consider what they could do to overcome this particular obstacle. The trainer then praises the participants for their ideas on how to bounce back from this setback. Later, the trainer asks the participants to write down on one side of a sheet of paper descriptions of setbacks they might encounter when they try to apply a skill they have learned, and to generate possible solutions for overcoming these setbacks on the other side of the paper. The participants then share these strategies with the rest of the group.[47]

Phase Three: Transfer and Maintenance

Transfer and maintenance of learnt skills is a particular challenge in social and emotional learning. When learners return to their natural environments, there are likely to be many cues and reinforcers that support the old neural pathways that training was designed to weaken. Further, there may be significant barriers to the use of some of the new social and emotional competencies that still have a fragile neural foundation.[48] Well-designed training programmes cannot be effective if the larger organisational system in which they are rooted is not supportive of the training goals. Recent research has pointed to several aspects of the organisational environment that seem to be helpful in facilitating transfer of social and emotional learning.

---

47. Heaney, C.A., R.H. Price and J. Rafferty (1995). "The Caregiver Support Program: An Intervention to Increase Employee Coping Resources and Enhance Mental Health", in L.R. Murphy et al. (eds)., *Job Stress Interventions.* Washington, DC, USA: American Psychological Association; Davis-Sacks, M.L., A. Weine and C. Heaney (1988). *The Caregiver Support Program: A Descriptive Account.* Ann Arbor, Michigan, USA: Institute for Social Research, University of Michigan.

48. The difficulty of transferring and maintaining social and emotional learning was demonstrated in a study of an assertion training program. Gains from the training had disappeared when the participants were tested two months following the end of training. The author concluded that long-term behavioral maintenance requires special intervention, such as training in self-management skills and restructuring the individual's natural environment (Ford, J.D. (1978). "Therapeutic Relationship in Behavior Therapy: An Empirical Analysis", *Journal of Consulting and Clinical Psychology* 46: 1302-14).

20. Encourage Use of Skills on the Job

There are many different ways that supervisors, peers, subordinates and others in the work environment can encourage learners to apply what they have learned. The best methods involve either reminding people to use the skills or reinforcing them when they do so.[49]

Reinforcement is a particularly good way to encourage trainees to apply their new skills on the job and to continue doing so. In the workplace, reinforcement by one's supervisor can be especially powerful.[50] Consider the difference in outcomes for two supervisory training programmes.[51] In both, the participants liked the programmes and successfully learned the new skills.[52] But follow up showed that the participants from the first programme applied their skills on the job, while those in the second did not.

The biggest difference between the two programmes was that the trainees in the first one were 'directed and encouraged by their supervisors to use the new skills'. In fact, two of the participants were removed from their jobs for not using the new skills.

Supervisors can reinforce the use of new skills on the job in less drastic ways. For instance, they can encourage trainees to use learnt skills on the job simply by cueing them to do so.[53] Also, a follow-up assessment of skills learnt during training can make the trainees feel more accountable and increase transfer of learning.[54] For example,

---

49. Rouiller, J.Z. and I.L. Goldstein, (1993). "The Relationship between Organizational Transfer Climate and Positive Transfer of Training", *Human Resource Development Quarterly* 4: 377-90.

50. Baldwin, T.T. and J. K. Ford (1988). "Transfer of Training: A Review and Directions for Future Research", *Personnel Psychology* 41: 63-105; Noe, R.A. (1986). "Trainees' Attributes and Attitudes: Neglected Influences on Training Effectiveness", *Academy of Management Review* 11: 736-49.

51. One program was described in Latham, G.P. and L.M. Saari (1979). "Application of Social-Learning Theory to Training Supervisors through Behavioral Modelling", *Journal of Applied Psychology* 64: 239-46. The other was described in Russell, J.S., K.N. Wexley and J.E. Hunter (1984). "Questioning the Effectiveness of Behavior Modeling Training in an Industrial Setting", *Personnel Psychology* 37: 465-81.

52. Russell et al, *op. cit.*: 477.

53. Rouiller and Goldstein, 1993, *op. cit.*

54. Baldwin and Magjuka, 1991, *op. cit.*

the airlines have 'check pilots' observe flight crews during flights and then give them feedback in order to encourage the crews to use the teamwork, communication and leadership skills that they previously learned.[55]

The behaviour of a supervisor or any high status person is crucial for the transfer and maintenance of new emotional and social competencies. The models to which learners are exposed when they, return to the work environment are even more powerful than those they encountered during training. Social and emotional behaviour seems to be especially sensitive to modelling effects, and high status persons are influential models for this kind of behaviour in the workplace.[56] For instance, in one supervisory training programme, the participants were taught to adopt a more supportive leadership style. After they returned to their jobs, only those trainees whose own supervisors had such a style transferred what they had learned to their jobs.[57]

In addition to modelling and reinforcement, reflection can help learners transfer and maintain what they have learned. It can be particularly helpful for supervisors to set aside some time periodically to help learners reflect on what they have done to apply the skills and to consider what have been the barriers and facilitating factors. Because self-awareness is a cornerstone of social and emotional competence, reflection can be especially valuable during the transfer and maintenance phase.[58]

---

55. Wiener et al. *op. cit.* For another example, see Komaki, J., A.T. Heinzmann and L. Lawson (1980). "Effect of Training and Feedback: Component Analysis of a Behavioral Safety Program", *Journal of Applied Psychology* 65: 261-70.

56. Manz, C.C. and H.P. Sims (1986). "Beyond Imitation: Complex Behavioral and Affective Linkages Resulting from Exposure to Leadership Training Models", *Journal of Applied Psychology* 71: 571-78; Weiss, H.M. (1977). "Subordinate Imitation of Supervisor Behavior: The Role of Modeling in Organizational Socialization", *Organizational Behavior and Human Performance* 19: 89-105.

57. Fleishman, E.A. (1955). "Leadership Climate, Human Relations Training, and Supervisory Behaviour", *Personnel Psychology* 6: 205-22.

58. For a good discussion of some of the recent work being done on managerial reflection as a development tool, see Daudelin, M.W. (1996). "Learning from Experience Through Reflection", *Organizational Dynamics* 24: 36-48; and Seibert, K. (1996). "Experience is the Best Teacher, If you can Learn from it: Real Time Reflection and Development", in D.T. Hall (ed.), *The Career is Dead: Long Live the Career*. San Francisco, USA: Jossey-Bass.

Although supervisors are especially salient sources of reinforcement and encouragement, other individuals and groups in the work environment can be important as well. For instance, in a supervisory skills programme, the supervisors' employees were trained at the same time as the supervisors.[59] This additional component of the programme helped create an environment that encouraged the supervisors to practise and use the new behaviours.[60]

21. Provide an Organisational Culture that Supports Learning

Transfer and maintenance of specific skills seems to be affected by the extent to which the organisation values learning and development in general.[61] Challenging jobs, social support, reward and development systems, and an emphasis on innovation and competition influence these perceptions and expectations.

The climate of the work environment is particularly important for transfer of social and emotional learning to the job. One study found that participants in a human relations training programme who returned to a supportive climate performed better on objective performance measures and were promoted more often than those in an unsupportive climate. Furthermore, these effects were not observed until 18 months after training, highlighting the importance of a supportive environment for the development of social and emotional competencies over time.[62]

---

59. M. Sorcher and R. Spence, 'The InterFace Project: Behavior modeling as social technology in South Africa, Personnel Psychology, Vol. 35, 1982, pp. 557-81.

60. R. K. Flemming and B. Sulzer-Azeroff, 'Peer management: Effects on staff teaching performance', Paper presented at the 15th Annual Convention of the Association for Behavioral Analysis, Nashville, TN, USA, 1990. Specially designed support groups, coaches, and mentors also can provide reinforcement and encouragement, as noted above. In one training program, the trainers paired up the trainees with someone who helped them with feedback and encouragement, following the end of training. Data on the program indicated that pairing up trainees led to greater transfer of training.

61. J. B. Tracey, S. I. Tannenbaum and M. J. Kavanagh, 'Applying trained skills on the job: The importance of the work environment', Journal of Applied Psychology, Vol. 80, 1995, pp. 239-52; P. Senge, The Fifth Discipline, New York, USA: Doubleday/Currency, 1990.

62. H. H. Hand, M. D. Richards and J. W. Slocum, 'Organizational climate and the effectiveness of a human relations training program', Academy of Management Journal, Vol. 16, 1973, pp. 185-95.

Phase Four: Evaluating Change

22. Conduct On-going Evaluation Research

Evaluation is essential for promoting effective training. Research suggests that many training programmes do not fulfil their promise.[63] Only through evaluation can poor programmes be improved and effective ones retained. By evaluation, we mean a process that focuses on continuous improvement rather than just a 'pass–fail' test in which individuals associated with a programme win or lose credibility. When an evaluation suggests that a programme falls short in achieving its goals, it should not be used to punish an individual or group. Rather, it should be used as a guide for improving the training that is offered. Evaluation should be linked to learning and the continual pursuit of quality.

Evaluation has received increased attention of late because of the recognition that training departments in modern organisations need to be held more accountable.[64] Instead of cost centres, training departments now are viewed as profit centres. Unfortunately, the field has been slow to meet this challenge. An October 1997 survey of 35 highly regarded 'benchmark' companies conducted by the American Society for Training and Development found that of the 27 companies that said they tried to promote emotional competence through training and development, more than two-thirds made no attempt to evaluate the effect of these efforts. Those that did attempt to evaluate their efforts relied primarily on measures such as reactions to training and employee opinion surveys.[65]

Good evaluation of social and emotional learning efforts has been especially rare. One reason seems to be a widespread belief that

---

63. Baldwin and Ford, 1988 *op. cit.*

64. Kraiger, K. and K.M. Jung (1997). "Linking Training Objectives to Evaluation Criteria", in M.A. Quinones and A. Ehrenstein (eds.), *Training for a Rapidly Changing Workforce: Application of Psychological Research.* Washington DC, USA: American Psychological Association. pp.151-75.

65. American Society for Training and Development, *Benchmark Survey*, Tannenbaum and Yukl, 1992 *op. cit.*, also found that few companies evaluate their training efforts, those that do rely on student evaluation sheets or anecdotes.

programmes designed to promote 'soft skills' cannot be evaluated. Although this may have been true at one time, we now have the tools necessary to conduct rigorous evaluations of most training programmes for social and emotional competence.[66]

It can be difficult to include every aspect of the ideal evaluation design in many organisations, but there are examples of evaluation studies that come close. One is a study of 11 management training programmes offered in a large pharmaceutical company.[67] The evaluators utilised pre- and post-assessments of those who went through the programmes, and these assessments included ratings of the participants' performance on the job by bosses, peers and subordinates. They also calculated the costs and benefits of the programmes. They found that three of the 11 programmes were worthless. On the other hand, five programmes had a return-on-investment ranging from 16 to 492 per cent; and one time management programme had a return-on-investment of 1,989 per cent. The four-year study cost $500,000, which was only .02 per cent of the $240 million that the company spent on training during that period. As a result of this evaluation, the company has eliminated the ineffective programmes and retained the ones that more than pay for themselves.

Another example was an evaluation of a supervisory training programme conducted in a forest products company.[68] This study used a control group and pre- and post-measures. The programme's impact on the supervisors' competence was measured through subordinate ratings and the study also assessed the programme's impact on absenteeism, turnover and productivity. The results showed first that the trained supervisors were using all of the interpersonal skills covered in the programme significantly more than did the controls during the six months following training. Second, the average daily production of the trained supervisors' employees,

66. Goldstein (1993), *op. cit.*; Spencer et al (1997), *op. cit.*

67. C. C. Morrow, M. Q Jarrett and M. T Rupinski, `An investigation of the effect and economic utility of corporate-wide training', Personnel Psychology, Vol. 50, 1997, pp. 91-119.

68. J. I. Porras and B. Anderson, 'Improving managerial effectiveness through modeling-based training', Organizational Dynamics, Vol. 9, 1981, pp. 60-77.

relative to controls, increased over 20 per cent. Third, turnover and absenteeism significantly declined among the employees of the trained supervisors, relative to the controls. The evaluation study thus provided strong evidence that the training programme had the desired effects on both supervisor competencies and the bottom line.

These two examples show that while it is not easy to evaluate social and emotional competence training programmes, it now is possible to do so with much greater rigour and precision than ever before. By making evaluation an integral part of the process, training programmes will gradually become more effective.

What are the Guidelines Worth?

Not all training programmes in social and emotional competence follow these guidelines. How much money currently is lost by training that does not follow these guidelines? We estimate that the figure is between 5.6 and 16.8 billion dollars.[69] We arrived at this estimate by starting with the commonly quoted figure of $ 50 billion spent on training each year. We then assumed that the average cost per worker for one week of training is $1,500. Dividing this figure into the $50 billion total gave us an estimate of the total number of workers trained, which is 33 million workers.

We next assumed that only a quarter of these workers receives training related to emotional competence. (The number probably is higher, but we wanted to be conservative in this estimate.) The rest receive technical and cognitive training. Thus, we estimated that adopting the guidelines should improve training for about 8 million workers.

Next we computed the economic impact of training. Several studies have suggested that on average, training improves worker performance by .4 to .6 of a standard deviation (SD).[70] To be on the

69. We are indebted to Lyle M. Spencer, Jr. for his help with this part of the research.

70. See Burke, M. and R. Day (1986). "A Cumulative Study of the Effectiveness of Managerial Training", *Jounal of Applied Psychology* 71: 232-45; Falcone, A.J., J.E. Edwards and R.R. Day (1986). *Meta-Analysis of Personnel Training Techniques for Three Populations.* Paper presented at the Annual Meeting of the Academy of Management, Chicago, Ilinois, USA; and Morrow, C.C., M.Q. Jarrett and M.T. Rupinski (1997). "An Investigation of the Effect and Economic Utility of Corporate-wide Training", *Personnel Psychology* 50: 91-119.

conservative side, we used the lowest figure, 4SD. Other research has suggested that for the average worker, an SD equals about 40 per cent of salary.[71] The average salary of an American workers is about $ 35,000. Thus the average economic impact of training currently is .4 SD x .40 x $35,000 = $5,600 per worker.

We next factored in the difference in effect size between training programmes that follow the guidelines and those that don't. We used the data from a recent study of training programmes in one large corporation, which found that programmes adhering to most of the guidelines improved the impact of training by about .3 SD over those that didn't follow the guidelines.[72] To be conservative, we then assumed that only about half the workers who are now trained (the lower half of the distribution) would do better by that amount if the guidelines were adopted. We also considered the estimated impact for weaker effect size differences of .1 and .2 SD. Thus, we estimated that if the guidelines were adopted uniformly, about 4 million workers would show an improvement of .1 to .3 SD in training impact. We then computed the total economic impact of training currently and compared it to the impact if the guidelines were adopted:

Current economic impact of training = 4 million workers x $5,600/ worker = $22.4 billion.

Impact if guidelines were followed = 4 million x $7,000 = $28 billion (assuming an improvement of .1 SD)

Difference = $28 billion - $22.4 billion = $5.6 billion.

The difference for an effect size improvement of .2 SD would be $11.2 billion, and the difference for the full .3 SD improvement would be $16.8 billion. Thus, using these figures, we estimate that American business currently is losing between $5.6 and $16.8 billion.

Conclusion

71. Hunter, J.E., F.L. Schmidt and M.K. Judiesch (1990). "Individual Differences in Output Variability as a Function of Job Complexity", *Journal of Applied Psychology* 75: 28-42.

72. Spencer, L.M. and C.C. Morrow (1996). *The Economic Value of Competence: Measuring ROI.* Paper presented at the Conference on Using Competence-Based Tools to Enhance Organizational Performance, Boston, Massachusetts, USA.

It is possible for people of all ages to become more socially and emotionally competent. However, the principles for developing this type of competence differ greatly from those that have guided much training and development practice in the past. Developing emotional competence requires that we unlearn old habits of thought, feeling and action that are deeply ingrained, and grow new ones. Such a process takes motivation, effort, time, support, and sustained practice, as the guidelines presented in this article make clear. The guidelines also suggest that the preparation and transfer-and-maintenance phases of the training process are especially important. Yet too often, these phases are neglected in practice.

Organisations increasingly are providing training and development that is explicitly labelled 'emotional intelligence' or 'emotional competence' training. However, the guidelines presented here apply to any development effort in which personal and social learning is a goal. This would include most management and executive development efforts as well as training in supervisory skills, diversity, teamwork, leadership, conflict management, stress management, sales, customer relations, etc.

Ideally, efforts to develop emotional competence would include all the elements we have identified here, but we realise that it often will not be practical to do so. Fortunately, the effect of adhering to the guidelines is multiplicative and synergistic: the more guidelines that trainers can follow, the greater and more lasting will be their impact.

If the current interest in promoting emotional intelligence at work is to be a serious, sustained effort, rather than just another management fad, it is important that practitioners try to follow guidelines based on the best available research. Only when the training is based on sound, empirically based methods will its promise be realised.

7

Yoga with Respect to Action

Skill in Action

Now a man comes and says to me, 'Swamiji, I have listened to your talks and I have decided to be a *karmayogi* from now on. I will receive everything as *prasada* of the Lord. Now I want your opinion regarding what I am planning to do. I have a neighbour who has a great deal of unaccounted money in the form of gold biscuits which he has hidden in a safe.'

'I know where the safe is, and also the combination of the lock, and I have decided to steal this gold. I have already made an underground tunnel from my house to the house of this neighbour and if I work for one more hour, I can enter the room where the safe is.'

'I am planning to carry out this operation tonight and I have decided to accept the result as *prasada*. If I get more than what I expect, that would be wonderful. If I get what I expect or less than what I expect, that would also be fine. And even if I get caught in the process, get beaten up and thrown into a prison, that would also be accepted as *prasada*:

'I have already sent my family away to a place which nobody knows and I am also planning to leave quietly as soon as this is over, so that no one will know my whereabouts. Since I am going to accept whatever result that comes as *prasada* of the Lord, can I be called a *karmayogi*?'

Lord Krishna must have expected this kind of a situation and so, defining karmayoga in terms of action, the Lord says in the *Gita*.

Yogah karmasu kausalam
Kausalam with respect to action is yoga.
(*Bhagavad Gita* II 50)

This is very important to understand. The Lord says that *kausalam* with respect to action is yoga. What is meant here by the word *kausalam*? This word is often translated as 'skill' and then this statement is translated as: skill in action is yoga. This translation is very misleading as skill means an ability to do something well. And so, according to this interpretation, all you have to do is to develop the skill in a given action, to become a *yogi*. 'But skill can be developed in any action if a person keeps doing it again and again. Even a murder can be committed skilfully such that no evidence is left behind. A bootlegger can be a very skilful person and so also a pickpocket.'

One can develop skill in talking, cooking, driving, in any action. If one keeps performing an action again and again, one develops skill in that action. In the olden days, bus conductors used to write the destination on the ticket itself. In course of time, a conductor could develop such a skill that he could write very clearly, standing in a moving crowded bus! So one can develop skill in anything.

Skill is not *yoga. A yogi* can be skilful in a given action because he is a person and so he can apply himself very well to a given task. He will be able to figure out the best method of performing a given action and so, it is likely that he would be able to perform a given action better than others. So a *karmayogi* can be skilful in performing an action, but the reverse is not necessarily true. While a yogi can be skilful, a skilful person is not necessarily a *yogi*. Therefore this man, who wants to steal gold from his neighbour, can be a skilful thief but he cannot be called a *yogi*.

People try to read into the statements of the *Gita* what they are obsessed with and so we get this kind of interpretation, namely, 'skill in action is *yoga*,' Efficiency is yoga', and so on. This is definitely born of some efficiency hang-up in the minds of people. But we must remember that the *Gita* is a scripture. It gives certain fundamental solutions to the problems of human life and that is why it has acquired the status of a scripture. It is not a handbook describing how to do things, giving simple solutions to our small silly problems. So *kausalam* has to mean something more than skill or efficiency.

Faculty of Choice

A human being possesses the faculty of choice. He has a free will and so he can choose to perform an action in whichever manner he likes. This is why Lord Krishna says: *Karmani eva to adhikarah*—you have a choice, a freedom in performance of an action. "When there is a freedom of choice, the choice can be right or wrong where right and wrong are determined with respect to an order. A thing becomes right or wrong when there is an order. Suppose all the traffic laws are withdrawn, then everybody is right. Driving one way becomes right or wrong when there are traffic laws. When I have a faculty of choice, I must have some norms for carrying out interactions with others around because I am born related to the world. Since I am related to the world, I have to interact with the world and such interactions should be governed by some common norms so that people are able to relate properly with one another. A response is proper when it is in keeping with the common norms. And these norms must be universally known.

If I am born with a faculty of choice, and I have no way of determining what is right and what is wrong in a given situation, that would be a defect in creation. It is like giving a person a sports car without brakes! A car without brakes is a manufacturing defect and similarly, a faculty of choice without the knowledge of the norms would be a defect in creation. Animals do not require any education with respect to the norms because that knowledge is built into them as instinct. A cow need not be told to be a vegetarian because it is vegetarian by its nature. A baby monkey tightly holds on to its mother when the mother is jumping from one branch to another, because the baby instinctively knows that loosening the hold means falling down and hurting itself.

This is the knowledge, not born of any education, because if it is gained through education, there will be some monkeys who would miss that education, and would be deprived of this knowledge which is very essential for survival. That would be a defect in creation. But that is not the case because a monkey instinctively knows how to survive. This is true of all living beings other than human beings, because they are not endowed with a faculty of choice. So, a cow is vegetarian instinctively. It will not eat a man. But a man can eat a cow! He has a faculty of choice and so he can be a herbivore or a carnivore or a multivore. Thus, when I am born with a faculty of choice, I must have some norms to go by in conducting myself. These norms, the universal order is called *dharma*.

Is *Dharma* Subjective?

There is a tendency these days to dismiss *dharma* as something that is purely subjective, something personal. But is that so?

If you like a particular flower, a particular fruit, that can be subjective because people have their individual likings and what is liked by one may not be liked by another. If a group of people share certain preferences, that may be cultural. People, living for a length of time in a certain area may develop certain common values and that is cultural. Thus people of Gujarat may like a certain type of cooking while people of Orissa may like an altogether different kind of cooking. In Gujarat they use groundnut oil in cooking while in Orissa, they use mustard oil. A person from one state may not like what a person from another state likes, and *vice versa*. There is nothing right or wrong about it. People are different, their choices are different and that difference is beautiful. But is *dharma* given to individual tastes and choices?

If I ask you whether you like to get hurt, physically or Mentally by another person, I am sure your answer will be: 'No'. And the answer will be the same if I ask that question to a member of the tribe living in the Andamans. If this question was placed before a person a thousand years ago, the answer would have been the same. Because no one likes to get hurt. Do you like to be lied to? Even a liar does not want someone else to lie to him. Do you like to be cheated? Even a thief does not want to be cheated by another one. Do you like to be hated by another one? Do you like to be an object of someone else's anger or jealousy? Do you like to be deceived? The answer to all these questions is going to be 'No'. There is no exception.

Now if I ask you: Do you like it that someone should share one's things when you are in need? That others should be friendly, sympathetic, understanding, accommodative towards you? The answer will be 'Yes'. There is no exception here, either.

When you want others to behave with you in a given manner, what kind of behaviour do you think others expect from you? Do you think the other person would want to get hurt by you? You figure that out. You know it very well that the other person does not want to get hurt by you, does not want to be lied to or hated by you.

Everyone is absolutely ethical as far as the behaviour of others towards him or her is concerned. We wish that even mosquitoes should not hurt us. Everyone is quite clear as to how the world should treat him or her. And everyone knows equally well as to what the world expects from him or her. Every thief knows that no one in the world wants to get his or her property stolen by another. No thief can say that he did not know this, because otherwise he would not use the cover of the night; he would simply walk into someone's house in broad daylight, pick up things and walk away. But that does not happen. That means that a thief also knows that people do not want to get their things stolen.

This only proves that these norms are not subjective; they are universal and therefore known to everyone. If these norms had to be learnt through a process of education, there would be some who would not be able to get that education. In that case, there would be some people who would love to be hurt, others who would like their property to be stolen, some others who would love to be ridiculed and yet others who would love to be objects of hatred and jealousy. But we do not find this in anyone, whether the person is educated or not.

Dharma is Universal Order

If you go to the Andamans where there is a tribe with some habits of the Stone Age and try to steal their property, I am sure you will get arrows shot at you! You go to any part of the world, even its remotest corners, and inquire, you will find that no one wants to get hurt, no one wants to be lied to, deceived or cheated. No one requires education in this regard. Everyone knows how others should treat him or her. Just as a monkey knows, without being taught by anyone, that it should not fall down because it hurts, so also the human being has a sense of this order, which one cannot go against without having to pay a price for it. One has to operate within the law if one does not want to get nabbed by it. It is an order sensed by common sense which is given to all of us. Everyone has the common sense of this order, which is like any other order in creation.

We find a variety of laws in the universe because of which things keep going. Even my physical body has all the disciplines of knowledge in it. There is, in the body, chemistry, biochemistry, electrochemistry, engineering, etc. When there is a fracture, they join the bones by bolts and nuts, just as they join pieces of metal. They are able to do all this because it can be done. Why can it be done? Because there is knowledge, because the body behaves in a certain manner, in accordance with certain laws. Hence a discipline of knowledge is nothing but an understanding of certain principles which already exist. This is what we call order. Therefore, there is always a possibility of disorder. There can be something wrong only when there is something right. And we all sense this order with our common sense. I will call it a moral order. You cannot plead ignorance of this order because you know exactly what you expect from others and you also know what they expect from you in general. This is what we call a universal order which we interpret in a given situation.

Hence your understanding, your assimilation counts here because interpretation of an order requires more knowledge than merely the knowledge of the order. Understanding of a law is one thing but much more knowledge is required to interpret that law. You have to think. The *Ramayana* and the *Mahabharata* present situations in which the moral order is interpreted dynamically. But first you should know that there is an order which you sense without being taught.

If I sense this order and want others to behave in conformity with it, then how come I ignore the order when it comes to my behaviour? Why do I deceive someone? Why do I cheat? Why do I lie? Why do I hurt someone? Because it takes a certain maturity, an understanding to conform to the values. It is because of a certain gain or a fear of loss that a person compromises, goes against the order which he or she knows exists. The order does not seem to matter when there is some gain or when a loss is to be avoided. That means, what a person gains by compromising the order is more valuable than the order. Hence, the basis for compromise is nothing but the priority of values, the importance or hierarchy of values.

When we have our likes and dislikes, we employ certain means to fulfil them. The question is: Do the means conform to the order or do they go against it? We should know this. If we are carried away by our likes and dislikes without considering the universal order, we have a problem of priorities. This is nothing but immaturity.

You are the Loser When You Compromise

Suppose you tell a lie to a friend and in the process, make some quick money. Let us say there is a house which you have bought for the purpose of investment. Now a friend of yours wants to buy it from you because it is convenient for him to live there. He offers to pay you 20 percent more than what you have paid for the house. Here is an opportunity for you to jack up the price because your friend trusts you and would pay whatever price you declare. So you tell a lie. You jack up the price and thus get ₹20,000 more than what is fairly due to you. Perhaps, ₹20,000 is valuable to you and speaking truth is not as valuable. This is the problem of priorities.

Money occupies a higher rank in the ladder of priorities. You have, no doubt, a value both for truth and money. You have a value for truth because you expect others to speak truth to you, but your value for speaking the truth is subservient to your value for money. This can be either right or wrong. You should have the maturity to understand whether this action is right or not.

There is a universal value and it is common to everyone of us. Like the law of gravity, *dharma* is also an order not created by anyone of us, but only commonly sensed by everyone without requiring any education. Hence your behaviour must necessarily conform to that order. If you go against the order, you get hurt in the process, which means that you end up being a loser. People think they are gainers or winners when they compromise the law, when they cheat someone. They generally say that business is business and religion is religion, and that the two should not be mixed up. They say that it is impossible these days to follow ethics in business.

If I go against this order, *dharma*, I must necessarily be a loser. A value can be called a value only if it has an intrinsic worth. If it is a value, I must be a loser when I compromise it, and if I am a loser, I must know it. Otherwise I am immature. I think I can get away by telling a lie when some gain is involved in terms of money, power, name, fame, better image, etc. People often tell lies when it comes to their age, income, qualifications, etc. While telling a lie, one thinks that one gains more than one loses. Thus, in the case of getting an extra ₹20,000 by telling a lie, you think that you are a gainer. A sum of ₹20,000 makes a lot of difference in your life and, therefore, money is more valuable to you than truth. This is where maturity is required. Common sense is not enough. We have to discover the value of a value.

Let us analyse as to what happens to a man who compromises truth for the sake of money. There must arise a conflict in his mind when he tells a lie because he knows what the truth is. What he knows is one thing and what he says is another. So there are two persons now: the knower I and the doer I. You know there are some who cover the wrinkles on their face with cosmetics, because they cannot accept their face with wrinkles. Here is a woman who has wrinkles on her face and she has covered them before going to a dinner. This cosmetic can cover the wrinkles for two hours. So this woman pulls out a mirror from her purse every 15 minutes to see if the wrinkles are still covered or not. She can cover the wrinkles all right but who can cover her knowledge of her wrinkles? You cannot cover the knowledge of what there is. You can cover it from others but you know it within yourself. This is what makes a Ravana out of a person.

As you know, Ravana had ten heads and each head thought differently. This is an imaginative depiction of sage Valmiki, of a man in conflict. A person becomes a split personality. This is an emotional problem. The one who thinks also is I and the one who acts also is I. There is only one I who is capable of acting in many ways. There is no distance at all between the knower and the doer. The knower protests against the actor but the actor shuts him up. This distance between I and I is not an ordinary distance. It is self destruction.

After all, why do you tell a lie? Because you want money. And you want money so you can buy things. And you want things so you can enjoy them. Hence, you tell a lie for your sake, for your enjoyment and not for the sake of money or things. But who can enjoy? The one who is together (one) as a person can enjoy things. With money, you can get the best of musicians to sing for you, but you will fall asleep while listening! Money can get you the music, but it cannot make you read. Books will adorn your shelves, and will perhaps be read by your friends and ultimately get lost! You cannot make more joy out of things than you are capable of. What can you enjoy when you are a split person? You cannot fulfil your resolves also because the one who makes resolves is different from the one who has to implement them.

You decide to get up at 5 o'clock in the morning. You set the alarm at night but when it rings in the morning you turn it off and go to sleep again. Why? Because the one who decided to get up early did not consult the one who actually had to get up. There is a split between the resolver and doer. You cannot have a self opinion about yourself because you are a split person. There cannot be a greater damage to the personality than this, that you cannot live up to your own resolves. Thus, a small lie destroys the person.

What kind of a bargain is this? You tell a lie for the sake of the money so you can enjoy life. But what is the use of money if you lose yourself in the process? Money can provide situations and opportunities, but who is the one to enjoy these things given to you? You. And that you is a split you, a splintered you. You cannot even enjoy gross things in life, let alone the profound and the beautiful which money can neither buy nor can make you see or enjoy.

The sight of stars does not cost money. In fact, things profound and beautiful do not cost anything. All that is required is you, a complete you. A person who is together is a complete person, and that person can learn and enjoy the world even without money. You may possess just a *kaupina* (loin-cloth), but you can still be happy. Who can deny you the cool breeze? Who can deny you the beauty of a flower? Who can deny you the birds? The whole of creation is bright and colourful. Who can deny you that? Or, who can deny you yourself? You do not even require the world, for being happy. All that is required is just yourself. The breath in your nostrils is good enough to make you feel full and complete. But in the process of acquiring money for your enjoyment, you have lost yourself, the very enjoyer. What a bargain! No one will go for such a bargain unless one is totally immature. Thus, you are the loser, every time you go against the order.

***Dharma* is *Kausalam* (Skill)**

When you go against the universal order, you certainly get hurt in the process. It is like rubbing against a margosa tree; you get scratched all over the body. When you rub against the order that is *dharma*, you get scratched in the process. You are mature to the extent you understand this and therefore Lord Krsna tells Arjuna in the *Bhagavad Gita* not to come under the sway of likes and dislikes. You may have likes and dislikes with reference to the means, but if your likes and dislikes go against the law of *dharma*, do not submit to them. Conform to the law of *dharma*. Likes and dislikes are your enemies. It is better to die than submit to them, if they are against *dharma*.

Go back to our friend who wants to rob his neighbour. We have to ask him: Do you like to be robbed by your neighbour? Are you going to approve of someone stealing your property? If not, that means there is an order. Respect that order. You are the gainer when you do that; you certainly will not lose.

We think that by following *dharma*, we are doing a favour, we are contributing to society. Not at all. If you think you are a good person who does not harm anyone, you are only doing a favour to yourself, not to the society or to the Lord or to anyone else. You are the gainer in the bargain. It is nothing but a part of your maturity. It is only your determination to conform to the law of *dharma*, knowing fully well that you are the gainer in the process, and that going against the order is only going to create problems for yourself.

This is what is meant by *kausalam* in the statement: Yogab *karmasu kausalam*. The difference about what is to be done and should be avoided in a given situation is *kausalam*. This is what should be done by me under this situation,'—that is *kausalam*. It makes me *kusala*, a *karmayogi*.

Our friend, who wants to rob his neighbour is not a *karmayogi*. It is not enough that I have *prasada*-buddhi with reference to the result of the action, but I should conform to the order of *dharma* while performing action. This *dharma* is not created by me. It is part of the creation of the Lord, and therefore *dharma* also is *isvara*. That is why you feel happy whenever you do something right because you are in contact with the Lord. I am in tune with the Lord whenever I perform an action in conformity with *dharma*. This is the ecology, the harmony of karma. I refrain from doing anything that disturbs the karmic ecology. Whatever I do is in conformity with the cosmic order, it is in order with the order where there is *dharma*, there is order, it is in order with the order. Where there is *dharma*, there is order, that psychological order relates to the *karta*, the performer of action.

Whether Lord Rama existed in human form or not, as far as I am concerned, He is the Lord because He is *dharma*. *Ramo virgrahavan dharmah*—Rama is the embodiment of *dharma*. It is *dharma* that has appeared with hands and legs and that is walking because you worship *dharma* as the Lord. There we invoke the Lord in the form of *dharma*. For us, Sri Rama need not have existed historically, but He is *isvara*, the *dharma*.

Worship the Lord by Your Actions

Dharma has entered into our psyche. If you have read or heard the Ramayana, you know what it takes to be a brother, a father, a husband, a wife and so on. And the Ramayana also presents before us what it takes to be a *raksasa*, a demon. So, we do not look upon *dharma* as something separate from the Lord; we do not say you reach the Lord through *dharma*—*dharma* itself is the Lord. Therefore, we invoke the Lord whenever we follow *dharma*. This is the Vedic vision of human life and the world. This vision is beautifully expressed in the following verse of the *Bhagavad Gita*.

Yatab pravrttibhutanam yena sarvamidam tatam
Svakarmana tamabhyarcya siddhim vindati manavah

[A human being achieves success (siddhi) by worshipping, through his own duty (svakarma), Him from Whom is this entire elemental creation, and by Whom is all this pervaded.]

(*Bhagavad Gita* XVIII 46)

By worshipping the Lord with *svakarma*, by action in keeping with the order, one gains *siddhi*, success. *Siddhi* is a beautiful word. We generally understand *siddhi* to mean some unusual power or some miracle, but here it means *karya-siddhi*, success in action.

Here, the Lord is presented not only as the author of creation but also as the one who pervades the entire creation. Just as a pot is pervaded by clay, its material cause, so also is the creation pervaded by the Lord. The entire creation, including this physical body, is pervaded by the Lord. One has to worship the Lord by *svakarma*. Whatever should be done in a given situation, in keeping with the law of *dharma*, is called *svakarma*, one's duty. In every situation, whether digging ditches, or driving a car or working in an office, you are required to function in a given manner. Generally what is to be done in a given situation is obvious. If this obvious action is performed, it becomes worship of the Lord.

It is not that the Lord has created this world and then retired. Creation is going on constantly. Even though Lord Visnu is presented as lying on a serpent bed in *yoga-nidra*, he is performing his task of maintaining the order in creation. Things take place by His very presence; no particular effort has to be made by Him and therefore, He is presented as lying on a serpent-bed. New is constantly being created since the old is being replaced by the new. We find things constantly changing and what is gone does not come back. There is a process of destruction and creation. There cannot be creation of the new unless the destruction of the old takes place simultaneously. A new second cannot be born unless the old second is gone. There cannot be a world without this element of kala, time and the nature of time itself is the past, present and future. Hence all the three deities, Brahma, Visnu and Rudra are working simultaneously.

Everything in creation functions according to its nature. A mango tree gives only mango fruits, not lemons! The trees breathe in carbon dioxide and breathe out oxygen. The behaviour of every element in creation is predictable according to set rules. Everything functions in conformity with the universal order and thus everything participates in the great *yajna*, the cosmic ecology. Every plant participates, every animal participates. They have the necessary instinct and behave in accordance with a set order.

I am also a participant in this *yajna* of creation. I am not intended to be a mere witness. I need not have been given the organs of action such as hands and legs, if I had been intended to be a mere witness, rather than a participant. So, as a human being I am also a participant in this cosmic ecology. I have been given a free will and a faculty of choice. Since I am given the freedom to choose, I must necessarily know what I am expected to do in the *yajna* of creation.

Lord Krishna says: "Worship the Lord by your action performed in keeping with the norm." Such instruction is not necessary for animals or other living beings because they are programmed to function in accordance with the order. But the human being has to figure out what is expected of him in a given situation at a given time and place, and for that he must have the knowledge of the norms on the basis of which he can choose his actions. This basis or the order is the cosmic order, the moral order based on free will. A cow does not require a scripture such as the *Gita* because every cow is ethical. There is no immoral cow. Even carnivorous animals do not deprive other creatures by hoarding. They appear to be free from greed. A mother animal may save for its young ones, but it does it within limits, whereas a human being wants to save not only for his children but for his grandchildren too! Thus, a human being can deprive others of their rights and requirements.

Animals and other beings instinctively follow the cosmic order and so their behaviour is predictable. When you come home, you can be sure that your dog will greet you wagging its tail, because you are its master. But if a man comes to you with a smiling face and shakes hands with you, you can never be sure that he is a friend; it is quite possible that a moment after shaking hands with you, he can pull out a gun and shoot you.

Do What Should be Done

No one can deny the knowledge of what is right and what is wrong. Everyone knows that he or she does not want to get hurt by others. This universal law is not produced by man. It is the creation of the Lord and it is not apart from the Lord. That is why we feel good whenever we do something good. Hence, one should follow the order. The end should not justify the means; the means must be in keeping with *dharma*, the order.

Some people feel that anything is justified for the sake of their ideal. There are even some devotees of the Lord who feel that anything is justified for the sake of the Lord. One such devotee was caught pushing drugs! When asked why he was doing such a thing, he replied that he was doing it for the sake of the Lord! After all, a drug addict is going to get his supply from somewhere and so, he may as well get it from me, so that the money can go to the Lord's work!' There was another incident in which some devotees were caught stealing flowers from someone's garden. Valuable roses were being regularly stolen and so the owner decided to find out who the thief was. Early morning next day, he found a group of people stealthily plucking the roses. One of them was caught and presented before a magistrate.

When asked why he was plucking the flowers from someone else's garden, the devotee replied, 'Because the flowers belong to the Lord'. 'But why should you pluck them?' `Because I want to offer them to the Lord!' `In that case you should buy the flowers and then offer them to the Lord. Why should you steal?' Actually, the culprits steal the flowers, present them to people waiting at bus stops, railway stations, etc., and having invoked their sentiments, sell them books and articles! It is dangerous when the end justifies the means.

The means should justify the end and not the other way around. Sometimes you are required to do things that are not in keeping with your likes and dislikes, but it has to be done in keeping with *dharma*. That is why the Lord says in the *Gita* that one should not come under the sway of one's likes and dislikes. *Dharma* should govern one's choice of actions and not one's likes and dislikes.

Suppose you are going for a business dinner. You have dressed carefully because this dinner is important to you. You are going to meet some people from whom you expect good business. Now, as you are walking on the road, an old man, just walking ahead of you slips and falls into a roadside ditch, full of mud. The old man cries out for help. You think: 'Well, if I help him, my clothes will be ruined and I will not be able to attend the dinner. So let me leave him to his fate. If he is lucky, someone will come along and help him.' And you walk away, leaving that man in the ditch. You have justified your action because of your priorities and thus, have not done what should have been done by you. You should have offered your helping hand to that man and taken care to save your clothes too. Even if your clothes got spoiled, you could have attended the dinner and explained the situation to the people there. If you had fallen down, you would have expected the other man to help and so helping in such a situation is *dharma*. You have violated the order of *dharma* and that is going to create a conflict in your mind. There is always a conflict whenever you go against *dharma*.

That you have likes and dislikes is not a problem. There is a problem only when you allow them to govern you. There is no problem if you allow yourself to be governed by *dharma*, if you surrender your will to *dharma*. That is what is called surrender. Surrender is not an action, it is *bhavana*, a condition of the mind. And this surrender is for our own growth, for our own maturity: If what you have to do in a given situation is not in keeping with your likes, bring your discretion into play and do what is right.

You become a participant in the cosmic yajna when your action is in conformity with *dharma*, with what is proper in a given situation. A great yajna is going on and you do what is to be done and avoid what should not be done. This order itself is the Lord and that is yoga. Conformity to *dharma* brings about a harmony in life; the mind remains free from conflicts, free from regrets. Do what is to be done—cross all the t's and dot all the i's. That is what we call yoga, the life of *dharma*.

Dharma Calls for Interpretation

Thus, *kausalam* with reference to action is conformity with the order of *dharma*. This conformity requires knowledge of *dharma* as well as an ability to interpret *dharma* in a given situation. Hence *kausalam* also involves an expertise in interpretation because *dharma* is law and no law is absolute. Every law has to be interpreted, taking into account the conditions existing in a given situation.

Let us take the example of this mandate: *Satyam vada*—speak truth. It often happens that the manner in which truth is spoken creates displeasure. So the mandate is qualified by saying: *Pryam vada*—speak what is pleasant. May you speak truth that is pleasant also. Further, what we say may be true, and may be pleasant also, but it may not serve any purpose. So it is said: *Hitam vada*—speak what is beneficial. May you speak truth that is pleasant and beneficial too.

Suppose a man comes to you seeking protection, saying, `I am being chased by another man, my life is in danger. Please give me protection.' You let the man inside the house and ask him to hide behind a cupboard. A little later, another man comes along, looking for the first man and wants to know if anyone had come here asking for protection. Now, what will you do? Will you speak truth and hand over the hiding man to this attacker or will you pose as being ignorant? If you speak the truth, the other man will surely lose his life, and therefore, either you have to tell a lie and declare yourself ignorant or, if you want to speak the truth, you have to assert that the attacker cannot go in unless he first kills you. Thus, this situation calls for an interpretation of the mandate of speaking the truth because one must speak the truth that is also beneficial at the same time.

We should know that no mandate is absolute. If mandates are absolute, nobody can conform to them. Every law has to be interpreted and there is nothing wrong in interpretation. Take the case of the law of gravity. Here on earth, a flower when dropped from the hand goes down, but that is not so in a spaceship. There it may continue to hang in the air or may go sideways. Thus, every law has to be interpreted. That is why we are taught *dharma* through the stories of the *Ramayana* and the *Mahabharata*. A number of situations are created and the mandates of *dharma* interpreted. Thus even today, we question whether it was proper for Lord Rama to strike Vali from behind or was it proper for Arjuna to kill Karna when the latter was without arms. Karna pleaded with Arjuna to spare him because he was unarmed. Lord Krsna asked Arjuna to strike Karna because he was not unarmed, he was disarmed! There is a lot of difference between being unarmed and being disarmed.

Thus, every situation calls for an interpretation of the law. The *Gita* itself is an interpretation of certain cosmic laws. Therefore, you have to interpret all the time, but when you interpret, be sure that you are not benefiting at the cost of someone else, because there is a general tendency to interpret a law in one's own favour.

Take the case of a doctor trying to fulfil the mandate of speaking the truth. Here is a patient who has just been operated upon to determine whether the tumour is malignant or not. The reports have come and the tumour has been detected as malignant. The patient asks the doctor as to what the reports have to say. What will the doctor tell him? If the doctor feels that the patient is not ready to face the truth, he will quietly declare that the reports indicate that the tumour is not malignant. Not only will he tell a lie but ask that the family members and the friends of the patient should also do the same. Perhaps later on, when the patient will be ready, the truth would be revealed to him. Would you say that the doctor is going against *dharma*? I would not say that because in this case the interpretation of *dharma* is not for the personal benefit of the doctor; it is for the benefit of the patient. So this is not telling a lie, it is managing the situation. Therefore *dharma* is not rigid, it is dynamic, and has to be interpreted. This capacity to interpret *dharma* is also a part of *kausalam*.

Conformity to *Dharma* is Maturity

So, *yoga* is not skill in action. It is the right attitude on your part which enables you to choose the action properly in keeping the *dharma*. You have to set aside your personal likes and dislikes and follow the order of *dharma*. If *dharma* in a particular situation is in agreement with your likes and dislikes, there is no problem. Your action will be spontaneous. It is like this fellow who was told by the doctor to eat plenty of karela (bitter gourd) because his blood test revealed a high level of sugar. Now this man loved karela but hardly had a chance to eat it because his wife did not like it and so avoided cooking it. But now, after the direction from the doctor, he could eat karela every day! Thus, if what you have to do in a given situation is what you like to do, there is no need for deliberation. But, if what you have to do is one thing and what you like to do is something quite different, then you have to be deliberate.

That is where *yoga* comes into play. There is some pain involved when you have to do something against your wish, but there is some joy also involved in it because you are able to conform to *dharma* and this conformity is the life of maturity. Everyone has to grow into that. In the course of time, the person is freed from the hold of likes and dislikes and his or her actions start becoming spontaneous. Conformity to *dharma* is emotional maturity.

Emotional Competence Framework

This generic competence framework distils findings from MOSAIC *Competencies for Professional and Administrative Occupations*.

Self-Awareness

- Emotional awareness
- Recognising one's emotions and their effects. People with this competence:
    - Know which emotions they are feeling and why
    - Realise the links between their feelings and what they think, do and say
    - Recognise how their feelings affect their performance
    - Have a guiding awareness of their values and goals.

Accurate Self-assessment

- Knowing one's strengths and limits. People with this competence are:
    - Aware of their strengths and weaknesses
    - Reflective, learning from experience

    - Open to candid feedback, new perspectives, continuous learning and self-development
    - Able to show a sense of humour and perspective about themselves.

Self-confidence

- Sureness about one's self-worth and capabilities. People with this competence:
    - Present themselves with self-assurance; have 'presence'
    - Can voice views that are unpopular and go out on a limb for what is right
    - Are decisive, able to make sound decisions despite uncertainties and pressures
    - Self-regulation.

Self-control

- Managing disruptive emotions and impulses. People with this competence:
    - Manage their impulsive feelings and distressing emotions well
    - Stay composed, positive and unflappable even in trying moments
    - Think clearly and stay focused under pressure.

Trustworthiness

- Maintaining standards of honesty and integrity. People with this competence:
    - Act ethically and are above reproach
    - Build trust through their reliability and authenticity
    - Admit their own mistakes and confront unethical actions in others
    - Take tough, principled stands even if they are unpopular.

Conscientiousness

- Taking responsibility for personal performance. People with this competence:
  - Meet commitments and keep promises
  - Hold themselves accountable for meeting their objectives
  - Are organised and careful in their work.

Adaptability

- Flexibility in handling change. People with this competence:
  - Smoothly handle multiple demands, shifting priorities and rapid change
  - Adapt their responses and tactics to fit fluid circumstances
  - Are flexible in how they see events.

Innovativeness

- Being comfortable with and open to novel ideas and new information. People with this competence:
  - Seek out fresh ideas from a wide variety of sources
  - Entertain original solutions to problems
  - Generate new ideas
  - Take fresh perspectives and risks in their thinking.

Self-Motivation

Achievement Drive

- Striving to improve or meet a standard of excellence. People with this competence:
  - Are result-oriented, with a high drive to meet their objectives and standards
  - Set challenging goals and take calculated risks
  - Pursue information to reduce uncertainty and find ways to do better
  - Learn how to improve their performance.

Commitment

- Aligning with the goals of the group or organisation. People with this competence:
  - Readily make personal or group sacrifices to meet a larger organisational goal
  - Find a sense of purpose in the larger mission
  - Use the group's core values in making decisions and clarifying choices
  - Actively seek out opportunities to fulfil the group's mission.

Initiative

- Readiness to act on opportunities. People with this competence:
  - Are ready to seize opportunities
  - Pursue goals beyond what's required or expected of them
  - Cut through red tape and bend the rules when necessary to get the job done
  - Mobilise others through unusual, enterprising efforts.

Optimism

- Persistence in pursuing goals despite obstacles and setbacks. People with this competence:
  - Persist in seeking goals despite obstacles and setbacks
  - Operate from hope of success rather than fear of failure
  - See setbacks as due to manageable circumstances rather than a personal flaw.

Social Competence

Social Awareness: Empathy

- Sensing others' feelings and perspective, and taking an active interest in their concerns. People with this competence:
  - Are attentive to emotional cues and listen well
  - Show sensitivity and understand others' perspectives

- Help out based on understanding other people's needs and feelings.

Service Orientation

- Anticipating, recognising and meeting customers' needs. People with this competence:
  - Understand customers' needs and match them to services or products
  - Seek ways to increase customers' satisfaction and loyalty
  - Gladly offer appropriate assistance
  - Grasp a customer's perspective, acting as a trusted advisor.

Developing Others

- Sensing what others need in order to develop and bolstering their abilities. People with this competence:
  - Acknowledge and reward people's strengths, accomplishments and development
  - Offer useful feedback and identify people's needs for development
  - Mentor, give timely coaching and offer assignments that challenge and grow a person's skill.

Leveraging Diversity

- Cultivating opportunities through diverse people. People with this competence:
  - Respect and relate well to people from varied backgrounds
  - Understand diverse world views and are sensitive to group differences
  - See diversity as opportunity, creating an environment where diverse people can thrive
  - Challenge bias and intolerance.

Political Awareness

- Reading a group's emotional currents and power relationships. People with this competence:
  - Accurately read key power relationships
  - Detect crucial social networks
  - Understand the forces that shape views and actions of clients, customers or competitors
  - Accurately read situations and organisational and external realities.

Social Skills

Influence

- Wielding effective tactics for persuasion. People with this competence:
  - Are skilled at persuasion
  - Fine-tune presentations to appeal to the listener
  - Use complex strategies like indirect influence to build consensus and support
  - Orchestrate dramatic events to effectively make a point.

Communication

- Sending clear and convincing messages. People with this competence:
  - Are effective in give-and-take, registering emotional cues in attuning their message
  - Deal with difficult issues straightforwardly
  - Listen well, seek mutual understanding and welcome sharing of information fully
  - Foster open communication and stay receptive to bad news as well as good.

Leadership

- Inspiring and guiding groups and people. People with this competence:

- Articulate and arouse enthusiasm for a shared vision and mission
- Step forward to lead as needed, regardless of position
- Guide the performance of others while holding them accountable
- Lead by example.

Change Catalyst

- Initiating or managing change. People with this competence:
  - Recognise the need for change and remove barriers
  - Challenge the status quo to acknowledge the need for change
  - Champion the change and enlist others in its pursuit
  - Model the change expected of others.

Conflict Management

- Negotiating and resolving disagreements. People with this competence:
  - Handle difficult people and tense situations with diplomacy and tact
  - Spot potential conflict, bring disagreements into the open and help de-escalate
  - Encourage debate and open discussion
  - Orchestrate win-win solutions.

Building Bonds

- Nurturing instrumental relationships. People with this competence:
  - Cultivate and maintain extensive informal networks
  - Seek out relationships that are mutually beneficial
  - Build rapport and keep others in the loop
  - Make and maintain personal friendships among work associates.

Collaboration and Cooperation

- Working with others towards shared goals. People with this competence:
  - Balance a focus on task with attention to relationships
  - Collaborate, share plans, information and resources
  - Promote a friendly, cooperative climate
  - Spot and nurture opportunities for collaboration.

Team Capabilities

- Creating group synergy in pursuing collective goals. People with this competence:
  - Model team qualities like respect, helpfulness and cooperation
  - Draw all members into active and enthusiastic participation
  - Build team identity, esprit de corps, and commitment
  - Protect the group and its reputation; share credit.

Section 2

8

Spiritual Intelligence

Spirituality exists in the hearts and minds of men and women everywhere, within religious traditions and independently of tradition. If, following theologian Paul Tillich, we define spirituality as the domain of ultimate concern, then everyone is spiritual because everyone has ultimate concerns. However, the term 'ultimate concern' can be interpreted in many different ways. Some people do not consider themselves or their concerns to be spiritual. Spirituality, like emotion, has varying degrees of depth and expression. It may be conscious or unconscious, developed or undeveloped, healthy or pathological, naive or sophisticated, beneficial or dangerously distorted.

Some current definitions of spirituality can be summarised as follows:

(a) Spirituality involves the highest levels of any of the developmental lines, for example, cognitive, moral, emotional and interpersonal;

(b) Spirituality is itself a separate developmental line;

(c) Spirituality is an attitude (such as openness to love) at any stage; and

(d) Spirituality involves peak experiences, not stages.

An integral perspective would presumably include all these different views, and others as well.

Spirituality may also be described in terms of ultimate belonging or connection to the transcendental ground of being. Some people define spirituality in terms of relationship to God, to fellow humans or to the earth. Others define it in terms of devotion and commitment to a particular faith or form of practice.

To understand how spirituality can contribute to the good life, defined in humanistic terms as living authentically the full possibilities of being human, it seems necessary to differentiate healthy spirituality from beliefs and practices that may be detrimental to well-being. This leads to the challenge of defining and cultivating spiritual intelligence.

Spiritual Intelligence: the Vital Part of Leadership

Research is finally validating what many of us knew all along—that there is more to great leaders than brains. What research is now validating is that great leaders use their hearts and souls, as well as their minds! But let's begin at the beginning.

In 1905, Alfred Binet and Theodore Simon developed the first modern intelligence test. Since that time we have been debating what 'intelligence' is, where it comes from and how to develop it.

Our 'Intelligence Quotient' or 'IQ' is generally thought of as our linear, analytical intelligence. Initially it was expected that IQ would be a strong predictor of success in careers. In fact it has turned out to be a weak predictor of success. IQ appears to be related to minimum standards to enter a given profession. But once you have chosen your career, what actually leads to success is far more complicated.

Daniel Goleman popularised the phrase 'Emotional Intelligence' with the publication of his book by the same title in 1995. In his book, Goleman cites research at Bell Labs that examined star performers and tried to determine what distinguished them from more average performers.

It appeared that star performers had stronger relationship skills than average performers. The Harvard Business Review published the results of the Bell Labs study in 1993. Business interest in the study of 'Emotional Intelligence' or `EQ' began in earnest.

Emotional Quotient (EQ) is actually a large collection of skills. Goleman has recently grouped these skills into four quadrants as shown below.

1. Self-Awareness

- Emotional self-awareness

- Accurate self-assessment
- Self-confidence

2. Other awareness

- Empathy
- Organisational awareness
- Service orientation

3. Self-management

- Self-control
- Trustworthiness
- Conscientiousness
- Adaptability
- Achievement orientation
- Initiative

4. Social Skills

- Teamwork and collaboration
- Developing others
- Influence
- Communication
- Leadership
- Conflict management

There is a fascinating relationship among these quadrants. Research shows that EQ begins in the Self-Awareness quadrant. The degree to which we are self-aware literally limits our ability to be aware of others or to manage ourselves. The last skills to develop are our social skills, being dependent on the other three quadrants. Self-awareness is dependent on listening to feedback. So a willingness to truly hear others is a prerequisite for high EQ.

It is interesting that Socrates gave the advice 'Know Thyself' approximately 2,400 years ago. Buddha (roughly 2,500 years ago) made the study of the mind (profound self-knowledge) such an elevated practice that it became a major world religion.

So what is the link to Spiritual Intelligence? Dana Zohar, a quantum physicist, gave a lecture at the Science and Consciousness conference in Albuquerque, New Mexico in April 2001. She was working on a new book on Spiritual Intelligence (or 'SQ'), and at that time, listed nine characteristics of SQ. The first of Zohar's points directly echoes the first quadrant of EQ-Self-Awareness, but goes beyond it to a sense of connection to the universe.

Spiritual Intelligence, according to Zohar, is:

1. *Self-Awareness*
   You know who you really are and you know that you are connected with the whole universe.
2. *Vision and Values-Led or Idealism*
   Children naturally want to serve and so do we. Vision and values-led is definitive of our humanity.
3. *Capacity to Face and Use Adversity*
   Owning up to our mistakes and adversity and using pain and tragedy to learn.
4. *To be Holistic*
   Seeing the connections between things. Being open to and interested in everything.
5. *Diversity*
   Thriving in and celebrating diversity. I look at you and see what is different in you and I say 'Thank God for that!'.
6. *Field Independence (Courage)*
   A term from psychology that means the courage not to adapt but to be independent.
7. *Tendency to Ask Why?*
   Questions are infinite. In Quantum Physics questions create reality.
8. *Ability to Reframe*
   Put things into a larger context of meaning.
9. *Spontaneity*
   This is not acting on a whim; it comes from the same Latin roots as response and responsibility. It is not conditioned by fear. It is appropriately 'responsive to' the world.

Jim Collins became famous in the world of business with the publication of his first book, *Built to Last: Successful Habits of Visionary Companies* (HarperCollins, 1994) co-authored with James Porras. In it, they described their in-depth research and their conclusions regarding 18 companies that were unique in their reputation in their industry, their resilience through hard times and their financial success over 50+ years. The central conclusion: truly great companies are Visionary and Values driven. This directly echoes Dr. Zohar's second characteristic of SQ.

In his latest book, Good to Great: *Why Some Companies Make the Leap and Others Don't* (HarperCollins, 2001), Jim Collins researched 11 companies that had made the transition from being good companies to being 'great' companies on par with the companies in 'Built to Last'. A key finding was that each company had what he calls level-5 Leadership'.

After poring over Level 5 leaders, one can realise that they seemed to demonstrate most or all of the characteristics described as 'SQ' by Zohar. In addition, they showed a profound personal humility and a powerful faith that they and their company would prevail in the end, regardless of the difficulties.

Self-awareness and cultivating inner strength (or faith) has a solid grounding in all of the major spiritual traditions. Jesus went into the wilderness to meditate and to hear the voice of the infinite Creator, as did Abraham, Moses and Mohammed. Buddhists and Hindus practise meditation for these purposes as well.

The implications for leadership are clear. High IQ does not guarantee a good leader. High EQ has been correlated with success. But does it alone create greatness?

Sustained and recognised greatness, even in the tough world of Corporate America, is obtained by something deeper. If a corporate leader is willing to deeply know himself and his place in the universe, he can reach the graduate school of SQ. With SQ comes the ultimate success—obtaining company success in such a way that customers, employees and society all benefit. And after creating a great company, the high SQ person sincerely deflects all praise onto the 'wonderful people of this organisation'.

Most of us are smart enough to realise that IQ doesn't mean very much. A complex quality like intelligence can't be reduced to a single number. And we're aware that some universities are starting to discount the value of SATs in college admissions because test scores are not always very good predictors of success in higher education. They do not measure a student's stick-to-it-iveness or motivation to work hard. They can't predict who's going to cheat. And they don't give very much insight into traits like sociability or ability to get along with others that are just as important as raw brain power in making one's way through life. Consequently, most educators now accept the concept of 'multiple intelligences'.

Multiple Intelligences

Intelligence is sometimes defined as the ability to manage cognitive complexity. In current usage, the distinction between intelligence and reason has been largely lost. For example, as defined in Webster's Dictionary (Mish, 1993), intelligence includes the ability to understand, to apply knowledge, to use reason skilfully and to manipulate one's environment. The view that intelligence comprises many different abilities is supported by current trends in neurology and cognitive psychology.

Among researchers who have identified various types of intelligence, Howard Gardner's (1993) pioneering work at Harvard on multiple intelligences has helped people understand that intelligence is multifaceted. His work is currently being applied in many schools across America. Gardner's research indicates that different kinds of intelligence develop relatively independently of each other, and proficiency in one area does not imply proficiency in another.

For example, linguistic skill with words can be differentiated from logical mathematical skill with numbers and from the spatial intelligence that perceives spatial relationships. Excellence in one area does not necessarily tell us anything about abilities in another. In addition, Gardner (1993) discussed kinaesthetic intelligence that enables a person to use the body in highly differentiated and skilled ways, such as dance or athletics; musical intelligence necessary for all different kinds of musical aptitude; intrapersonal intelligence that implies awareness of one's own thoughts and feelings; and interpersonal intelligence that enables us to relate to others empathically. He does not discuss spiritual intelligence as a separate line of development.

Intelligence Core Components (High-end States)

1. *Linguistic Sensitivity* to sounds, structure, meanings and functions of words and language (writer, orator).
2. *Logical-Mathematical Sensitivity* to, and capacity to discern logical or numerical patterns; ability to handle long chains of reasoning (scientist, mathematician).
3. *Spatial Capacity* to perceive the visual–spatial world accurately and to perform transformations on one's initial perceptions (artist, architect).
4. *Body-kinaesthetic Ability* to control one's body movements and to handle objects skilfully (athlete, dancer, sculptor, surgeon).
5. *Musical Ability* to produce and appreciate rhythm, pitch and timbre; appreciation of the forms of musical expressiveness (composer, performer).
6. *Interpersonal Capacity* to discern and respond appropriately to the moods, temperaments, motivations and desires of other people (counsellor, political leader).
7. *Intrapersonal Access* to one's own feelings, life and the ability to discriminate among one's emotions; knowledge of one's own strengths and weaknesses (psychotherapist, religious leader).
8. *Naturalistic Ability* to perceive the environment and ecosystems; knowledge of relationships in nature (naturalist, environmentalist).

Daniel Goleman's (1995) research on emotional intelligence, based primarily on intrapersonal and interpersonal intelligence, indicates that success in many areas of life depends on emotional skills as much as on cognitive capacities. Emotional intelligence includes self-awareness and self-control, as well as the ability to get along well with others. Getting along with others implies an ability to listen, to communicate, to accept feedback and to emphathize with different points of view. (Refer *Spiritual Intelligence: The vital part of leadership*).

According to Goleman and others, different kinds of intelligence are associated with different areas of the brain. Although little research has been done to isolate areas of the brain associated with spirituality, numerous studies in meditation research indicate that significant physiological changes result from even limited practice

1. Shapiro and Walsh, 1984;
2. Walsh and Vaughan, 1993;
3. Murphy and Donovan, 1999;

Studies that measure the effects of intensive, long-term practice point to significant psychological benefits in addition to deepening emotional and spiritual sensitivity.

An interesting anecdote about Emmanuel Swedenborg, the 18th century scientist who became a visionary mystic and founded the Swedenborgian church, says that when Swedenborg suffered a stroke that left him paralysed on one side of his body, he lost his visionary capacity (Wulff, 1991). This certainly suggests that a spiritual gift may be associated with specific areas of the brain. However, the fact that spiritual experiences have physiological correlates in the brain does not necessarily mean that they are caused by the brain. Presumably neurophysiology plays a role in all experiences, but referral to brain and bodily processes does not help us fully comprehend spiritual experiences or evaluate their significance.

In recent years, numerous empirical studies have supported the idea that certain spiritual beliefs and practices are positively associated with physical and mental health (Richards, 1999). In addition to exploring the relationship of spirituality to health and healing (Dossey, 1993), researchers are also investigating the impact of spiritual beliefs on the dying process (Gallup, 1997). Practical applications of spirituality are finding their way into the mainstream practice of medicine and alternative methods of healing (Boyle, 1999) and distinctions between religiousness and contemporary spirituality are being clarified (Wuthnow, 1998).

Views of Business Community on SQ

In the business community worldwide, SQ has already become a practice after being a buzzword for a long time. It is being touted as the best formula for success in business, in one's profession and in life. But it has roots in a part of our lives that has never been considered of relevance to these fields. It is Spirituality Quotient (SQ).

Spirituality Quotient (SQ), its proponents say, is the ultimate intelligence, the one that enables us to give value and meaning to our lives. It allows us to look beyond material success to our larger purpose in this world. It is the foundation of both Intelligence Quotient and Emotional Quotient.

For long it was believed that a person's intellectual intelligence, measured as IQ, was an indicator of what that person would achieve in life. Experts devised a variety of tests to find out an individual's IQ score. This statistically derived number was said to indicate mental abilities that could be used to obtain academic skills and knowledge, and to solve logical problems. It was assumed that the higher the IQ score, the greater the person's success in life. Those with high IQ scores got preferential treatment in academic institutions and in the job market.

But then it was observed that a high IQ score was no guarantee for success, happiness or even sanity. Nor, it was seen, was a low IQ score a hindrance to achieving material, emotional or spiritual fulfilment. In fact, experts realised that even individuals with a high IQ score could be miserable failures in life, or in their interaction with fellow human beings.

Most of history's worst tales are about smart individuals who ended up harming others. The inability of rational intelligence to solve many of life's crucial problems is well illustrated in our times by stories of treachery, crime and violence perpetuated by those who are otherwise known to be bright and successful people.

This has prompted psychologists to look for something other than IQ to account for success and happiness. And they soon came up with Emotional Intelligence or EQ, a term used to describe the ability to understand one's emotions and the emotions of others and to act appropriately on the basis of this understanding. EQ is said to merge empathy, compassion, motivation and the ability to respond skilfully to joy and pain. EQ, it is argued, is necessary for the use of IQ.

But, over the past decade, as the pressures of modern life grew, it has been realised that even EQ was inadequate to deal with the situations individuals were facing in their professional and personal lives. This is because while EQ enables one to adjust one's feelings according to the situation, it does not have the power to transform negative feelings into positive ones. That requires SQ, the spirituality quotient.

The 'discovery' of SQ in the HRD field is a belated acknowledgment of a truth that our sages have known long ago: that all of life's problems are essentially spiritual problems and require a spiritual remedy. When one learns to recognise the spiritual roots of a problem, one can find more holistic and rewarding solutions to them using spiritual intelligence than mere IQ

The validity of SQ demonstrates another truth: that lasting success and happiness cannot be achieved at the expense of morality. This is because moral virtues are the original qualities of the soul, and each deed that lessens these qualities leaves the soul that much more hollow. What makes business sense must also make moral sense if it is to bring lasting happiness to all. That is the best way to conduct business and the business of life, as many organisations are now discovering.

People with strong spiritual intelligence look at interconnections and the whole self—the mind, the body and the soul. People account typically for up to 85 per cent of an organisation's overheads but their value as an intangible asset far exceeds this figure. A growing trend has emerged in the work place for people to seek meaning there, to work for and deal with organisations whose values and beliefs tie in with their own and who have integrity and respect for them as people and not treat them as just numbers. The leader with SQ is able to understand and tap into this powerful source of energy.

Spirituality Becoming Integral Part of Corporate Life

Today, people are finding that there's more to life—and business—than profits alone. Money as the single bottom line is increasingly a thing of the past. In a post-Enron world, values and ethics are an urgent concern. The hottest buzz today is about a 'triple bottom line,' a commitment to 'people, planet, profit'. Employees and the environment are seen as important as economics. Some people would say it's all about bringing your spiritual values into your workplace. Some time back, a poll by KRC Research for Spirituality, published on 17 November 2003 in *USA Today*, found that 6 out of 10 people say workplaces would benefit from having a great sense of spirit in their work environment.

What is spirituality in business? There's a wide range of important perspectives. Some would say that it's simply embodying their personal values of honesty, integrity and good quality work. Others would say it's treating their co-workers and employees in a responsible, caring way. For others, it's participating in spiritual study groups or using prayer, meditation or intuitive guidance at work. And for some, it's making their business socially responsible in how it impacts the environment, serves the community or helps create a better world.

Some business people are comfortable using the word 'spirituality' in the work environment, as it is more generic and inclusive than 'religion.' Instead of emphasising belief as religion does, the word spirituality emphasises how values are applied and embodied. Other people aren't comfortable with the word spiritual and prefer to talk more about values and ethics when describing the same things that others would call spiritual. However, there are some people who will talk about God as their business partner or their CEO.

There's some fear about spiritual beliefs or practices being imposed by employers, but to date this has been extremely rare. On the other hand, some observers warn about the potential for superficiality and the distortion of spiritual practices to serve greed.

Key spiritual values embraced in a business context include integrity, honesty, accountability, quality, cooperation, service, intuition, trustworthiness, respect, justice and service. The Container

Store chain nationwide tells workers they are 'morally obligated to help customers solve problems'—they're not just to sell people products. The CEO of Vermont Country Store, a popular national catalogue company, honoured (instead of fired) an employee who told the truth in a widely circulated memo, and so increased morale and built a sense of trust in his company.

Research on Spirituality and the Bottom Line

Are spirituality and profitability mutually exclusive? Bringing ethics and spiritual values into the workplace can lead to increased productivity and profitability as well as employee retention, customer loyalty, and brand reputation, according to a growing body of research. More employers are encouraging spirituality as a way to boost loyalty and enhance morale.

A recent study done at the University of Chicago by Prof. Curtis Verschoor and published in *Management Accounting* found that companies with a defined corporate commitment to ethical principles do better financially than companies that don't make ethics a key management component. Public shaming of Nike's sweatshop conditions and slave wages paid to overseas workers led to a 27 per cent drop in its earnings several years ago. And recently, the shocking disregard of ethics and subsequent scandals led to financial disaster for Enron, Arthur Anderson, WorldCom, Global Crossing, and others.

Business Week magazine reported on recent research by McKinsey and Company in Australia that found that productivity improves and employee turnover is greatly reduced when companies engage in programmes that use spiritual techniques for their employees.

In researching companies for his book, *A Spiritual Audit of Corporate America*, business Professor Ian I. Mitroff found that 'Spirituality could be the ultimate competitive advantage'.

A study reported in MIT's *Sloan Management Review* concluded that `people are hungry for ways in which to practise their spirituality in the workplace without offending their co-workers or causing acrimony'. The word 'spirituality' is used generically and seems to emphasise how one's beliefs are applied day-to-day, rather than 'religion', which can invoke fears of dogmatism, exclusivity and proselytising in the workplace.

Research by UCLA business Professor David Lewin found that 'companies that increased their community involvement were more likely to show an improved financial picture over a two-year time period'. A two-year study by the Performance Group, a consortium of seven leading European companies such as Volvo, Monsanto and Unilever, concluded that environmental compliance and eco-friendly products can increase profitability, enhance earnings per share and help win contracts in emerging markets.

Investment returns on the Domini 400 Social Index (publicly traded, socially responsible, triple bottom line companies) have outperformed the S&P 500 over a ten-year period ending last year.

Business Week reported that 95 per cent of Americans reject the idea that a corporation's only purpose is to make money. Thirty-nine per cent of US investors say that they always or frequently check on business practices, values and ethics before investing. The Trends Report found that 75 per cent of consumers polled say they are likely to switch to brands associated with a good cause if price and quality are equal.

Growing Movement

A proliferation of book titles (currently over 500) reflects a growing national movement to bring spiritual values into the workplace: *The Soul of Business, Liberating the Corporate Soul, Working from the Heart, The Stirring of Soul in the Workplace, Jesus CEO, What Would the Buddha Do At Work?, Spirit at Work, Redefining the Corporate Soul The Corporate Mystic, Leading with Soul, etc.* Some books on this theme, such as Stephen Covey's pioneering *The Seven Habits of Highly Effective People*, have sold millions of copies.

There are several national newsletters and associations based on spirituality at work, as well as dozens of national conferences on this theme, including the one I organised in Washington in 1998 with over 50 leaders, including many from local businesses such as Marriott International and Riggs Bank.

The prestigious American Management Association held a conference on 'Profiting from a Values-Based Corporate Culture' on how to tap into the fourth dimension of spirituality and ethics as crucial components for success. To the surprise of many, this movement is beginning to transform corporate America from the inside out. Growing numbers of business people want their spirituality to be more than just faith and belief—they want it to be practical and applied. They want to bring their whole selves to work—body, mind and spirit. Many business people are finding that the bottom line can be strengthened by embodying their values. They can 'do well by doing good'.

People at all levels in the corporate hierarchy increasingly want to nourish their spirit and creativity. When employees are encouraged to express their creativity, the result is a more fulfilled and sustained workforce. Happy people work harder and are more likely to stay at their jobs.

A study of business performance by the highly respected Wilson Learning Company found that 39 per cent of the variability in corporate performance is attributable to the personal satisfaction of the staff. Spirituality was cited as the second most important factor in personal happiness (after health) by the majority of Americans questioned in a *USA Weekend* poll, with 47 per cent saying that spirituality was the most important element of their happiness.

Across the country, people increasingly want to bring a greater sense of meaning and purpose into their work life. They want their work to reflect their personal mission in life. Many companies are finding that the most effective way to bring spiritual values into the workplace is to clarify the company's vision and mission, and to align it with a higher purpose and deeper commitment of service to both customers and community.

Why Spirituality is Popular

"Why this sudden interest in spirituality at work?" Researchers point to several key factors. Corporate downsizing and greater demands on the remaining workers has left them too tired and stressed to be creative—at the same time the globalization of markets requires more creativity from employees.

To survive into the future, organizations must offer a greater sense of meaning and purpose for their workforce. In today's highly competitive environment, the best talent seeks out organisations that reflect their inner values and provide opportunities for personal development and community service, not just bigger salaries. Unlike the marketplace economy of 20 years ago, today's information and services-dominated economy requires instantaneous decision-making and building better relationships with customers and employees.

Also, spending more time at work means there is less time available for religious activities. The New York Times recently reported that a growing number of companies are allowing employees to hold religion classes at work. This accommodates busy professionals who are pressed for time and are afraid they have abandoned their faith. Many people are feeling more comfortable in the public expression of their faith.

Another factor in the popularity of spirituality at work is the fact that there are more women in the workplace today, and women tend to focus on spiritual values more often than men. The ageing of the large baby boom generation is also a contributor, as boomers find materialism no longer satisfies them and they begin to fear their own mortality.

Ninety-five per cent of Americans said they believed in God or a universal spirit, and 48 per cent said they talked about their religious faith at work that day, according to a 1999 Gallup poll published in *Business Week*.

Prayer and Meditation in the Workplace

Many people use prayer at work for several reasons: for guidance in decision-making, to prepare for difficult situations, when they are going through a tough time, or to give thanks for something good. Timberland Shoes CEO, Jeffrey B. Swartz uses his prayer book and religious beliefs to guide business decisions and company policy, often consulting his rabbi. Kris Kalra, CEO of BioGenex uses the

Hindu holy text, the *Bhagavad Gita*, to steer his business out of trouble.

The *ABC Evening News* reported that the American Stock Exchange has a Torah study group; Boeing has Christian, Jewish and Muslim prayer groups; Microsoft has an on-line prayer service. There is a 'Lunch and Learn' Torah class in the banking firm of Sutro and Company in Woodland Hills, California. New York law firm Kaye, Scholer, Fierman, Hays and Haroller features Talmud studies. Koran classes, as well as other religious classes, are featured at defence giant Northrop Gumnan Wheat International Communications in Reston, Virginia has morning prayers open to all employees, but not required. Spiritual study groups at noon are sometimes called 'Higher Power Lunches', instead of the usual 'power lunches.'

The *Los Angeles Times* reported that Marketplace Ministries of Dallas placed freelance chaplains at 132 companies in 38 states. Fellowship of Companies for Christ International based in Atlanta has 1,500 member companies around the world. They promote 'the importance and practice of prayer in company decisions; a commitment to excellence; following Jesus' example of focusing on people, not things. 'Do unto others in the workplace as you would have them do unto you,' is what they strive for. Fast food companies, such as Taco Bell and Pizza Hut, hire chaplains from many faiths to minister to employees with problems, and credit them with reducing turnover rates by one half.

In addition to prayer and study groups, other spiritual practices at companies include meditation; centering exercises such as deep breathing to reduce stress; visioning exercises; building shared values; active, deep listening; making action and intention congruent; and using intuition and inner guidance in decision-making. According to a study at Harvard Business School published in *The Harvard Business Review*, business owners credit 80 per cent of their success to acting on their intuition.

Apple Computer's offices in California have a meditation room and employees are actually given half hour a day on company time to meditate or pray, as they find it improves productivity and creativity. A former manager who is now a Buddhist monk leads regular meditations there. Aetna International Chairman Michael A. Stephen praises the benefits of meditation and talks with Aetna employees about using spirituality in their careers. Avaya, a global communications firm that is a spin-off of Lucent/AT&T, has a room set aside for prayer and meditation that is especially appreciated by Muslims, as they must pray five times a day.

Medtronic, which sells medical equipment, pioneered a meditation centre at headquarters 20 years ago, and it remains open to all employees today. Prentice-Hall publishing company created a meditation room at their headquarters which they call the 'Quiet Room', where employees can sit quietly and take a mental retreat when they feel too much stress on the job. Sounds True in Colorado, which produces audio and video tapes, has a meditation room, meditation classes and begins meetings with a moment of silence.

Employees can take Personal Days to attend retreats or pursue other spiritual interests. Greystone Bakery in upstate New York has a period of silence before meetings begin so people can get in touch with their inner state and focus on the issues to be discussed.

LOTUS founder and CEO Mitch Kapor practises Transcendental Meditation and named his company after a word for enlightenment. A research project by Professor Richard Davidson at the University of Wisconsin at Pomega, a biotechnology company that had a very high-stress workplace, found that mindful meditation training produced astonishing results in reducing stress and in generating positive feelings.

Paula Madison at WNBC TV in New York City prays before each show and says she became the number one news show in the area when she increased coverage of spiritual stories. Apparel manufacturer Patagonia provides yoga classes for employees on their breaks, as does Avaya Telecommunications. A Spiritual Unfoldment Society has been meeting regularly at the World Bank for years, with lectures on topics such as meditation and reincarnation.

Executives of Xerox have gone on week-long retreats led by Marlowe Hotchkiss of the Ojai Foundation to learn a Native American model of council meetings and experience vision quests. The Vision

Quests inspired one manager with the idea to create Xerox's hottest seller, a 97 per cent recyclable machine.

The CEO of Rockport Shoes, Angel Martinez, talks openly of the spiritual mission of his company and encourages employees to spend work time envisioning ways to express their deepest selves in their work. Companies such as Evian springwater have successfully used spirituality in their advertising, as for example: 'Your body is the temple of your spirit.'

The Service-Master Company, with six million customers worldwide, provides cleaning, maintenance, lawn-care and food services, and puts its spiritual values upfront in its annual report. It begins with a biblical quote, `Each of us should use whatever gift he has received to serve others, faithfully administering God's grace in its various forms.'

People are the Most Important Resource

Increasing numbers of business people find that the key area for applying spirituality is in how employees are treated. Southwest Airlines, one of the only airlines staying profitable since the 9/11 terrorist attacks, says that 'people are our most important resource'. Company policy is to treat employees like family, knowing that if they are treated well, they in turn will treat customers well. They have a 'University for People' directed by Rita Bailey, and their policy is to hire people based on their attitude and then train them for skills, rather than the reverse. Unlike other airlines, negotiations between management and employees for pay raises and benefits are much shorter and easier as both sides come to the table wanting to hand write a win/win contract. They have been named many times as one of *Fortune* magazine's '100 Best Companies to Work For.'

Aaron Feurenstein, CEO of Malden Mills in Lawrence, Massachusetts, which produces popular Polartec fabrics, believes labour is the best asset a company has. He says a company has an equal responsibility to its community and to itself, and since his town has high unemployment, he kept all 3,000 employees on his payroll after a major fire destroyed three out of its four factory buildings. Workers repaid his generosity with a 25 per cent increase in productivity and 66 per cent drop in quality defects.

Anita Roddick, founder of The Body Shop, with stores all over the world, purposely built a soap factory near Glasgow, Scotland because it was an area of high unemployment, urban decay and demoralization. She made a moral decision to employ the unemployable and put 25 per cent of the net profits back into the community because she said this is what 'keeps the soul of the company alive'.

Nearly 100,000 Marriott International employees worldwide dedicate a day of service to their local communities each year in their 'Spirit to Serve' programme. Timberland, the popular New Hampshire based shoe company, pays employees for 40 hours of volunteer work annually.

Ohio-based Zero Casualties Inc., an urban apparel maker, donates seven per cent of its profits to inner city charities. The company has created a marketing campaign based on its values of 'no drugs, no violence, no racism'.

IBM funds child care centres at 60 of its locations. Intel offers 22 weeks of maternity leave. The Men's Wearhouse, one of *Fortune* magazine's 100 Best Companies to work for, supports homeless men in re-entering the job market.

Tom Chappell, CEO of Tom's of Maine, which produces soaps and toothpastes, stays mindful of profit and the common good by giving away 10 per cent of its pre-tax profits to charities. Tom's gives employees four paid hours a month to volunteer for community service, and uses all natural ingredients that are good for the environment. After studying at Harvard Divinity School, Chappell re-engineered his business into a sort of ministry, saying, 'I am ministering—and I am doing it in the marketplace, not in the church, because I understand the marketplace better than the church'.

Saturn auto manufacturing says the key to their success is their experiment in corporate democracy and participatory governance. Empowered teams make most company decisions.

60 Minutes did a television show on SAS, a billion dollar computer software company that has low absenteeism and only 3 per cent turnover, which saves them $80 million each year in training and recruitment. Their secret? A no-lay-off policy, 35 hour workweeks, flex time, and on-site amenities such as a gym, a medical clinic and massage therapists.

Spiritually oriented materials on personal change have been used in employee training for several years at the Bank of Montreal, and Boatman's First National Bank in Kansas City regularly provides spiritually oriented training for its top executive group.

Consulting firms using spiritual approaches are doing a booming business. The Enlightened Leadership International in Colorado has been teaching top executives at major companies such as GTE, Georgia-Pacific, and Lockheed Martin how to focus on what's positive, instead of the problems, because `our beliefs create what we experience.' Other major firms such as the Covey Leadership Center and the Centre for Generative Leadership teach Fortune 500 executives how to align their company's mission with their deeper values.

Managers and union workers of Southern California Con Edison attend sessions called The Heart Shop' with pianist Michael Jones to cultivate compassion for each other, creativity and a new intelligence of the heart. Boeing set up a series of week long training with poet David Whyte for 600 of its top executives to unleash feelings, take risks, and be excited by change, instead of being terrified of it.

NYNEX established an Office of Ethics and Business Conduct to encourage employees to live by a set of core values: quality, ethics and caring for the individual. This new focus led to an increase in profits, productivity and product and service quality, as this affected how the company is perceived by customers and stakeholders.

Judy Wicks, founder of the highly successful White Dog Cafe in Philadelphia, uses her restaurant as 'a tool for the common good' by raising money for the hungry and sponsoring seminars on racism, the environment and social change. Thanksgiving Coffee Company invests a share of its revenues in community development among the Central American villages that grow its coffee beans. It pays Fair Trade prices for coffee from small farmers cooperatives, which is often three to six times as much as regular prices.

Protecting the Environment for Future Generations

Many companies see their commitment to the environment as their spiritual mission. A 1995 Vanderbilt University analysis found that in 8 out of 10 cases, low-polluting companies financially outperformed their dirtier competitors. Ray Anderson, founder of Interface Carpets, the world's largest commercial carpeting manufacturer, trained 8,000 employees in environmental sustainability, with the goal of reducing pollution to zero per cent in the next few years. Instead of buying a carpet, you now rent a carpet, and when it wears out, you bring it back to be recycled, and are given a new recycled one. Anderson estimates that his company has saved $185 million on waste-reduction efforts alone.

Home Depot recently introduced a line of wood products grown through sustainable forestry practices. British Petroleum renamed itself Beyond Petroleum as it is developing alternative forms of fuel and lobbying governments on the scientific, economic and moral reasons for climate change so they will sign the treaty on global warming.

Starbucks Coffee has partnered with Conservation International to work with its farmer/suppliers in Mexico to promote water and soil conservation and reduction of chemical fertilisers and pesticides.

By reducing, reusing and recycling, Fetzer Wine has reduced its garbage by 97 per cent. It buys recycled paper, cans and glass for its products, had switched from petroleum to biodiesel fuel, and farms its own grapes organically.

At Hewlett-Packard, each product has a steward whose job is to minimise its ecological footprint by reducing packaging, reducing toxic materials in the product, increasing recycling, etc.

Mitsubishi Electric American specified that their suppliers could not provide them with paper or timber from old growth forests. Once they set the example, almost 500 other companies followed their lead and together they saved four million acres of forest.

In 1986, the Caux Round Table, based in Minnesota, pioneered a list of Principles for Business, an international code of ethical values formulated by senior business leaders from Japan, Europe, and the

United States and Canada. And recently, 300 multinationals joined the UN Global Compact, pledging to support human rights, labour standards and environmental protection.

The spirituality in business movement is one of the hopeful signs that business, as the most powerful institution in the world today, may be transforming from within. What is emerging is a new attitude towards the workplace as a place to fulfil one's deeper purpose. As World Business Academy co-founder, Willis Harman remarked: 'The dominant institution in any society needs to take responsibility for the whole, as the church did in the days of the Holy Roman Empire.' Each day, more and more business people are helping to create a better world by being more socially responsible in how they treat people and the environment. They are proving that spirituality helps, rather than harms, the bottom line.

Exhuming Spiritual Intelligence

Spiritual intelligence is concerned with the inner life of mind and spirit and its relationship to being in the world. Spiritual intelligence implies a capacity for a deep understanding of existential questions and insight into multiple levels of consciousness. Spiritual intelligence also implies awareness of spirit as the ground of being or as the creative life force of evolution. If the evolution of life from stardust to mineral, vegetable, animal and human existence implies some form of intelligence rather than being a purely random process, it might be called spiritual. Spiritual intelligence emerges as consciousness evolves into an ever deepening awareness of matter, life, body, mind, soul and spirit.

Spiritual intelligence, then, is more than individual mental ability. It appears to connect the personal to the transpersonal and the self to spirit. Spiritual intelligence goes beyond conventional psychological development. In addition to self-awareness, it implies awareness of our relationship to the transcendent, to each other, to the earth and all beings. Spiritual intelligence is related to emotional intelligence as far as spiritual practice includes developing intrapersonal and interpersonal sensitivity. Paying attention to subjective thoughts and feelings and cultivating empathy is part of increasing awareness of the inner spiritual life.

Spiritual intelligence depends on the capacity to see things from more than one perspective and to recognise the relationships between perception, belief and behaviour. Most people are expected to take responsibility for behaviour but not for beliefs or perceptions, although these are intimately interconnected. Refining any form of intelligence requires training and discipline, and spiritual intelligence is no exception. We rely on spiritual intelligence when we explore the meaning of questions such as 'Who am I?' `Why am I here?' and 'What really matters?'. Perhaps spiritual intelligence can also help a person discover hidden wellsprings of love and joy beneath the stress and turmoil of everyday life.

Different Ways of Knowing

Definitions of spiritual intelligence seem incomplete if they do not include different ways of knowing. In a recent survey of grassroots spirituality, Robert Forman (1997) reported that people from many different traditions tend to view spirituality today as being experiential rather than conceptual, and clearly trans-rational. Contemplative practices, such as meditation, seem particularly relevant for refining spiritual intelligence because it depends on familiarity with at least three distinct ways of knowing: sensory, rational and contemplative.

These three ways of knowing appear to be an integral part of the spiritual intelligence that some people demonstrate. The Dalai Lama, for instance, is evidently very familiar with different ways of knowing and seems to be continuously aware of multiple levels of consciousness. I have heard him give extraordinarily complex and sophisticated lectures on the nature of consciousness, and I have seen him respond to hostile questions with grace and dignity.

His demeanour of friendliness and compassion never wavers. He seems to practise what he preaches when he says, 'I consider human affection, or compassion, to be the universal religion. Whether a believer or a non-believer, everyone needs human affection and compassion because compassion gives us inner strength, hope and mental peace. Thus, it is indispensable for everyone' (as cited in Grey, 1998, p. 177).

Descriptions of various levels of consciousness provide useful maps for differentiating spiritual intelligence from other types of intelligence (Wilber, 1995). Wilber (1999) pointed out that although many of us have had peak experiences that access expanded states of transpersonal consciousness, we can, with practice, evolve into having constant access to the witness or pure awareness that is aware of all levels. This awareness can be maintained through waking, dreaming and sleeping states because it is always already present in all three states. He says: 'Spirit is not an altered state of consciousness or a non-ordinary state. There is only Spirit . . . within which different states arise' (p. 322).

From another perspective, Islamic scholar Seyyed Hossein Nasr (1989) said, 'Intelligence is a divine gift which pierces through the veil of maya and is able to know reality as such' (p. 146). In this context, intelligence refers to the capacity of distinguishing truth from illusion, which implies more than just being sensitive to subtle energies and spiritual phenomena.

Ideally, spiritual intelligence would enable us to see things as they are, free from unconscious distortions. In contrast to wishful thinking or grasping for certainty, exercising spiritual intelligence implies facing existential realities such as freedom, suffering and death, and grappling with the perennial quest for meaning.

For many people, spiritual intelligence also implies aesthetic sensitivity and appreciation of beauty. Physically, spiritual intelligence is sometimes associated with sensitivity to subtle energy currents in the body. Practices such as meditation, yoga and martial arts that quiet the mind can expand awareness and refine perceptual sensitivity to energy, sound, light and subtle levels of consciousness.

Since ancient times, spirituality has been an integral part of human life. Societies have started believing that everyone has the potential for developing spiritual intelligence, just as everyone has a capacity for intuition, thinking, sensing and feeling (Vaughan, 1979). However, these capacities develop and become more reliable when we pay attention to them. Whereas some people try to ignore spiritual issues, others choose to cultivate spiritual sensitivity. Because people now have access to a wide variety of spiritual teachings, intelligent discernment is needed to make wise choices and avoid some of the entrapping seductions of spiritual illusions (Anthony, Ecker and Wilber, 1987; Deikman, 1990; Vaughan, 1995).

Spiritual Intelligence and Psychological Health

Spiritual intelligence can generally be associated with psychological health, although some forms of spirituality may be dysfunctional or pathogenic (Deikman, 1990). When spiritual beliefs foster denial and projection and contribute to fear and conflict, they can be destructive and seriously problematic. For example, when a cult leader exerts control over people through manipulation of fear and guilt, the community may exhibit the characteristics of a dysfunctional family. It can sometimes take a person years to recover from having made a spiritual commitment without discernment.

Conventional religion often provides a person with a sense of security and belonging, serving as a social support to its members. Among those who have been disillusioned by conventional religion, spirituality is more likely to be inner directed. A person may still belong to a group, but with the development of spiritual intelligence, the circle of empathic identification expands to all people and takes the well-being of the whole into account. When we recognise our interconnectedness and interdependence, it becomes possible to view the world from multiple perspectives.

Developing spiritual intelligence includes and transcends personal growth, extending to the farther reaches of healthy psychological development. It begins with cultivating authenticity and self-awareness and develops with practice to a concern for all beings. Some personal characteristics that could be associated with spiritual intelligence are the traditional virtues of veracity, humility and charity, which could also be described as authenticity, respect for differences and the willingness to engage in service to others.

Well-developed spiritual intelligence could also be associated with the absence of defensiveness and hostility as well as an inclination to kindness and generosity. Of course, these traits can also be found in psychologically healthy people who do not consider themselves particularly spiritual. In other words, they can be considered necessary but insufficient conditions for spiritual intelligence.

In medicine, we are used to finding answers or at least searching for solutions to problems. SQ is about questions more than answers. It lives in stories, poetry and metaphor; in uncertainty and paradox.

One of the qualities of SQ is wisdom. This includes knowing the limits of your knowledge. Other ingredients are values such as courage, integrity, intuition and compassion. With SQ, more is less; so as you learn, the process may involve unlearning what other people have taught you. That last sentence has great significance. There is often so much unlearning to be done in our journey towards a life that is meaningful, fulfilling and fun.

Recognising that Spiritual Intelligence could cover an enormous range of concepts, the article focuses on two elements, intuition and compassion. It defines intuition in this way:

> Your intuition is part of your unconscious intelligence, and it complements rational thinking and decision making. Antonio Damasio, a neurologist, who studied the links between cognitive and emotional intelligence, believes that intuition is the 'glue' that holds together our conscious intellect and our intelligence action.

How do we develop that intuition?

Intuition can flourish where there is space and time for reflection. If you are often under stress, you will find it difficult to be intuitive even though we all have this potential.

To develop your intuition, it will help to expand your ability for 'relaxed attention'. Have you had the experience that the harder you try to achieve a task, the more difficult it becomes? There is a difficult way that involves worry, increasing effort and frustration at your delay in making a decision. The easy way is to ease off, take a break and trust that your intuition will help you find a new direction.

Rather than focus on having compassion for others, the article focuses on compassion for oneself.

It's hard being a doctor if we feel that we have to give all the time.

We are bound to meet patients we don't like, and sometimes we are at risk of making mistakes or being abrupt or rude or feeling stressed. So let's forget about the patients for a moment. Ask yourself whether you are compassionate with yourself. To help find the answer to this, ask yourself some of these questions:

- Are you in the sort of job you love?
- Do you look after your body? Take enough exercise? Eat a healthy diet?
- Do you nourish yourself with healthy relationships?
- Are you living in a healthy and safe environment?
- Do you forgive yourself when you make 'mistakes'?

One of the principles of holism is that we are all connected. It then follows that if you have compassion for yourself, you will be able to be compassionate to your patients (whether you like them or not).

Developing compassion for oneself can be a huge factor in moving forward in creating the life you want. So many people are out there beating themselves up, and wonder why they feel strained, drained, and empty.

Spiritual Intelligence (SQ) Skills

Higher Self/Ego Self Awareness

1. Awareness of own worldview
2. Awareness of life purpose (mission)
3. Awareness of values hierarchy
4. Complexity of inner thought
5. Awareness of Ego Self/Higher Self.

Universal Awareness

6. Awareness of interconnectedness of all life
7. Awareness of worldviews of others
8. Breadth of time/space perception
9. Awareness of limitations/power of human perception
10. Awareness of Spiritual laws
11. Experience of transcendent oneness.

Higher Self/Ego Self Mastery

12. Commitment to spiritual growth
13. Keeping Higher Self in charge

14. Living your purpose and values
15. Sustaining your faith
16. Seeking guidance from Spirit.

Social Mastery/ Spiritual Presence

17. A wise and effective spiritual teacher/mentor
18. A wise and effective change agent
19. Makes compassionate and wise decisions
20. A calming, healing presence
21. Being aligned with the ebb and flow of life.

Solving logical or strategic problems involves the use of rational intelligence. Psychologists who devised tests to measure rational intelligence termed their measure 'Intelligence Quotient (IQ)', their hypothesis being that the higher the IQ, more is the rational intelligence. Initially the IQ included only verbal and mathematical–logical capabilities. Howard Gardner's 1983 book Frames of Mind refuted the narrow IQ view and extended the concept to include spatial capacity, physical fluidity, musical capability, inter-personal intelligence, intrapersonal intelligence, etc. The operative word in his view of intelligence was 'multiple'. While the utility of IQ in identifying potential performers is not disputed, according to renowned psychologists IQ contributes only about 20 per cent to the factors that determine life success, which leaves 80 per cent to other forces. As Gardner in one of his articles observes: 'One's ultimate niche in society is determined largely by non-IQ factors, ranging from social class to luck'.

In the mid-1990s, Daniel Goleman popularised the 'Emotional Quotient (EQ)'—a degree of emotional intelligence, awareness of one's own and other people's feelings such as empathy, compassion, motivation and the ability to respond to pain or pleasure appropriately. His basic hypothesis was that for an effective use of IQ, EQ is a necessity. He writes: 'In a sense we have two brains, two minds—and two different kinds of intelligence, rational and emotional. How we do in life is determined by both—it is not just IQ, but emotional intelligence that matters'. The millennium contribution in the area of intelligence was from Danah Zohar and Ian Marshall who coined the term `SQ' for 'Spiritual Intelligence'.

They argue that SQ is the basic foundation for an effective use of EQ and IQ. They also refer to it as the soul's intelligence. While rational, logical thinking gives one's IQ and the associated habit-bound pattern, recognising emotive thinking gives one the EQ, and the creative, insightful, rule-making, rule-breaking thinking with which we reframe and transform our previous thinking gives one the SQ. On a scientific plane, the brain's serially connected neural tracts and neural networks are associated with the IQ and EQ, respectively.

Singer's work on the unifying neural oscillation offers the first evidence of SQ. Just as the whole can be greater than the sum of its parts, SQ allows one to add a larger, deeper and richer context to the present. She evolves a model of SQ based on the six petals of the lotus and its centre, corresponding to the seven *chakras* described by Hinduism's *Kundalini Yoga*. Can we identify, measure and improve on our SQ, and thereby effectively use our EQ and IQ?

The Indian philosophical treatises—the *Upanishads*—attribute perception to the mind, conception to the intellect and 'illumination' to the Self. They speak of the ascent from Intellect (IQ) through meditation. Meditation is the route to the highest knowledge (illumination), when self-realisation, which is integration of inner self or spirit into the cosmic spirit, occurs. For instance in the Sahaja Yoga mode of self-realisation it is propounded that the body is not the whole self. The vehicle of influence is the subtle body, parallel to the physical body, wherein there are seven *chakras*, the chief nerve centres; three tracks of nervous energy called nadis, and the latent energy coiled within called *Kundalini*. When *Kundalini* rises from the base of the spine, it integrates the seven main *chakras* and the subtle experience manifests itself in a flow of cool vibrations, which can be felt on the hands and also over the crown of the head like a cool breeze. It is through these vibrations that we gain a new awareness beyond thought, beyond emotions; with this subtle awakening we become sensitive to the state of our *chakras* and those of others.

This degree of sensitivity to the state of our *chakras* and those of others can be termed SQ. Our EQ is enhanced with the rise of SQ as each chakra, when cleaned with the *Kundalini* energy, enhances our ability to emote.

For instance, as per *Sahaja Yoga*, the first *chakra* enhances your ability to be 'child like', the second enhances creativity/aesthetics, the third inculcates a feeling of satisfaction, the fourth helps you control anger, the fifth improves your communication skills so that you do not offend others, the sixth enables you to forgive, while the seventh, the crown chakra allows you to integrate all these qualities so that the whole is greater than the sum of its parts.

Corporates are also increasingly leaning towards spiritual awakening programmes, retreats, ethic camps, soul searching camps and transcendental meditation workshops for the spiritual development of their employees. The renewed interest in spiritual training can be traced to the rigours and complexities of the modern, competitive working environment, which breeds stress, tension and complexes among employees.

Mangeshda's Institute of Spiritual Awakening, founded by Mangesh Vadhavkar, who is popularly called Mangeshda, has designed a number of programmes to help modern-day man lead an active life, realising his hidden spiritual potential.

With 43 centres in India and abroad, the Institute of Spiritual Awakening conducts unique personality development programmes like Self-Recognition and Development (SRD), Stress Management, Core Enlightenment, Meditation, Reiki and *Satsangs*.

'The Self Recognition and Development programme encourages a person to develop his own personality, and bring out the unique qualities lying unrealised in him. Every individual has some good traits as well as bad traits. Instead of copying others, the course teaches one how to develop one's good traits and overcome the bad ones,' says Mangeshda. 'Self-contemplation of "What I am" changes the whole perspective towards life,' he explains.

The programme includes practical sessions on public speaking and interactive role-play to understand the roots of problems. These sessions break open the grip of complexes, nervousness, tension and stress and help to build self-confidence.

The training is primarily on how to preserve energies and use them to develop the innermost potential of the body, mind and soul. Understanding and practice of the same enables one to tackle any kind of negativity and face tough situations with ease in day-to-day life. The SRD programme caters to the overall development of persons of all ages.

The Core Enlightenment programme is an intense residential training course. Here, the participants are taught to totally disconnect themselves from the outer world, work over their negative emotions hidden deep within and prepare themselves to experience tranquillity and peace of mind. The special meditation techniques are simple, effective and effortless so that anybody can easily practise them. There are no restrictions of posture, dress, time, place, etc. The institute has also brought out meditation cassettes to enable people to practise the art at home.

The institute has designed its stress management programmes in such a manner that anyone and everyone can learn to reduce stress and enjoy life. The *Satsangs* are spiritual discourses by Mangeshda. Instead of being mere followers, he exhorts people to come forward and experience unity with the Divine Energy.

An Analysis of Spiritual Intelligence

The first inference I germinated was that spirituality is not rituals and cults of a particular religion. However, in some of the hues God has not been yoked to spirituality but I believe that God is the centre of all purposes. I believe we shouldn't treat God as an independent entity; rather He is a component of this world. I would treat God as a common denominator of all good in this world. We possess catholic geographic identities, religious sects and customs but we all weep, laugh, cry, enjoy for a cause.

It is very perceptible from our ambience that day-by-day competition is getting more and more fierce. The last century witnessed the metamorphosis of social behaviour. The world has evolved as a destination that is highly networked thereby enabling the business community to take over politics directly or indirectly. No country can project itself as an island. This change has exponentially boomed during the last 20 years. We have explored a plenitude of areas of consumption and so is the case in respect of jobs. Unlimited job roles are there but it all has increased in tandem with the population behemoth.

During the last 20 years, companies and enterprises were striving for market share, and profits, and were never reluctant to exploit nature, earth and all natural resources by any means. Companies attained the highest level of brutality towards the environment. This caused the emergence of a number of regulatory bodies. People invited a lot of impositions towards themselves. All these regulatory bodies are the concomitant of the renascent spiritual approach of people. This phenomenon seems quite weird apriori but enough analogies and evidences are present to prove it.

We can easily contend that human abilities have ameliorated singularly during the last century and in the last 20 years when distances of egotism were sifted out among humans, the human ego began to clash. This brought about a ruthless conflagration of intelligence. This was actually a war of Intelligent Quotient (IQ) but soon it became saturated. The main cause of this saturation of intelligence was complacency. The war made human beings very belligerent and attracted unbridled emotions. The new concept was bound to dawn that one who is emotionally intelligent or who can control and balance emotions, will win the race.

During the recent past, interdependence has increased so much that one could not hold to a personal stance that the way one is emotionally intelligent is absolutely right. For example, all the corporate titans, who were actually driving the technological force, believed that their emotions towards society are very controlled and without creating any clamour or hue and cry, they are driving society but soon they realised that they alone cannot stand tall in front of other companies and that's why a number of collaborations, M&As, took place. This realisation also brought out that the sole aim of earning profits could not sustain a company; there had to be a way out, and then emerged Spiritual Intelligence.

In may opinion, spiritual intelligence motivates a person intrinsically because it has no measure and is very purposeful, whereas EQ restricts one's thinking level. Since acute emotions are always connected with personal beliefs or persons, they confine one's orbit; whereas spiritual intelligence subsumes all entities uniformly thereby allowing a person to be a calmer, consistent performer and self-healed in a variety of situations. It widens one's vision and creates a broad perspective. Even in the previous examples we have observed that employees working in any company, who are on the path of spiritual intelligence, either work out their own development via meditation or they work for society as a whole but not for individuals. The family may be their indispensable priority but social service gives them tremendous impetus. This was quite evident in some of the cases of companies that was depicted in financial terms.

If we could see the future job scenario, we could find it attracting new definitions of cut-throat competition which, even now, is already a dog-eat-dog situation. Previously, skills demarcation in a pool of candidates was an easy task for interviewers but now more and more skilled candidates are appearing and through my personal experience I can really impugn their selection. It is all happening because candidates are still being scaled on IQ and EQ. I have found that pretence is now very easy. One can mould himself or herself according to situations in a very easy manner as far as the behavioural aspect is concerned but the reality is much behind that. Sycophantic employees are getting promotions, pretentious students are getting more praise from teachers.

The way out is Spiritual Intelligence. This can be the only criterion for assessors to judge persons because the Spiritually Intelligent person is aware about the sole purpose of the task to be done, he is aware of the subsystems and supersystems between which he is working, aware of the ramifications of his deeds; he possesses a long-term vision.

Take the case of the structure of organisations. We have three classifications of organisations today. One, multinational companies (MNCs) which have reached diverse parts of the globe and sustain a great uniformity in quality and product lines. These companies possess high IQ (Intelligent Quotient). The second are transnational companies (TNCs). These companies share the resources of other countries. They make the host country realise that we have to cope with each other. Their products also have uniform quality, the only difference being that those are made from local physical resources. These companies are emotionally intelligent because they independently continue their operations but allow the host country to share the pie.

Third are metanational (MeNCs) companies. Companies share resources but MeNCs share knowledge apart from resources. Sharing knowledge shows that companies are spiritually intelligent because they have a broad perspective of the future. The world has already become so interdependent that no company can do it alone, be it Microsoft, HP, Mittal Steel or any other. Each one of them is into mergers, acquisitions and collaborations. These companies are not just eyeing profits because profits alone will not enable them to survive. It would ultimately be society. If society realises that this company has direct impact on the individual, be it direct or indirect from the company's perspective, it would sustain itself and survive successfully. These companies are simultaneously involved in social concerns along with the commercial.

There is no doubt that spiritual Intelligence is the need of the hour. A spiritually intelligent person always seeks for purpose of any task before carrying it out; he is pliable. Leadership comes as a concomitant of SQ in a person. Their goals are not for their life time only. Their enjoyment doesn't hamper others' activities.

Envisioning a networked world is also a corollary of spiritual intelligence by monolithic enterprises. Ultimately humanity has no place other than earth to share. SQ is a lifestyle not a score. A person having a higher IQ can do very well in statistical or quantitative exercises, that's why it was embraced in the recent evolution of human being preponderated by technology. When technology got its generic platform or, say, a prerequisite standardisation, managing individuals became more important. Here we started promoting EQ. But ultimately when interconnection becomes inevitable we will have to withdraw our attention from individuals. This attitude automatically gives us leadership qualities. This broad vision is spiritual intelligence.

Guidelines for Best Practice

The following 22 guidelines represent the best current knowledge about how to promote emotional intelligence in the workplace. They apply to any development effort in which social and emotional learning is a goal. This would include most management and executive development efforts as well as training in supervisory skills, diversity, teamwork, leadership, conflict management, stress management, sales, customer relations, etc.

These guidelines are based on an exhaustive review of the research literature in training and development, counselling and psychotherapy, and behaviour change. The guidelines are additive and synergistic; to be effective, social and emotional learning experiences need not adhere to all of these guidelines, but the chances for success increase with each one that is followed.

The guidelines are divided into four phases that correspond to the four phases of the development process: preparation, training, transfer and maintenance, and evaluation. Each phase is important.

Paving the Way

- *Assess the organisation's needs*
  Determine the competencies that are most critical for effective job performance in a particular type of job. In doing so, use a valid method, such as comparison of the behavioural events, interviews of superior performers and average performers. Also make sure the competencies to be developed are congruent with the organisation's culture and overall strategy.
- *Assess the individual*
  This assessment should be based on the key competencies needed for a particular job and the data should come from multiple sources using multiple methods to maximise credibility and validity.
- *Deliver assessments with care*
  Give the individual information on his/her strengths and weaknesses. In doing so, try to be accurate and clear.

Also, allow plenty of time for the person to digest and integrate the information. Provide the feedback in a safe and supportive environment in order to minimise resistance and defensiveness. But also avoid making excuses or downplaying the seriousness of deficiencies.

- *Maximise learner choice*
  People are more motivated to change when they freely choose to do so. As much as possible, allow people to decide whether or not they will participate in the development process and have them set the change is goals themselves.
- *Encourage people to participate*
  People will be more likely to participate in development efforts if they perceive them to be worthwhile and effective. Organisational policies and procedures should encourage people to participate in development activity and supervisors should provide encouragement and the necessary support. Motivation also will be enhanced if people trust the credibility of those who encourage them to undertake the training.
- *Link learning goals to personal values*
  People are most motivated to pursue change that fits with their values and hopes. If a change matters little to people, they won't pursue it. Help people to understand whether a given change fits with what matters most to them.
- *Adjust expectations*
  Build positive expectations by showing learners that social and emotional competence can be improved and that such improvement will lead to valued outcomes. Also, make sure that the learners have a realistic expectation of what the training process will involve.
- *Gauge readiness*
  Assess whether the individual is ready for training. If the person is not ready because of insufficient motivation or other reasons, make readiness the focus of intervention efforts.

Doing the Work of Change

- *Foster a positive relationship between the trainers and the learners*
  Trainers who are warm, genuine and empathic are best able to engage the learners in the change process. Select trainers who have these qualities and make sure that they use them when working with the learners.
- *Make change self-directed*
  Learning is more effective when people direct their own learning programme, tailoring it to their unique needs and circumstances. In addition to allowing people to set their own learning goals, let them continue to be in charge of their learning throughout the programme and tailor the training approach to the individual's learning style.
- *Set clear goals*
  People need to be clear about what the competence is, how to acquire it and how to show it on the job. Spell out the specific behaviours and skills that make up the target competence. Make sure that the goals are clear, specific and optimally challenging.
- *Break goals into manageable steps*
  Change is more likely to occur if the change process is divided into manageable steps. Encourage both trainers and trainees to avoid being overly ambitious.
- *Provide opportunities to practise*
  Lasting change requires sustained practice on the job and elsewhere in life. An automatic habit is being unlearned and different responses are replacing it. Use naturally occurring opportunities for practice at work and in life. Encourage the trainees to try the new behaviours repeatedly and consistently over a period of few months.
- *Give performance feedback*
  Ongoing feedback encourages people and directs change. Provide focused and sustained feedback as the learners practice new behaviours. Make sure that supervisors, peers,

friends, family members—or some combination of these—give periodic feedback on progress.

- *Rely on experiential methods*
  Active, concrete and experiential methods tend to work best for learning social and emotional competencies. Development activities that engage all the senses and that are dramatic and powerful can be especially effective.
- *Build in support*
  Change is facilitated through ongoing support of others who are going through similar changes (such as a support group). Programmes should encourage the formation of groups where people give each other support throughout the change effort. Coaches and mentors also can be valuable in helping support the desired change.
- *Use models*
  Use live or videotaped models that clearly show how the competency can be used in realistic situations. Encourage learners to study, analyse and emulate the models.
- *Enhance insight*
  Self-awareness is the cornerstone of emotional and social competence. Help learners acquire greater understanding about how their thoughts, feelings and behaviour affect themselves and others.
- *Prevent relapse*
  Use relapse prevention, which helps people use lapses and mistakes as lessons to prepare themselves for further efforts.
- *Encourage use of skills on the job*
  Supervisors, peers and subordinates should reinforce and reward learners for using their new skills on the job. Coaches and mentors also can serve this function. Also, provide prompts and cues, such as through periodic follow-ups. Change is also more likely to endure when high status persons, such as supervisors and upper-level management, model it.

- *Develop an organisational culture that supports learning*
  Change will be more enduring if the organisation's culture and tone support the change and offer a safe atmosphere for experimentation.

Spiritual Intelligence—The Ultimate Intelligence

Spiritual Intelligence, first published in 2000, is another milestone publication about how the mind works. It is an unusual book, deceptively easy to read, considering its content, and may owe its relatively undeserved obscurity to inadequate promotion.

Spiritual intelligence is described as 'the intelligence with which we address and solve problems of meaning and value, the intelligence with which we can place our actions and our lives in a wider, richer, meaning-giving context, the intelligence with which we can assess that one course of action or one life-path is more meaningful than another.'

The authors contend that in the early part of the 20th century, IQ, or rational intelligence, was the big issue. More recently, emotional intelligence (EQ) has been identified as a requirement for the effective use of IQ

Now there exists much scientific data that points to the presence of a spiritual intelligence (SQ), the ultimate intelligence that serves as a necessary foundation for the effective functioning of both IQ and EQ.

What is SQ? introduces the concept as an expansion of psychology as a science and posits the need for a new psychological model of the human self and of human personality. In doing just that, the authors draw on mystical and mythological structures found within human spiritual thought, both ancient and modern, carefully pointing out that SQ is not necessarily about being religious, but rather it is an internal and innate ability of the human brain and psyche. How SQ is used is described; what indicates when it is highly developed and how to improve its level.

The Scientific Evidence for SQ deals with the anatomy and functioning of the brain. It summarises present knowledge of the subject, including the studies in neural oscillations that point to a third kind of thinking of which the brain is capable—unitive thinking.

A fulsome chapter is devoted to the significance of the brain's 40 Hz neural oscillations; what different brain wave patterns mean; and the more profound question of where does consciousness come from. The chapter dealing with the 'God spot' in the brain, identified by neuro-biologists Persinger and Ramachandran, and the varieties of spiritual experiences emanating therefrom, lead the authors to make some intriguing connections with human behaviours.

A New Model of the Self utilises the lotus symbol 'as the ultimate symbol of the spiritually intelligent self—the obvious way to combine the great Eastern and Western traditions of the self with the latest insights from science.'

Each layer of petals depicts one of the three basic human intelligences: the outer petals representing six ego types; the middle layer representing the associative conscious and unconscious components, and at the centre the Deep Self which is the main focus of this book.

Using SQ describes how we become, or as Western society has become, spiritually stunted and the symptoms of that condition. It gives guidance about the recovery of SQ and using it to be able to live with uncertainty yet find inner poise. 'Uncertainty can inspire us because it creates conditions in which we must make a choice. It gives us our freedom and sets the conditions for our responsibility.' Our SQ serves as an inner compass.

Can we improve our SQ? Uses the Lotus of the Self symbol to lay out six spiritual paths that any one of us might follow in living a life with greater heart—and you might be on more than one path at any one time. It lays out seven steps one can take to greater Spiritual Intelligence; ways to assess one's own SQ; and concludes with a helpful chapter on how to be, become, or remain spiritually intelligent in what is for the most part a spiritually dumb culture.

9

The Self is Complete

Hurt and Guilt

All psychological or emotional problems are centred on I, the self. When you say, 'I am frustrated,' is that frustration possible without I being involved? Will there be frustration if I is removed from frustration? I am frustrated, the mind is not frustrated. In fact, it should get frustrated because of you! It is wrong to say, 'My mind is giving me trouble.' The mind does not give you trouble, you are the trouble. 'I' is involved in frustration, 'I' is involved in despair. It is not the mind that is sad, I am sad. In fact, all your problems are centred on 'I'. By educating yourself, 'I' becomes more enlightened and mature. The problems are under control to a certain extent for a mature person, but not totally.

All your problems, namely, frustration, despair, sadness, etc., can be reduced to two: 'I am hurt', and 'I am guilty.' When we think about it, we find there is no third problem.

I am guilty. Of what? Of what I did or did not do. 'I should not have done that. Why did I do it?' `I should have done that. Why did I not do it?' Certain incidents are so well rooted in our memory that they keep coming back. The more you try to avoid them, the more they come back. You cannot avoid thoughts for you cannot avoid memory. A thought will be forgotten if you forget to remember but that does not happen. The more you try to avoid a thought the more it comes back. It is silly to try to avoid anything in the memory. Memory is memory. The more you try to avoid, the more reality you are giving to it. You are giving a new lease of life to the dead past. What is past, is past anyway. All that remains, is just memory. But the problem is that 'I' is involved. I is involved in every guilt. I is involved in every hurt: Why did he do this to me? How can he do it to me? Why me, of all the people?

Remember that it is you who allows the world to hurt you. I can hurt you only to the extent you allow me to hurt you. It is like hypnotising; you can get hypnotised by me only if you allow yourself to be hypnotised.

One man wanted to hypnotise me. He put one person to sleep and now turning towards me, said, 'I can hypnotise you, I can put you to sleep.' I agreed. I lay down and he started saying, 'You are going to sleep now . . . . You do not hear my words . . . . You are dead to this world . . . . You are dead to this room . . . . You are dead to time . . . . You are dead to everything . . . . You are going to sleep now . . . . You are sleeping now . . . I was lying down with my eyes closed. He lifted my hand and it fell down. 'See, he has gone to sleep.' I opened my eyes and asked, 'Who has gone to sleep?' He was shocked.

He said, 'Well, you did not receive my message.' I said, 'I did receive your message. Do you want me to repeat all that you said?' He said, 'No, no . . . . You received the words all right, but not the message. You did not try to sleep.' I said, 'If I have to try to sleep, where do you come in, in putting me to sleep?'

The world can hurt you only to the extent you allow it to hurt you. And `world' includes your family, relatives, friends, even gods. All of them can hurt you only to the extent you permit yourself to be hurt.

No One Can Hurt You

Vedanta goes a step further. It says: No one can hurt you. *Nayam hanti na hanyate: Atma*, I, neither hurts nor gets hurt. If you listen to the teaching well, you will discover the self to be *akarta*, actionless. Atma is free from action. It never performs any action that gives a guilt complex. Whatever there is, is just in your memory, just impressions. God has given us memory not for self-judgement. It is given to just remember the necessary things in life, so that you will not fail to recognise your wife and child when you return home or that you do not ask for another lunch the same day!

Memory is not you. You have picked up impressions in life, some of them pleasant, some of them unpleasant. It is only maturity to recognise the fact that all events cannot be pleasant. Life is a mixture of the pleasant and the unpleasant. A mature person is the one who accepts in one's stride, both the pleasant and the unpleasant in the journey of life. Memories are just memories, whereas the T in you is simple awareness.

Self does not perform any action. When you are looking at me, it is not the self that is looking. The self that is behind the eyes, behind the mind is simple awareness. What action does it perform? It is mind that moves, thinks, wishes and wills, and all actions take place on account of that. Awareness just blesses the mind, makes things stick and that awareness is T. It performs no action whatsoever and hence you are ever free from guilt because guilt is centred on T which is actionless.

And there can be hurt only if someone can objectify the T. But who can objectify T. You are the only one who can objectify the whole world, but the world cannot objectify you. Is it not true? You are the T and everything else is the object of T. This body, the sense organs, the mind, time, space—everything is the object of knowledge of T and T is the only subject in creation. There is no second subject at all. Who can objectify the T to hurt you? *Nayam hanti na hanyate*—neither hurt nor guilt is possible in atma, the Self.

There is a relative absence of hurt and guilt for a mature person. He does not permit the world to hurt him because the world can hurt only that person who wants the world to behave in a particular manner. If you accept people as they are with their limitations, their insecurities and their fears, then you become understanding and sympathetic. If someone is trying to cheat you and you know that, and you allow the person to cheat you; that means you are stronger. You know that you are big enough to allow this cheating to take place. It is like a threadless screw. You go on driving the screw but it keeps turning. Nothing happens to it because it is threadless. I do not mean that you should be a loose screw or something. What I mean is that the world cannot hurt you if you understand it rightly.

This is not arrogance or pride. You are only inviting problems when you are proud: 'No one can hurt me.' If you have an ego, there will be another one who will have a bigger ego. I am not talking about ego. I am saying that you should try to understand the other person. Why should he accuse you? Why should he bother you? Why is he frightened of you? Why is he jealous of you? What makes him so? The moment you ask these questions, you become an enquirer, you become understanding and sympathetic, and in the process, you also learn how to deal with that person. Sometimes you have to keep a distance, sometimes you have to be patient. You can do that according to your disposition, as long as you are not hurt.

Thus, you should become mature and maturity is inner growth. It has to be initiated by you, not by God because you have a free will. And you can never be the loser. You may lose some money in the process of becoming mature, but so what? At least you are together as a person and when you have acquired this maturity, you will be able to understand the truth that the self, `I', is *purna*, complete, whole.

You are Whole

You are complete, whole. The whole cannot be made up of patches. Just as infinity does not consist of finite numbers, so also whole is always whole and not something separate from me. Therefore, as the self, you are a whole person. You come across this whole person whenever you are happy. Whenever you are listening to music and feel happy, there is the music that you love and also you, the person you, whom you love. Both are loved in the experience of happiness. At that time, your likes and dislikes do not interfere, meaning that the wanting self, the struggling self, the small self does not present itself. Then you find that the situation has changed and you form a complete circle. It is this circle that is called *purnatvam*, wholeness. This circle can be manifest in any situation that makes you happy.

You are watching the stars, you are pleased. You do not want the stars or anything else in the situation to be different from what they are. When you are pleased with a situation, the situation and you become a complete circle. At that time, you are in fact, experiencing yourself because the whole is you. It is a thing to be understood. Experientially *purnatvam*, wholeness is known to you. You do not need a new experience of the whole. It is the confusion that is the problem and not the lack of experience.

The Self is to be Understood

Another problem regarding *Vedanta* is that people think that Vedanta is intellectual knowledge and having gained that knowledge, you should practise. Practise what? If practise is required, it is the practice of study of Vedanta. *Atma va are srotavyah*: The self must be listened to. It is a manner of listening. When you are listening to the *Gita*, you are not doing anything intellectual because it is everything. The *Gita* is *pramana*, a valid means of knowledge. The words of the Gita are a mirror that shows you what you are. When you want to see your face, you require a mirror because your eyes cannot objectify your face. When you see your face in the mirror, it is with your eyes that you see it, but you still require a mirror. So also, when you listen to the Gita, it is with your intellect alone that you understand, but you require the mirror in the form of the words of the Gita. The person who uses the intellect is the person who is using this means of knowledge and that person is whole, *param brahma*. The word 'whole' serves as a mirror to get you back to yourself and you are never tried of looking at yourself in the mirror.

You look at yourself in the mirror in the morning even though you have already looked at yourself yesterday. The first thing that a person does in the morning is to look at oneself in the bathroom mirror. And thereafter, one takes the opportunity of looking at the self in every shining surface he comes across. When this physical body, with all its limitations is so much loved by a person, what to talk of that self that is *ananda*, full, and the mirror that reflects this complete self? No one will ever be tired of looking at this mirror that does not tell me that I am a sinner. Lord Krishna says:

Api cedasi papebhyah sarvebhyah papakrttan ah
Sarvam jnanaplavenaiva vrjinam santarisyasi

[Even if you be the worst sinner among all the sinners, still you will cross over with ease all the sins with the raft of knowledge alone] (*Bhagavad Gita* IV 36)

If you are the greatest sinner who has committed all the crimes in the book and even more, even then you will cross this ocean of sin with the raft of knowledge and that knowledge is the *Gita*.

There is no new experience required here. It is the understanding of the experience that is required. The self is always experienced. You are able to listen to me because the self is ever shining. It has to be understood that the self is the whole. The understanding requires the inner maturity.

I should live the life of *yoga* in order to be mature. The *Gita* is *yogasastra* too because it talks about *yoga*, the means to gain inner maturity.

What I have talked here so far is all based on the *Gita*. For a yogi who has a mature mind of what is known as *suddhantahkaranaim*, there is something to be understood. Understanding the self is the very end of life. What you are seeking in life all along is self-acceptance, and that is possible only when the self is acceptable; otherwise you cannot appreciate the teaching.

When I say you are a happy self, it is not positive thinking, it is proper thinking. Positive thinking does not take you very far because when there is positive thinking, negative thinking is invariably involved in it. If a man has a very low image of himself—thinks of himself as useless—and if he is told that he is useful, that may help him. But ultimately, the positive thinking is only as valid as the negative thinking. However, when I say you are already acceptable, it is not just positive thinking because it is a fact; self is acceptable, is *purna*. The *purnatvam*, the acceptability is experienced by you whenever you are happy, and that is to be understood.

You Must Study the Scriptures

Our scriptures, namely, the Upanishads, the Gita, are the mirror. It is fascinating to study them. There is nothing intellectual in that study, if the study is carried out in a proper manner. For example, you are paying attention to me right now. There is nothing intellectual in that. I am using all the reasoning to ward off your irrational conclusions about yourself. You have to see the reasoning and knock off the irrational conclusions. How irrational the conclusions are has to be recognised as such. In the absence of proper reasoning, everything appears rational. What *sastra*, the scripture does is that it brings to light all the wrong conclusions and then knocks them off.

The way of the *sastra* is not replaceable by any other method. No *yoga* can replace the study of the *sastra* and so it is said:

Sannyasya sravanam kuryat

[Give up everything and listen to the scriptures]

Sravanam means *sastra-vicara*, enquiry into the truth with the help of the *sastra*. *Sastra* is a mirror for you and you must seize the opportunity to study the scriptures and expose yourself to them. It is all in your blood, in your culture, in your upbringing. You may not know that you have already imbibed a number of things. You have to know. Sri Hanuman had to be told by Jambavan that he could lead and carry out the given task. He had to be told and similarly you also have to be told. You have it in you. There are a number of things in our religious culture but you have to know them and that is what you do by the study of our scriptures, the *Gita* and the *Upanishads*.

10

Introspect to Improve

'Don't find fault with others. Rather learn to see your own faults.'

Holy Mother Sri Sarada Devi

Such is the importance of introspection in our lives that the subject merits a separate discussion of its own. We understood in the preceding chapter that introspection is the watching of one's thoughts and emotions with a view to finding the source of all our distractions and mental turmoil.

It is the examining of one's thoughts to see and discriminate which of them are good, having a positive effect on us and which of them are bad. One may even say that introspection is the art of thinking about one's own thoughts!

When a schoolboy fares badly in his exams, his parents often tell him to introspect and find out the reason for his poor performance. Similarly, when someone commits an evil act, we advise him to introspect to realise what he has done and how he may avoid repeating the mistake in future. Evidently, introspection is a very useful tool for one's betterment! But isn't it surprising that most of us don't even know the meaning of this word, leave alone the technique of using it for self improvement?

As we shall see, introspection is crucial if we are to have a happy, fulfilling life. It is exactly because we are lacking in this power that we often find ourselves to be in a miserable condition.

All humans suffer from two kinds of sufferings—physical sufferings (such as diseases, sprains, etc.) and mental sufferings (such as depression, lack of concentration, etc.). For the first, we usually visit a doctor and hope that he will give us a cure for our disease. However, one usually finds that the doctor first insists on a battery of tests—blood tests, x-rays, CT scans, etc.—so much so that we get irritated and ask if he is ever going to treat us instead of just sending our already tired bodies to all departments of the hospital! The truth is that the poor doctor is only doing his job. He must first find out what is wrong with us before he can provide the cure.

This process of finding the cause of the disease is known as diagnosis. In fact, once the diagnosis is completed successfully, the disease is already 70 per cent cured in most cases. Similar is the case of mental ailments. We must first diagnose exactly what our problem is before we try to find a cure. And just as in the case of physical diseases, mental diseases are 70 per cent cured the moment we find the cause of the disease through accurate diagnosis. The diagnosis of mental ailments is known as introspection.

However, the crucial difference between mental sickness and physical sickness is that in physical sickness, the doctors, nurses and hospitals are there to help us. But in mental sickness, nobody else can really cure us—we can get some guidance from people like psychologists or psychiatrists but ultimately it is our own efforts that will help cure us. We must be our own doctor and make full use of introspection, which is the most effective tool available to US.

In fact, introspection is also a form of prevention because when we practice introspection regularly, we become strong enough to ward off mental diseases even before they make their appearance in our minds. This makes introspection even more important since prevention is better than cure! And why do we need to look for outside support, when our mind itself has the capacity to look within itself and analyse its own preoccupations.

So it is clear that introspection is critically important in our lives and needs to be done daily on a regular basis. For this, we need to practice watching our thought flow. This should be practised ten minutes in the mornings and evenings daily. We should simply watch our thoughts without reacting—no censure, no criticism, accepting the way we are and making no efforts to change just yet—just watching the thoughts flowing in and out of our mind, like a gateman watches people enter and leave by the gate. Once you know the preoccupations of your own mind, you can guide it to your own advantage.

Introspection also builds mental strength to face life's great challenges. All of us have to face great tragedies at some time or the other. For some, the experience may come early in life, while for others, it may come later. Perhaps someone's parents pass away at an early age or perhaps another person is suddenly widowed after 20 years of happy, blissful marriage. In any case, we see how a particular individual emerges through such tragedies stronger and purer than before, while another simply collapses and in some cases, it even turns to alcoholism or drug abuse and doing so ends up as a mere shell of a human being.

The former case is the effect of practising the art of introspection, where the person concerned was able to realise that he must shake off his sorrow and move on with his life, that he must use this tragedy as an opportunity to strengthen himself and build his character and so emerge with a better personality. In the second case, the person concerned did not care to examine the source of his sorrow and so simply got washed away by the tidal wave of grief that had overcome him.

One method of strengthening this habit of introspection is to analyse the very world we live in. Most of us take this world for granted and imagine that others see and feel the same way as we do. This is incorrect—in fact, each one of us lives in a different world. This can easily be seen by the fact that same objects produce different emotions in different people. A father may feel deep love and affection when he sees his own child's toy lying by the road in front of his house, whereas a stranger may see the same as a dirty doll worthy of being kicked into the drain! Again, we see how babies have no idea of the value of money and may even tear a 500-rupee note into pieces without giving it a second thought. Yet things considered useful by a baby such as a piece of bread or an old and broken toy are usually seen as useless by us.

Even the same person at different times sees things in a different way. For instance, the same mother is the best mother in the whole world when she lovingly serves food or puts her child to bed, but to the child she becomes the worst mother in the world when she is angry and slaps and scolds the child. Or consider how a young couple who married against the will of their parents, professing undying love for each other, end their marriage a few years later in a bitter divorce, claiming that they are sworn enemies and will destroy each other in court! These examples show us that in reality, it is our mind that sways us by its whims and fancies and that most of the time, we are under its firm control and have no say in our own lives.

In fact, we only imagine that the world around us influences us in various ways. In reality, it is our mind that projects its thoughts and feelings onto the world around it and this is what causes us to perceive some objects as good and others as bad. We believe that the world must run according to our plan—that we must be successful in all our endeavours, that all people must be polite and sympathetic towards us, etc.

When reality dawns on us and we realise that this is not true, we often become disheartened or cynical. By introspection, we can realise that the world has no power to influence us. Rather, it is our mind that is making us happy or sad by projecting the respective qualities on the world around us.

Thus, we see that through introspection we are able to find the real cause of our suffering, which is our uncontrolled mind. In most of us, the mind acts as an agent of the lower self (that aspect of our personality that tries to drag us down into bad habits, evil emotions, etc.) and is a great foe of the higher self (that aspect of our personality that tries to inculcate good habits, pure emotions, etc.). The mind is a very treacherous foe and knows innumerable ways to trap and deceive us. Sometimes it may appear very cooperative and, just when we least expect it, suddenly spring a trap and destroys all our good intentions. The only way to control such an undisciplined and harmful mind is to practise introspection at all times.

The positive, mind-controlling power of introspection can be seen even in our ordinary lives. In most of the cases, a normal student has not developed the capacity required to control his mind. He wastes his time in playing, watching TV, gossiping, etc. But when he suddenly becomes aware of the approaching exams that are only a month away, realisation dawns on him that he will fail unless he studies hard.

During that one month, he allows nothing to distract him from his studies. He even refuses his mother's call for food and instead sticks to his studies simply because through introspection he realises what danger he was in and also realises exactly how his mind must be controlled if he has to clear the exam. What this student did during the one crucial month before the exam, we need to do at every single moment of our lives.

It is well known that if we are fully convinced of the utility of a particular path or action, then we will put forward our best possible efforts to succeed. This is seen in the case of the smoker who suddenly realises one fine day how harmful his habit has been; from that day on, he will make every effort to quit his habit. If we look around us, we will find many people who have given up a bad habit or have taken up a good habit because somehow they were convinced that such an action would truly benefit them. Our problem is that we are lacking in faith in the prescribed methods to correct and fulfil our lives. That is why it becomes absolutely essential to convince ourselves that introspection is critical if we are to live happy lives.

Before we can perform any action, there are two steps that must take place—firstly, there must be a tendency in us to perform that action and secondly, we must consent for the action to get performed. It is only when both these stages have been passed that we can perform any action. According to our scriptures, when the tendency to act arises, it emerges in a bubble form in our mind. At this stage the emotion is easy to control and overpower. However, the bubble soon forms into a wave and is then almost impossible to control. For example, there is a stage when we begin to feel annoyed at someone or something and then comes the stage when we are anger itself, with a red face, flaring nostrils, etc. It is only because we gave our consent to the anger in bubble form to erupt into the wave of anger that it overpowered us.

The trick is to stop our feeling at the bubble stage itself and so prevent any occurrence of the wave of emotion. The catch is that this bubble-to-wave conversion takes a fraction of a second and this is all the time we have to prevent an evil tendency from overpowering us and putting us in a position of great danger or embarrassment.

This requires the practice of introspection. There are both good and bad tendencies existing within us, due to the influence of our past actions, our environment, etc. We must not get disheartened by our bad tendencies and should stand firm and refuse to allow them to control us.

A German philosopher has said that the tendency to sin is not a sin; it is the consent to sin that is a sin. What he meant is that through the effect of past actions or environment, etc., we may feel the urge to commit bad actions. This urge in itself is not a sin—it is only when we consent to the urge and go ahead and carry it out, that the sin is committed. For instance, your parents ask you to do some household errand at a time when you want to go out and be with your friends. You may be reluctant to comply and may get the impulse to lie to your parents and excuse yourself with one or the other pretext. Even though this thought of lying to your parents has appeared in the mind, yet the sin has not been committed. It is only when you give in to the thought and actually avoid the work by making an excuse that the sin is committed. Firmly placing this before us, we must at all times fight off all evil tendencies and should make all efforts to purify our lives. We must refuse to give our consent to evil tendencies no matter how many times or how forcefully they make their appearance in our consciousness.

As mentioned in the last chapter, a little bit of introspection will reveal that there exists a basic tragedy in our lives which is our inability to do that which we know to be right and helpful, and our inability to avoid that which we know to be wrong and harmful. This realisation will help build our resolve to improve our lives by the practice of good and helpful actions.

In the end, we must remember the law of *karma* that says that the fruits of actions will surely come to us, sooner or later. If we perform righteous actions, we will be rewarded and will enjoy peaceful, fulfilled lives. But if we perform unrighteous or evil deeds, we will suffer and will feel miserable and wretched all over lives. We must learn to stand up and face our weaknesses. We must take responsibility for changing our lives. So many times we make feeble excuses such as, 'My friend influenced me to behave that way' or 'I don't know how it happened', etc. We ourselves are reponsible for our actions—we must acknowledge this and must recognise that as we sow, so shall we reap. A *shloka* in our scriptures says that the effects of our actions will surely find us one day just as a calf finds its mother amongst a herd of a thousand cows.

We must be awake at all times through the practice of introspection. Beginners may find it useful to maintain a daily diary with two columns—one for time wasted and one for time utilised in rightful activities. Fill this diary at the end of each day and analyse your entries. This will give an insight into how we waste our time and will enable us to put forward energies in the right direction to effect a change in our lives.

When we introspect, we find that our lives are changed and that suddenly we find greater peace and happiness in this very place that seemed such a hell earlier. This is what Swamiji meant when he said that we must Arise, awake and stop not till the goal is reached.'

There is a beautiful mantra, which we can use in our lives—*Introspect daily, detect diligently, negate ruthlessly, substitute wisely, grow steadily, be happy*. What this means is that we must go through continuous introspection, detect the source of our suffering; once detected we must negate this ruthlessly and substitute it wisely with good thoughts and ideas.

By doing so, we will grow steadily and will eventually attain happiness. Having understood introspection—its importance and its advantages—it must be clear to us how through practice of SDM, we can strengthen the ability of introspection in our lives for our own betterment as well as for those around us.

Manage Your Thoughts

'Difference is the first sign of thought'

'We are what our thoughts have made us; so take care of what you think. Our thoughts make things beautiful, our thoughts make things ugly.'—Swami Vivekananda

The importance of introspection can further be understood by the practice of SDM and can be further strengthened by learning the art of 'managing' our thoughts.

We live in an increasingly 'managed' world. Advertisements and newspaper articles are full of how management experts are devising new and wonderful ways of managing the environment we live in. These 'Management Gurus' are managing our businesses, hospitals, schools and even our relationships with people around us. But unfortunately, the hustle and bustle of life has made us oblivious to the first principle of management—namely, thought management or the management of one's own self!

Sceptics among us may ask as to how 'Thought Management' is actually related to self-management. We are so busy in living our lives that we never even stop to think about what is going on in our minds. We never realise the vital importance that thoughts play in shaping our lives. Then there are many unwanted thoughts that plague us all the time and which need to be weeded out of our minds.

Thoughts are the root cause of all the suffering in our lives—this may seem hard to believe at first, but is absolutely true! The science of 'Thought Management' is there to help us with techniques for building control over our thoughts. The following facts supported by verifiable examples give us an insight into this science of 'Thought Management':

1. *The first fact states that before we perform any action, there is and there must be a thought that provides the impulse for that action.*

   This means that if we can control or manage our thoughts, then we can control and manage our actions. The following two illustrations may convince us of the point being made.:

   (a) What is the state of our minds before an exam? For most of us, there is a late realisation that exams are approaching and unless we take drastic measures, there is every chance of a disaster coming our way. We then push aside all thoughts and engage ourselves in our studies.

No outside distraction—no matter how tempting—is allowed even a faint entry into our minds. When our mother tells us to eat food, we get annoyed and say, 'Not now! I have to study.' Here we are being forced to manage our thoughts due to the fear of failure of exams. Just imagine if we had such superb control on our thoughts all through the year, then all our dreams and ambitions would come true so easily and naturally!

(b) Consider another example: Suppose your friend suddenly slaps you one day. What will your thoughts be like then? First there may be some embarrassment at the humiliation, then there is a desire for revenge and at last anger may overtake you so powerfully that a fight ensues right in the middle of the street, just like little schoolboys quarrelling among themselves! If either of you had been able to manage your thoughts at the initial stage itself, let's say either through negotiations or by forgiving the other, then it would have been possible to prevent the situation from worsening.

2. *The second fact of Thought Management states that it is not the world around us that affects us—it is our attitude to the world around us which affects us.*

When we are in a good mood, then no matter how dirty or crowded the environment around us, we are most likely to feel peace and calm. On the other hand, when we are in a bad mood, then even if we are located in a beautiful hill station or are sitting by the side of a beautiful lake, we may feel great disturbance within. The following illustration supports our fact:

There were once two prisoners who were locked in the same cell. The cell had two windows—one overlooked a dirty drain and the other opened out to a beautiful scene giving full view of the sky above and hills below. One of the prisoners developed a habit of sitting by the first window and as the days went on, the dirty scene outside caused impure thoughts to arise in his mind and so he went lower and lower into depression. On the other hand, the second prisoner used to look out of the second window and, in time, the beautiful scenery made him develop good, peaceful thoughts in his mind and he gradually became a reformed person. This is the impact that thoughts have on us.

It is important to realise this vital importance that thoughts play in our lives, since it is only then that we will awaken to the importance of control of thoughts. Once we know the true relation of thoughts to ourselves, then we will not be very disturbed by the same thoughts as before.

3. *The third fact of Thought Management states that there is a definite relation between thoughts and mind—in fact the mind is nothing but a flow of thoughts.*

   It is like the case of water and a river. Not any water is called a river—only when water flows can it be termed a river. Similarly, only when there is a flow of thoughts can the mind be said to exist. If the flow of thought ceases then the mind does not exist. This means that the control of thoughts is the same as control of the mind.

   During deep sleep, there is a total absence of thoughts and the mind ceases to function temporarily. Then we feel great peace and say, 'I don't know anything, I just slept well.'

   There is saying in Hindi '*Chinta Chitta Hai*' which means that thoughts are like a burning fire. Just as a fire burns away a dead body, thoughts burn away a living body. This is the immense power of thoughts!

4. *The fourth fact of Thought Management states that if we wish to establish our mastery over our thoughts, we need to resolve to make proper use of our eyes and ears.*

   It is a common complaint amongst spiritual aspirants that they do not get much benefit and remain much the same as before, even though they read so many scriptures and conduct so many different practices such as *Pranayama*, etc.! The principal reason is that such people don't pay any attention to the management of their thoughts. Swami

Vivekananda has described their condition in a rather humorous quote:

'Before we can crawl half a mile, we want to cross the ocean like Hanuman! It cannot be. Everyone going to be a Yogi, everyone going to meditate! It cannot be. The whole day mixing with the world with Karma Kanda, and in the evening sitting down and blowing through your nose! Is it so easy? Should Rishis come flying through the air because you have blown three times through the nose? Is it a joke? It is all nonsense.' (Complete Works, Vol. 3, *Lectures from Colombo to Almora, The Future of India*).

What we need is proper thought management that will enable us to purify ourselves and achieve some peace in life.

The essential thing then is to control the thoughts. Everything else will follow. Even reading of scriptures is useful only so far as it helps us control our thoughts. Latu Maharaj (Swami Adbhutananda), a disciple of Sri Ramakrishna was an illiterate all his life. Yet, he achieved immense wisdom and spiritual enlightenment!

Even without reading a single scripture, he was able to attain everything that the scriptures talk about.

The main reason why we suffer from such unruly and undisciplined thoughts is because we have all this time been taking in unwholesome thoughts through our eyes and ears. It is something like the case of today's polluted rivers where all the filth from the cities is being dumped in them unchecked. And then we lament that the water is so unclean and toxic!

If we wish to establish our mastery over our thoughts, we need to resolve to make proper use of our eyes and ears—the taking in of unwholesome thoughts must stop immediately. Everyday we go to school or college or office and indulge in gossip, discuss sinful things with our friends and after coming home, we expect our minds to be pure and disciplined—this is impossible. Have you seen what happens when the master gives his dog full freedom to do whatever it likes? It soon becomes wild and bites and chases everyone and perhaps one day bites its own master. The position of our mind is exactly like that. Now that we have spoilt our mind and the thoughts occupying it, we must resolve to start the process of bringing it under control from this very moment. The eyes and ears should be used to expose ourselves to noble and uplifting thoughts that will purify and elevate our minds.

5. *The fifth fact of Thought Management states that in order to control the mind, we must know the goal of life.*

   People generally believe that the goal is just sensual pleasure and so they give unbridled freedom of enjoyment to their minds and senses and later reap bitter fruits like the master of the dog mentioned before. It is absolutely necessary to have right ideas before we can develop wholesome thoughts and be able to manage our thoughts efficiently. We have already established in the chapter on 'Introduction' that the goal of life is uninterrupted peace, happiness and bliss. And unless we realise ourselves that the goal is to enjoy uninterrupted peace, we will not find enough motivation to change our ways.

6. *The sixth fact of Thought Management describes the general nature of our thoughts.*

   Having established the importance of thought management, let us see how to achieve this. Just as in any other field of management, if we wish to become management experts in the management of our thoughts, we need to have a thorough understanding of the nature of these thoughts. Any given thought has two aspects to it—one is *aham vritti* (subject) and the other is *idam vritti* (object). *Aham vritti* is that part of the thought that relates to us and idam vritti is that part of the thought that relates to whatever is perceived as non-self, that is, everything except self. For instance, in the sentence, 'I see a red ball', the *aham vritti* is what relates to the self, to me. So here the perceiver of the ball is my self, which is *aham vritti.*

That what is outside of me *Idam vritti* (non-self) that is, the red ball. So every thought is the mixture of *aham vritti* and *idam vritti*. There is a constant struggle in our minds between those two aspects.

7. T*he seventh fact of Thought Management are the three key characteristics of our thoughts.*
   (a) *Quantity of thoughts*
   By quantity of thoughts is meant the frequency of thoughts, or in other words, the number of thought-eruptions per second. For most of us, this is very high.
   (b) *Quality of thoughts*
   By quality of thoughts is meant the nature of thoughts, that is, good or bad thoughts, pure or dirty thoughts, selfish or selfless, and so on.
   (c) *Direction of thoughts*
   Finally, by direction of thoughts, we mean the path or flow of thoughts. Thoughts tend to flow in one direction—if we are angry, then everything around us will anger us, if we are happy, then everything around us will seem joyous.
8. *The eighth fact of Thought Management establishes three basic principles that relate to the above mentioned seventh fact.*
   (a) The first principle under this eighth fact is: The higher the frequency of thoughts, the more are the sufferings we have to endure.
   This is evident if we analyse the number of thought-eruptions when we are disturbed. When we are angry or excited there is a sudden increase in the number of thoughts and as a result, we loose all control and commit acts that cause embarrassment or harm. When the quantity of thoughts is high we suffer mental disturbance and suffer symptoms such as lack of sleep, bad digestion, headache, high blood pressure, tension, etc. In fact, the source of emotions such as depression, dejection or remorse is due to higher number of

thoughts. In extreme cases, high frequency of thoughts can also cause insanity.

Here it is good to remember that the reverse is also true, that is, if thoughts are present in lesser numbers, we experience peace and become calm and quite. This is why we feel peace when we practice watching thought flow.

It should also be remembered that the greatest results are achieved only when we work with a calm and quiet mind. In order to enjoy success in our endeavours, it is essential to keep a calm and quiet mind by reducing the number of thoughts.

(b) The second principle under this eighth fact is: For peace of mind, it is essential to practise detachment.

Suppose there is a loose thread hanging from our shirt and we try to pull it. What happens? If the thread is still attached to the cloth at the other end, pulling it will cause creases and will spoil the shirt.

The right approach is to cut the other, end of the thread also so that it is free and then the thread will slide out easily. Similarly, if we try to pull away our mind from all the thoughts that have been plaguing us without first detaching ourselves from the very objects that cause these thoughts, we will face not only failure but also will become prey to all sorts of mental ailments.

It is important to note here that when some particular thought is bothering us, there must be some object behind that thought—there cannot be a thought without an object behind it.

Let us say, I want to get over the feelings of lust or greed. At the same time, if I watch such stuff on TV that is full of nothing but this, then—no matter how hard I try—I will never succeed in removing those feelings.

One must first cut off the attachment to the object, only then an effort at ‘pulling out the thread’ will be successful. Many people don’t understand this and attempt to practise meditation. 'When they sit down with closed eyes, they find that the number of thoughts has suddenly increased! Why?

Because their minds are so full of various thoughts, desires, etc. that when the eyes are closed, these thoughts get an opportunity to come out in the open. Getting scared, they jump off their seats and say 'I don't need this meditation and other things! It is absolutely ineffective!'

Actually speaking, it is not that meditation is ineffective, it is just that their practice is not wholehearted and sincere. This is why when as beginners we sit for meditation, we feel as if we are being pulled off the seat of meditation. The reason being, we are not detached from the objects of attachment and so are unable to meditate.

This is also why some people feel so much of tension in the face and neck when they sit to meditate. The solution is to first detach yourself from the objects of attachment and then attempt meditation—it will be so natural, so peaceful!

Like a good goldsmith, we need to know exactly where to hammer to reform ourselves. In this case, we must use the hammer of detachment to remove the bondage we have with various objects of sense enjoyment.

This practice of detachment is needed to control the quantity, quality and direction of thoughts. It is said that if we really wish to enjoy life, we must have this power of detachment.

(c) The third principle under this eighth fact is: It is only what is not normal that causes tension—what is normal and natural can never cause tension.

How much do we weigh? For most of us, it may be sixty to seventy kilos—do we ever feel that our body is a burden? Never! In spite of carrying around so much of flesh and bones all the time, we never say, 'I am tired of carrying my body.'

But what happens when we pick up a two-year old child? The baby may weigh only ten kilos, but in a matter of minutes we get tired and put down the child and tell him to walk on his own. Why this difference—in one case, 70 kilos is no burden, in another ten kilos is a burden within five minutes!

This is because our own body weight is normal and natural for us. The weight of the child is not a natural weight for us.

Similar is the case of the mind. The nerves have the capacity to carry a certain load—beyond that we feel tension. For some, may be three hours of study causes no tension, others may feel the tension in only one hour.

Consider how you feel when you indulge in your favourite hobby—say, kite flying or hiking or playing chess. Do you feel any stress even after two hours of such activity? No! This is because the mind and body are united in this particular task and you engage in it cheerfully.

However, when we are studying or are working in the office, how do we feel? After only an hour of work, there is tension and headache. In this case, the mind and body are not united in the work and so the load feels unnatural and causes tension.

The higher frequency of thoughts is not a natural state for the mind—this is why we feel tension, depression, etc. To reduce this frequency, we must practice detachment ruthlessly. All old habits, friends, gossip, etc. must go or we shall never ever achieve peace in our lives.

9. *The ninth fact of Thought Management explains methods to manage thoughts along each of the three characteristics mentioned earlier under the seventh fact.*

(a) For reducing the quantity of thoughts, we need to follow the three steps outlined below:

(i) *Discipline*: Discipline means carrying out one's activities in a planned, and systematic manner, according to a regular time table. Someone said that no one is so pitiable as the man who has no systematic plan in life and who spends every moment thinking about what he will do next. When we are disciplined, we don't waste time because we don't need to plan and re-plan our activities.

The mind becomes automatically calm when we discipline it and don't conduct ourselves according to its whims and fancies.

Even if practising discipline all through the day is difficult, we must make a commitment to practise discipline for four to five hours a day. For these few hours everyday, we must follow a set routine.

(ii) *Keep yourself busy all the time:* This is one of the most effective ways of reducing the frequency of thoughts. When we are busy in some activity like finishing a deadline at work or trying to study hard before an exam, where is the time to spend on idle thoughts? In order to keep busy, one must practise *dharmam chara,* that is, the practising righteously.

Around 50 or 60 years ago, common people in general were relatively much happier than they are today! They would spend all their free time in housework. Some would even refuse the help of servants saying that they wanted to serve their families out of love.

As a result of being busy, they had no time for gossip or TV and were relatively full of peace. Nowadays, people simply run after leisure and free time and then waste all that time in filling up their heads with stupid and sinful thoughts.

Being busy also means being alert—how alert we are when we drive a car! No other distracting thoughts are allowed into the mind—the one and only thought is how to drive and reach our destination safely.

So if we do all our activities remaining similarly alert we may, to a large extent, be able to keep out unnecessary thoughts from our minds.

We suffer various temptations because we are not busy enough. The busier we are, the less time we waste on such useless activities that can only cause mental unrest.

One of Sri Ramakrishna's great monastic disciples, Swami Ramakrishnananda, used to sit and do mathematics when he was free—simply so that his mind did not have the time to go here and there. Being a Sadhu, he was well versed in controlling the mind!

(iii) Practice: The principles being outlined here are available to all. Then why is it that one section of people is able to benefit immensely transforming their entire lives while the other, that includes a vast majority of people, is unable to do so?

It is simply because most of the latter are not serious enough and do not want to practise these things. Those who are serious, those who really want to improve themselves will do so; the others will only hear lectures and read books and will never improve.

Is not it astonishing that we can't implement one small decision in our lives and yet we want to read the Gita and the Upanishads and achieve all the high things that are written there. Of course, knowledge and reading are useful to some extent, but the main thing is practice, which we do not want to do.

Practice is the essential thing, otherwise we may read the Ramayana till we are on our deathbed and still stay the same! It is like the case of the boy who regularly attends all his classes, yet fails to practise when he goes home. Can you imagine what will happen to him at the time of his exams—naturally he fails!

(b) Next, let us look at the quality aspect of thoughts. Thoughts can be either good or bad depending on their nature. Due to good thoughts, we feel inspired to read holy books or listen to inspiring lectures by holy persons and due to bad thoughts, we wish to visit places such as the Bandstand (a popular seafront area in Mumbai frequented by 'fashionable' people).

The following tips help to control the quality of the mind:

Association with good objects and ideas and rejecting bad objects and ideas.

(a) Whether our thoughts are good or bad depends on the objects we associate with. If we spend the whole day associating with good things, our thoughts will naturally be good and if we spend the day associating with bad things, our thoughts will be bad. Of course, 'good' or 'bad' is determined by one's own value system and what may be good for me may be bad for you.

For instance, Vaishnavas do not eat meat, onions, garlic, etc., but in Bengal people offer fish to God. So we need to define good and bad universally—that is, we need do define them in such a manner that the definition will be applicable to all, and the goal is the ultimate goal of every single person, that is, uninterrupted peace.

Therefore all that takes us closer to our goal, that is, which elevates the mind and makes it more peaceful must be considered good.

(b) We see that all great souls in our history have this power of keeping absolutely calm no matter what the external circumstances may be like. This quality needs to be developed within ourselves if we are to control the quality of our thoughts.

It will not come about in a few days and will need lots of practice and patience. However, the practice of even a little of this calm-headedness will go a long way towards making our thoughts pure.

(c) Our thoughts have a tendency to flow in one direction and we often find it hard to change this direction. We are like a small child learning to ride a cycle. As long as the cycle is going directly in one direction, the child is fine, but when he tries to change the direction, he promptly falls down! The problem with us is that we have all this time been exposing ourselves to bad influences through our eyes and ears. The only remedy is to expose ourselves to noble thoughts and ideas.

There is the famous story of Saint Eknath who changed the whole course of his son's life by using this technique. The boy was going astray through the influence of evil company and by exposing him to holy ideas, Saint Eknath was able to reform his son.

We are careless about choosing our companions and so we suffer. In fact, our scriptures say that in this matter there must be no compromise—if we find a friend is disturbing our mind, we must cut off all contact with that friend no matter what the cost. This is because bad company has tremendous power to snatch away all our good qualities; if someone with a few good qualities keeps the company of those with bad tendencies, very soon he is likely to be brainwashed by his companions and will become just like those people. It is said that it is better to live in the forest with hill tribes than to live with a fool in heaven!

In a similar fashion, *Satsanga* or good company has tremendous power to build an unseen fort or wall around us so that unwanted thoughts cannot reach us.

However, our problem is that we practise only *weekend Satsanga*, which in reality is *weakened Satsanga*! This is our condition and that is why there is no improvement. We like everything to be cheap—we pay ₹5,000 to go and attend some seminar on spirituality and believe that everything will be fine after that. In reality, since there is no practice, there is no improvement. Money cannot buy us this goal of peace.

Satsanga does not mean that one has to always visit temples or *ashramas*—even reading of good books or listening to good music and bhajans is considered *Satsanga* as it has an elevating influence on the mind. So one may visit temples and ashrams on weekends when there is some free time and during the rest of the week, *Satsanga* can be practised through the reading of holy material or by listening to bhajans, etc.

Sankaracharya in a *shloka* from his famous *Bhaja Govindam has said Satsangatwe nisangatwam, nisangatwe nirmohatvam, nirmohatve nischaltatvam, nischaltatve jeevanmukti'n'*—meaning that through *Satsanga*, one attains non-attachment, from non-attachment comes freedom from delusion, from freedom from delusion comes self-satisfaction (that is, freedom from desires) and from self-satisfaction one realises the goal of one's life. Such is the true power of *Satsanga*.

Why are we so very busy all their lives? What will rushing about here and there in a mad hurry achieve for us? Unwanted thoughts such as greed or lust compel us to run about. Those who are really serious about improving will somehow find the time to practise *Satsanga* every single day—in the form of listening of bhajans, reading good books, etc.

These crucial points can be summarized as SDM—*Satsanga*, Discipline and Meditation. The meaning of SDM is that we must diligently practise *Satsanga*, Discipline and Meditation regularly. *Satsanga* and Discipline have already been explained above and Meditation means practising the watching of thought flows for at least 10 minutes in the morning and evening. Like water has a tendency to run from a higher place to a lower place, our minds have a tendency to run from a higher state to a lower state. This is why we need to practice SDM regularly to keep the mind at a higher plane. There are some great souls whose condition is such that their minds always go upwards even without any effort on their part, but such people are very rare.

It is pertinent to assert the importance of this practice, once again. It is only practice and nothing else that will help us. Otherwise all this reading and attending lectures on self development, spirituality, etc. will prove to be a hollow exercise producing no results. There is an example of a gentleman who was very fond of reading the Gita everyday. When a friend's close relative died, he consoled him with words from the Gita—(2.11) 'You grieve for those who should not be grieved for, yet you spell words of wisdom.... Death is simply changing bodies and the soul never dies.' Of course, the friend was not at all consoled and went away to find some more effective cure for his grief. Later, when the gentleman's own relative died, he himself started weeping. When his friend came to see him, the gentleman again repeated those some words—but this time with tears streaming down his cheeks! You may see how despite having so much knowledge of sacred scriptures, he was completely unable to control his own mind!

Another related example is that of a parrot and a sadhu. Once a sadhu saw a parrot sifting on a tree and a hunter approaching to spread his trap. The sadhu thought that if he gave the parrot some instructions, it would be able to save itself from the hunter. He told the parrot—'I will give you four mantras and if you repeat them, you will be saved.' The four mantras were:

1. The hunter come and spread his net
2. The hunter will spread the seeds
3. Birds will con* and eat the seeds
4. The hunter will bundle the net and carry off the, birds.

The parrot diligently repeated the four mantras and the sadhu was satisfied that the parrot would be saved. When the hunter came and spread his net and put out the seeds, the parrot repeated the first two mantras.

However, even while repeating the third mantra, 'Birds will come and eat the seeds, birds will come and eat the seeds . . .', it flew down to the net and started eating the seeds and when the hunter bundled the net and carried off the parrot, it kept on repeating, 'The hunter will bundle the net and carry off the birds'!

So many of us are like the parrot in this story—we have read so many books and have heard so many lectures that we are filled to the brim with all sorts of knowledge and spout high philosophy all the time. But when the time comes to implement the philosophy in our lives, we are found woefully inadequate since we lack the necessary practice.

10. *The tenth fact of Thought Management examines a subtle aspect, namely, the movement of the mind along three parameters.*

(a) *The mind moves in time:* One moment the mind is thinking of the present and the next instant it is thinking of some event that occurred five years back—may be someone visited America then and the mind suddenly recalls related incidents. Or maybe, while working in the office one is reminded suddenly of some particular incident from one's childhood. These are all examples of the mind travelling in time.

(b) *The mind moves in space (that is, hops from place to place):* One may be sitting in one room, say in the class room or in the office, but the mind is thinking of home or of some favourite place like the cinema. This is an example of the mind travelling in space.

(c) *The mind moves amongst objects*: Sometimes the mind thinks of rasagulla and at other times it thinks of rasmalai! Some may find that they are always thinking of their child or their spouse, etc.

11. *The eleventh fact of Thought Management presents methods through which the movements of mind mentioned under the tenth fact can be controlled.*

    The technical names of the methods used to control such movements of the mind are *Dharana, Dhyana* and *Samadhi.*

    (a) *Dharana:* When the mind is controlled from running apace, it is called dharana. When we sit to meditate, we cannot control the mind even for a second. It is constantly running here and there. To practise dharana effectively, it is recommended that we concentrate the mind in one place, that is in the region of the heart—this is not the same as the physical heart, but there is also a spiritual heart located in the same region. Gradually, one will acquire the power to dictate to the mind that it must stay in the heart and not roam here and there while one is meditating. This will take a long time, but at least the practice can be started now.

(b) *Dhyana*: When the mind is controlled against running after objects, it is called *dhyana*. We see that the mind runs after so many different objects—now it is thinking of that boy's shirt, then it thinks of my own shirt, then it is thinking of some particular food. We need to concentrate the mind on one object and hold it there—it is only when this is achieved that true meditation can be said to have started.

This object of concentration has to be chosen carefully—after all, our scriptures say that whatever we think of, we become; in fact if the object of concentration is not good, the mind will be ultimately ruined by constantly thinking about it. The scriptures again provide the solution and according to them, one must concentrate the mind on a holy object—something to which the mind is attracted with devotion. Those who have taken initiation are given one particular *Ishta* or Chosen Diety and they concentrate their minds on that particular object.

Like in the case of *dharana, dhyana* too will take a long time to perfect—the important thing is to keep up the practice and to have patience. When a war is going on, the outcome depends on the soldiers' performance, which in turn depends on the training they have received during peace time. Here too, it is the training we give to our minds that will determine the final outcome. How we live the daily 24 hours of our life determines the training of the mind. If we live an undisciplined life with excessive indulgence in sense pleasures, we will not achieve success no matter how long we sit in meditation.

(c) *Samadhi*: Finally, when the mind is controlled from travelling in time, it is called *samadhi*. May be someone has visited foreign lands a few months back—what is his state in the present? He is constantly thinking of and comparing the present situation with his experiences in those months during his visit abroad. Our common experience suggests that the influence of time on our minds is relatively less when we are deeply engrossed in some activity like studying for an exam or watching some favourite serial on TV—there is no awareness of time when one is involved in these activities. When the mind is prevented from travelling in time for a longer period of time, it is called *samadhi*. *Samadhi* is such a state that it cannot be explained—only those who have experienced it know what is like. It is said that Brahmana can never be defiled by the tongue—it can never be spoken of, it can only be experienced.

These three things—*dharana, dhyana, samadhi*—relate to a very advanced state of personality development. For the time being, we have to mainly concern ourselves with controlling the quantity, quality and direction of thoughts through SDM. Many people say that they want to practice *dhyana* or *samadhi* but unfortunately they do not even know how to manage their thoughts—first we must learn to manage our thoughts and only then can we even attempt to practise these things.

Summarising the Utility of Learning

The Facts of Thought Management

Our body is like a machine that can be used to extract bliss from this world. If we use it properly, we live in peace, else we live in agony, depression, frustration, etc. Just as we need to use a manual to make proper use of any machine, we need the help of the manual of religion to make proper use of this body. It is only religion that can teach us these useful principles, tips and tricks that can enable us to live a happy and peaceful life. *Sadhus* and *Rishis* live a happy peaceful life since they have the power to dictate to their minds. Once we are able to dictate to our minds in a similar way, we too will enjoy peace.

We need to develop the power of discrimination to distinguish between two types of peace in our lives. One kind comes after the fulfilment of some desire. When we achieve some dream job or gain admission to a dream college, we feel great peace at achieving the goal for which we had been struggling so hard. But this peace is temporary. It is like the peace on the streets after a riot. Everything appears calm and quiet, but at any moment another riot can start. This peace will disappear the, moment fresh desires erupt in the mind. This is not what we are looking for. What we want is permanent peace—uninterrupted bliss. For this second type of peace that is permanent, we need to reduce the frequency of thoughts, practise detachment and exercise regularly.

No one but our own selves can help in this matter. And we have to achieve this just as we strive to achieve our many academic and professional achievements. Management of thought will help us develop the right attitude, bringing us all the desired good qualities.

It is said that life is all about adjustment and adapting to different situations—we may desire something, but due to external situations it may become impossible to fulfil that desire. If one has the power of adjustment then mental balance is maintained—if not, then there is tension and suffering. For instance, suppose we want to go to some place by bus. On reaching the bus stop, we find that we have missed the bus. What will be the state of the mind? If we can adjust and accept the situation, we will calmly try to find another means of reaching our destination. If we cannot adjust, then we will get irritated and will shout to our mother or sister saying 'It is because of you that I have missed the bus—you have spoiled the whole day!' In essence, this kind of control is what we seek to achieve through thought management. If we can control our thoughts (and hence our mind), then we will be able to adjust to all of life's problems and so will enjoy peace even when others are suffering from so much tension and stress.

We conclude the discussion on the topic with yet another charming story of a king who once fell ill. All the best physicians in the country couldn't cure him, no matter what they tried. Finally, someone suggested that if the king were to wear the shirt of a happy man, he would be cured at once. The king immediately ordered his ministers to fetch the shirt of a happy man. The ministers were surprised—they had thought that as the most powerful man in the kingdom, the king would be the happiest! Anyhow, they at once set out to find a happy man. But alas! No matter how hard they tried, they just couldn't find a man who said he was happy. Someone suggested that a certain rich man was happy—but when he was asked for his shirt, even he said that he was not happy.

Finally, one of the ministers stumbled across a man sitting in meditation near a river. The man had a serene glow on his face and appeared to be truly happy and peaceful. The minister at once ran up to him and asked him for his shirt. At this the man looked surprised and said that he had no shirt! In fact, he had no possessions whatsoever! However, the man agreed to visit the king and said he would cure the king. When he met the king, he said: 'Look! I have no possessions, not even a shirt to cover my back. Yet I am happy. And you, who own uncountable riches are so unhappy! The reason is, I have controlled my thoughts while you have not. Control of thought, 0 king, is the only way to happiness. Nothing else can help.' At this the king realised his folly and devoted the rest of his life to spiritual practices and control of the mind. Like the king, we too must awaken and realise that it is these wretched thoughts that are barring us from the kind of permanent peace we desire, and the achievement of which is our birth right. Any true seeker of peace must attain the ultimate goal of life—uninterrupted peace by controlling and managing his thoughts through regular and continuous practice.

Practise! Practise! Practise!

The mind naturally tends towards evil deeds. It is lethargic in doing good work.... That is why I say that perseverance and tenacity are necessary for success in all good work.'

> It is very necessary to have a fixed time for these things. For it cannot be said when the auspicious moment will come. It arrives so suddenly. No one gets any hint of it beforehand. Therefore, one should observe regularity, however busy one may be with duties.... Even in the midst of the most intense activity, one should at least remember God and salute Him.
>
> *—Holy Mother Sri Sarada Devi*

One ounce of practice is worth a thousand pounds of theory' 'Practice makes us what we shall be.'

—Swami Vivekananda

Practice is the essential thing. We have emphasised the importance of practice again and again in the preceding chapters. We consider the life and teachings of Holy Mother Sarada Devi as a living embodiment of Practical Vedanta only because, rather than merely lecturing, she dutifully and silently practised the age old Vedantic truths in her own life.

The objective of this book will also be achieved only if readers set out and practise SDM, after convincing themselves of its importance in their respective lives.

To reiterate, the goal of our life is uninterrupted peace, happiness and bliss. The key to this goal lies in control of the mind. And it is the verdict of our countless sages and our numerous scriptures that it is only through practice that one can control the mind.

If we examine the lives of great men—be they scientists or philosophers or sages—we find that the key to their success lies in practice. Such people have the ability and dedication to practise their calling with such sincerity and devotion that success is guaranteed in whatever they do. Even in our ordinary lives, practice is essential for any achievement. For example, we see how much a student must practise his lessons in order to pass exams. In fact, it is through practice that we have mastered such talents as the ability to walk or write—we have practised these so much that we consider them almost part of our nature.

For a true seeker of peace, practice is of utmost importance in attaining his goal. Looking into our lives, we find that the real reason for our unhappiness is that we do not have control on our minds. It is because of this lack of control that we cannot focus and achieve our goals. It is because of this that we get into unnecessary quarrels with all around and it is because of this that we cannot stop ourselves from doing what we know to be harmful. The indiscipline and misbehaviour of our mind also causes us to lose our power of concentration.

Many people complain of stress in their lives. Properly analysed, it will be clear that stress is due to an uncontrolled mind. A thoroughly disciplined mind will never grumble or groan under heavy pressure but will instead channelise all energies at hand towards solution of the problem. In fact, it can be said that most of life's sufferings are due to an uncontrolled mind.

In order to control the mind, our first step should be to devote at least ten minutes every morning and evening to watching the flow of thoughts in our mind. During these ten minutes, we should sit down, preferably in a cross-legged position with eyes closed and straight back. After ensuring that no part of the body is moving except for the purpose of breathing, we are required to simply watch the thoughts as they enter and leave our mind without reacting to them and without brooding on them—just as if they are scenes flowing past on a television screen.

Another example is that of a watchman—he sees so many people come and go all day without reacting to them. But if he sees his wife, then he immediately gets up to talk to her—this is like brooding on our thoughts and must be avoided. Through steady practice of this exercise, we will find that our mind is getting purified slowly and we are gradually inching towards the peace we seek so desperately.

We see that there is not much success in controlling the mind as long as people don't practise enough—they simply don't realise the importance of practice. Most people start off with every good intention but after a few days of practice, they get bored or disheartened and give up. However, the same people will practise thoroughly when they want to achieve some material goal such as getting admission to a college of repute. What then is required is the right attitude, which is possible only when our mind is under control. Since practice is needed to control the mind, we can say that practice leads to a healthy attitude in life.

The 'Introduction' briefed us on the twofold philosophy taught in the *Vedas*—one is the philosophy of *Pravritti*, action, the other is the philosophy of *Nivritti*, withdrawal from action, that is, meditation; both are needed to establish a stable world order. Outward-going energy is *Pravritti*, inward-going energy is *Nivritti*. These two are needed to ensure to provide all beings' true material prosperity as well as spiritual growth and fulfilment. *Pravritti* also refers to our external nature and to the various jobs and social skills that we have learnt and acquired. *Nivritti* refers to our internal nature.

Most of us have developed our external aspect—we acquire several academic degrees, respectable jobs, cars, houses, etc. However, internally most of us are like new born babies—either zero or underdeveloped! Moreover, at least in this respect, there is not much of a difference between the illiterates and us. The apparent difference between the two is only external. As far as mental peace is concerned, both are equally afflicted and suffer in similar fashion.

Internal development makes a person cultured and refined. The external achievements and appearances are a mere sham and of little use in achieving peace of mind. Rather, they only add to our tensions and worries. Just as we need both physical legs to keep our balance, we also need both aspects of our personality to be developed for a balanced life.

We have understood in the preceding chapters that when one is suffering from a physical ailment, then diagnosis is critical in order to find a cure for it and that there are two kinds of suffering in our lives—physical and mental. For physical diseases, we go to doctors for a cure. But when we are suffering internally, who is going to help us? Who will be the doctor then? For mental ailments, no doctor is available outside—we must cure ourselves. By being a doctor to ourselves, we will be able to control the mind. In order to do this, we need to inculcate the practice and power of introspection. We recollect that introspection is nothing but examining one's thoughts—or 'thinking about' one's thoughts. Introspection requires practice with patience and perseverance to know the cause and cure of mental sufferings.

Good teachers teach their students to practise reading the question again and again in order to fully comprehend the problem and be able to find the solution. This is because by repeatedly reading the question, the exact problem is revealed gradually to the student and he is able to solve it with the help of his understanding based on past practice. Similarly, as said earlier, we can find at least 70 per cent of the solution of our suffering, once we know its cause through regular practice of introspection.

This practice has tremendous power that can be seen in this example. A person has a habit of smoking a cigarette at 11 every night. One night, he discovers that he has run out of cigarettes and he immediately resolves to walk two miles to the railway station in order to buy his cigarettes. And only a few minutes earlier, he had refused when asked to go out to do some urgent family work on the pretext that he was tired and moreover his favourite serial was being shown on TV! Another example is to see how some people have the habit of going to the Bandstand (a popular seafront area in Mumbai frequented by 'fashionable' people) in the evenings. At the same time each evening, they will automatically go there, no matter how urgent their other work may be.

So, we see the effectiveness of practice in building habits. If one does a certain kind of activity regularly for a lengthy period, the practice affects the mind and nerves turning the very activity into a habit and making it a part of one's nature. Later, the same activity becomes an involuntary action. Once learned, such actions then don't need any effort on our part, like swimming, cycling, etc. For instance, some people who have learnt how to play the tabla automatically move their hands as if playing a tabla whenever they hear any music; the practice is so deeply ingrained in them that their hands are automatically attuned to moving in that fashion.

Practice is also a very effective way of eliminating our bad habits and forming new, positive ones. Whatever we practise for a long time becomes a habit and eventually a part of our nature. The thoughts we entertain and the actions we perform are a result of practice. Thinking and behaving in a particular way when practised repetitively, becomes a habit. In fact, personality with all its characteristics is the sum-total of all our habits. Therefore, whatever we are today is because of our thoughts and actions practised in the past. Such is the power of practice!

Our *Shastras* say that if one takes up any practice, one should do it at all times—it should not be missed even for one day. The danger is that if the practice is missed even for one day, the mind will invent some excuse or the other to skip practice in the future as well.

We are not able to improve our lives because we suffer from a lack of interest in making the right efforts, a lack of interest in keeping up the practice. That is why we meet a failure in so many of our endeavours. Did the doctor ever dream that he would become a doctor when, as a child, he was struggling to learn his A B C? It took him almost 15-20 years of hard practice to make himself a doctor. When even wild beasts at a circus, such as lions or tigers, can be trained to perform tricks, why can we not control our minds? One must have enough patience and perseverance to practise steadily for a long time. The problem is that we don't practise and therefore, keep suffering.

Practice is like the waves of the ocean, repeatedly smashing against a rock and slowly but steadily eroding it away until only a few pebbles are left; even these get slowly worn out into fine sand particles. Just as repeated rubbing of buckets on the cemented platform under a hand pump slowly wears away a portion of it, repeated practice slowly but surely wears away our mental weakness and gives us enough strength to control our minds. Most people are like walls built of mud that often crumble at the slightest touch. However, practice makes us strong like walls of cement that can withstand huge forces and stress.

Knowingly or unknowingly, we all are practising one thing or another at a given time. Some practise so that they can have successful careers and business while some may practise ruining themselves by repeatedly indulging in bad activities! We, therefore, need to practise while being aware of its importance and effectiveness. After making ourselves aware of the importance of practice, we need to maintain our practice with all thoroughness and sincerity. There must be no excuse, no compromise; those who compromise cannot get the desired results.

The *Bhagavad Gita* encourages us and says (2.40) 'In this, there is no loss of attempt: nor is there any adverse effect. The practice of even a little of this dharma protects one from great fear.' It is up to us to put in even this small amount of effort so that we can reap a glorious harvest for the rest of our lives.

Control Your Anger

At one time, Mother's niece, Radhu was pestering her for some favour. Since Mother did not have the required money to fulfil her desire, she refused and Radhu, becoming furious struck Mother in the back with an egg-plant. As the vegetable stuck her, Mother bent her back in pain and the place became red and swollen. But unmindful of this, she turned to the Master and said with folded hands, 'Master don't be offended at her; she is ignorant.' So great was the Mother's control on anger!

Holy Mother Sri Sarada Devi

Swami Gambirananda, 'Radhu'

'Vengeance is bad. Disarm anger with love. Anger is not cured by anger, nor hatred by hatred. Dissolve anger by love'.

—*Swami Vivekananda*

There is an old precept that says anger is a great sin; from our very childhood we are taught not to be angry. We see before our very own eyes how much damage this emotion can cause—countries go to war, families break up ruining the lives of several generations, senseless murders are committed—all this simply due to anger, which can be both individual or collective. In retrospect, it is found that in most cases the resultant destruction could have been avoided had the people involved somehow curbed their anger and tried to solve the matter calmly and amicably.

Even in our own lives, we can find many occasions where our anger has caused us trouble, such as quarrels within the family, unpopularity at the office, loss of friends—the list simply doesn't end! Obviously, it is of paramount importance then that we learn to control our anger and channelise our energies in a more productive way.

Anger may be defined as an emotion or a feeling. In other words, it is the expression of emotion. Anger can also be called a form of concentrated lust. Hindrances or obstacles in the fulfilment of our desires cause us to be angry. These hindrances can arise from three sources:

1. *Conflict between Man and Nature,* that is, due to external factors which may be unavoidable, accidental, or uncontrollable such as earthquakes, hot weather, etc.
2. *Conflict between Man and Man*, that is, due to reasons such as disagreements, disharmony, discord and other differences with fellow humans.
3. *Conflicts within Man*, that is, continuous conflicts that go on within each one of us in the form of mental turmoil, depression, etc.

Whatever may be the source, the effects of anger can be very negative and destructive. Whatever we do in a fit of anger is harmful to ourselves and to others and is a sheer waste of our energies. This is why the *Mahabharata* wisely cautions us—'An angry person commits mistakes that lead to his own destruction.' This can be demonstrated through several examples:

(a) A certain family had a mongoose as a pet. Once the mother had to go out on an errand and left the little baby in the care of the mongoose. After the mother had left, a snake entered the house and realising that it could be a threat to the baby, the mongoose at once jumped at it and fought and killed it. Naturally, its mouth became bloody due to this. When the mother returned, the mongoose ran joyfully towards her, expecting to be appreciated for its efforts. But when the mother saw the blood on its face, she thought that the mongoose had harmed her baby and in a fit of anger picked up a stone and killed the mongoose on the spot! Only later when she went into the room where the baby was peacefully sleeping did she realise her grave mistake. So under the influence of anger, we lose all power of discrimination and commit terrible crimes.

(b) Anger is the reason why we fight and quarrel with each other. When anger is very intense, it can cause the affected person to indulge in terrible crimes like robbery or violence. In fact, a person can even commit murder under the influence of anger!

(c) An angry person utters all kinds of expressions such as 'I will kill you,' 'I will break his head', etc. This kind of utterance only worsens the situation and leads to further escalation of anger and violence on both sides.

(d) Anger can also distort the perception of persons and can make things appear different from what they actually are.

There is a story of how Sri Hanuman once took some white flowers to be red when he was possessed by anger. He insisted to all around that those particular flowers were red until Sri Rama told him that they were in fact white and that it was only his anger that had distorted his perception. Similarly, in our anger we see people as more evil and obnoxious than they really are and so may react in ways that may cause great harm and destruction. Consider for instance how a husband who otherwise loves his wife more than anything else, shouts at her in a fit of anger. Goaded by his anger, he even goes to the extent of demanding an immediate divorce!

(e) Anger can unsettle the mind of even a great sage. Once Sri Ramakrishna asked Swami Brahmananda, one of his direct disciples, to prepare a betel roll for him. Swamiji refused saying that he had never done such a thing and he did not know how. Swami Abdhutananda, another direct disciple who was present, was incensed at this disobedience of his Guru and started shouting at the top of his voice at Rakhal who calmly bore those insults. At this Sri Ramakrishna smiled and said that Rakhal was the more perfect devotee as he had perfect control on his anger—even though he had disobeyed his Guru.

(f) Whenever there is turmoil within a family, its cause can be traced to anger. When family members feel angry they express it in terms of shouting or passing sharp remarks that cause disturbance and turmoil in the family.

These illustrations clearly show that anger is the cause of sorrow and as such it is our number one enemy. Control of anger is a must if we are to enjoy a really happy, peaceful life.

The following scale provides an apt measurement of the level of one's progress in controlling anger and also the depth of one's anger:

1. Anger lasts for a few seconds in a higher class of people.
2. Anger lasts for two hours in a little lower class of people.
3. Anger lasts for a full day in still lower class of people.
4. Anger lasts till death in wicked persons.

It is said that anger is directly proportional to our desire. Where desire is strong, anger is relatively stronger and where desire is less, anger is relatively lower. Suppose you want to visit your friend's house—but at that moment your father asks you to to do some work in the house. How much anger will you show? But if you are planning to go to the market to buy something and your father disturbs you then, your anger will be relatively less. This is because the desire to visit the friend's house is stronger than the desire to go to the market.

The basic method of anger management is the use of the God-given tool called the intellect, which we can use to control our emotions. Animals do not have this tool and so they have no self-control and start fighting at the slightest provocation. Unfortunately we humans often behave just like animals and do not use our intellect adequately. This should not be so. Just as a river when guided by dams is a constructive force and when unguided is destructive, our emotions when checked by the intellect are a positive force which we can use to achieve all our goals in life.

However, when emotions are left unchecked, they get expressed in the form of passions such as anger, causing great damage and destruction. Intellect should not be confused with academic learning. If it were so, then all the greatest scientists and engineers would be perfectly self-controlled, but we see that many of these so-called great people are in fact very ill tempered! Intellect is that faculty of discrimination, which we use to distinguish between right and wrong. If every emotion is passed through intellect before we express it, we will never commit a mistake. Of course, this is a very high state of an individual's personality, which is why we need to practise to achieve it.

Dr. Samuel Johnson (1709-1784) was one of England's great literary figures and the compiler of the first comprehensive English dictionary. A certain Mr. Boswell approached Dr. Johnson for counsel over some insult and his temper was calmed down by Dr. Johnson's words: Today's insult will become insignificant after one year.' This shows that if we take a few moments to introspect and analyse our anger, we will go a long way towards practising effective anger control.

The following few tips will help us control our temper:

(a) Practise waiting for five minutes before reacting in a fit of anger. We may find after five minutes that our anger was unreasonable and that where we once wanted to shout and scream, only a few words will suffice!

(b) It is better to simply leave the place if the surroundings are not conducive to anger control. Sometimes a change of setting can immediately distract the mind and bring in some amount of calmness.

(c) Go and stand before a mirror and examine the expressions that appear on the face in a fit of anger. The ridiculous expressions we produce in a fit of anger will clearly highlight how anger has overpowered us and has robbed us of our normal composure and dignified behaviour.

(d) Think about the damage caused by anger before giving expression to it. When properly analysed, anger is simply not worth the immense damage it causes us and those around us.

(e) Convince yourself again and again that the world cannot move as per your calculations. It moves in its own way. We labour under the misconception that the world is designed to suit our purposes and when we find things going against our wishes, we get annoyed and irritated. If we realise that the world will go its own way irrespective of what we wish, we will find that our irritation at the world will automatically be reduced.

In addition to these simple techniques, there are two other more subtle but very effective techniques that can be used to control anger.

(f) Practise concentration on the feeling of anger: Suppose you are angry with some person. Now try to observe carefully the condition of the mind. First, his face and whole body will appear to your mind. Then will arise a special kind of feeling, which is called anger. One is the object of anger, which is the person. The other is the feeling of anger. If you try to concentrate on the feeling of anger, without focussing on the object of anger, the anger melts away. Try this and see the immense effect—it may require a little practice initially, but is one of the most effective techniques. By this technique, we can conquer any passion.

(g) Stop guessing about the person: Suppose you are angry with say Ram Babu. Then you start imagining about Ram Babu: 'He behaves like this, I know him very well from the beginning. I know he will act this way. I should not encourage him by overlooking his faults. He should be punished. I have my faults. But his faults are more than mine. I will say something directly or indirecly . . .' Actually, this kind of imagination or guessing stimulates and strengthens the feeling of anger. The more you imagine, the more powerful will be your anger. Stop imagining or guessing and the intensity of anger will be less.

It is important to note that to be able to practise these things correctly, we need to remain aware and alert right at the moment when anger arises in us. Mostly, the moment the spark arises, we tend to fire! But through practice, this has to be controlled. We must learn not to react at the spur of the moment; there must be a gap between the impulse of anger and the expression of anger, otherwise there is no chance to control it. This kind of control can be effectively achieved though the practice of SDM (*Satsanga*, Discipline and Meditation).

It is true that sometimes anger may be justified to set things right. When a child wants to play with fire, his parents scold and even slap him—this is constructive anger used for a good purpose. This kind of anger is controlled by us. The other destructive form of anger is such that it controls us—this is to be avoided.

It is said that we waste two-thirds of our energy in useless emotions such as anger. Even people who are doctors or engineers use only one-third of their energy! By controlling anger, one gradually learns to tap the remaining two-thirds of energy stored within each human being. Just imagine what all we could achieve if we had access to the remaining two-thirds of our energy. All our dreams and projects may then come true!

There are very few who use their intellect or *buddhi* and break out of the bondage of this action–reaction mechanism. These are the only people who can claim to be true humans and are worthy of respect and emulation. It is only by practising control of our minds that we can be more human and less animal-like, thus developing better values in life. The various steps in developing higher values are:

1. Control of mind
2. Assimilation of right ideas
3. Creation of higher values
4. Continuous effort towards the higher goal.

Through control of anger, we get the strength to control our other passions and so are able to make progress towards our ultimate goal—which is uninterrupted peace or bliss.

Curb Your Jealousy

Jealousy is the bane of our national character.
Jealousy is the central vice of every enslaved race.
—Swami Vivekananda

Jealousy too, just like anger or greed, is the expression of emotion. Jealousy is the fear or apprehension of superiority; it is a state of mind where one fears the superiority of others. A jealous person always feels uneasy and uncomfortable.

The cause of jealousy is comparison of oneself with others leading to an inferiority complex. It can also be said that the cause of jealousy is the desire for importance. We wish to be 'somebody' and when there is a hindrance in achieving that importance, we feel jealous.

For instance, when a schoolboy stands first in his class, his other classmates may be jealous of him since they too wish to enjoy the position and respect of being first in the class.

In fact, it can be said that jealousy is the root of all evils. Instead of counting our own blessings and striving to achieve our goals; we waste all our time in trying to find defects in others. So it is the greatest enemy of our happiness. Swami Vivekananda has said: 'Jealousy is a terrible, horrible sin.' A jealous person is never at ease. He will be in a constant rage of discontent. Such people can never appreciate the good qualities of others and are always trying to find fault. When they are unable to find faults, they even indulge in injustice and deceit to ruin their enemy's reputation. They seem to find some sort of joy in doing these things.

In this modern era of competition and stress, many people suffer terribly from jealousy. Some suffer from it at the workplace and cannot bear to see their co-workers being praised by their boss. Others suffer jealousy at home and cannot bear to see their relatives doing well. For such people, their entire life is spent in this petty hatred and they are unable to achieve any peace in life.

A woman was once terribly upset when she heard that her brother-in-law's son had obtained admission into a good medical college. She went about the neighbourhood telling people how the medical profession had become degraded in modern times and that no talented child would like to waste his life in pursuing such a career. The reality behind this was that her son too had tried to secure admission in a medical college, but had failed to do so. It was the woman's jealousy that caused her to say those things. Actually due to jealousy, we see things not as they truly are, but as we are.

Generally we feel joy upon seeing the joy of others and conversely, we feel sorrow upon seeing the unhappiness of others. For instance, when we run into a beggar on the street, most of us are moved by pity and share in the beggar's sorrow. A jealousy-stricken person, however, feels quite the opposite. He feels joy when his enemy is in trouble and feels sorrow when his enemy prospers. This is the perverse nature of jealousy.

Jealousy can turn the head of even good, virtuous people. It can wash away all our good qualities and fill us instead with poison. This is evident from the following example. Two ascetics were once practising sadhna (spiritual exercises) by the banks of a river. Pleased by their devotion, God decided to grant them each a boon. He appeared before one of the ascetics and asked him what he wanted. The man replied that he wanted double of whatever was given to the other ascetic.

The other ascetic got to know of this and when God appeared before him, he asked God to make him blind in one eye as this would make the first man blind in both eyes! Not being satisfied with this, the half-blind man dug a pit in front of the blind man's house so that he would fall in and kill himself. If this is the impact jealousy has on men who could please God Himself, think what a terrible effect it has on lesser mortals like us!

The moment we start hating others or are jealous of others, we give them the right to exercise all kinds of control over us—they control our sleep, hunger, blood pressure and happiness. Because of our jealousy-induced unhappiness, we are unable to digest our food or sleep peacefully. It is as if we have given the key of our happiness to our enemy. Wouldn't he jump in joy if he knows this! In any case, jealousy cannot stop his progress. The only effect of jealousy is that it ruins our peace and burns us. While our enemy progresses, we burn ourselves through hatred.

Jealousy as an emotion is found even in children. If the mother loves or favours any one child, the other gets jealous and impatient. To avoid such situations, parents should be absolutely impartial in the treatment of their children.

If we want to remove this evil of jealousy, we must first understand that jealousy is a mental disease. Many of us are unaware of the evil effects of jealousy. Unless we awaken to its real nature as a fatal disease, we will not take any steps to cure it. It is only when we know that we are sick that we visit a doctor for treatment. In this case too, once we know that jealousy is a disease, we must try to remove it slowly. A person who wastes his energy in hatred instead of working for his own betterment is a fool.

The following simple tips can help in removing or at least curbing jealousy.

1. One should realise the evil effects of jealousy and guard oneself against it. You should not give the key of your happiness to others. In any case, your jealousy cannot stop the progress of others. By spreading jealousy, you are only hurting yourself by wasting your energy.
2. Jealousy is nothing but fear of a sense of inferiority, which appears when one compares oneself with others. Through jealousy we fail to see the good qualities of others and imagine ourselves to be the best. We must stop comparing and must accept the truth. Stop posing as 'somebody'. Try to be bold enough and stop your imagination to save your energies for your own betterment. If you must compare, compare with yourself. Try to see where you were a month ago and where you stand today. Such comparisons will be beneficial both in controlling jealousy and in motivating you to strive harder to achieve your goals.
3. We must learn to appreciate the good qualities of others. Many people cannot stand anyone else being praised and immediately try to pull him down by saying things such as, 'Why do you praise him like this? I have heard that he has done many bad things,' etc. In reality, such people only manage to degrade themselves and slowly lose all credibility with those around.
4. One must try to be content with what one already has. It is no use worrying about whatever possessions or positions other people enjoy. What we deserve is bound to come to us and what we do not deserve, even if we try to gain it by some crooked way, will not stay with us. Instead of frittering away our energies in useless jealousy and hatred, we should use that energy to work hard so that we may rightfully enjoy the fruits of our labour. Swami Vivekananda has said (*Complete Works of Swami Vivekananda*, Vol. 9, "The First Step Towards Jnana"): 'What you have earned by your past actions, none can take away from you'.

If you have deserved wealth, you can bury yourself in the forest and it will come to you. If you have deserved good food and clothing, you may go to the North Pole and they will be brought to you. The polar bear will bring them. If you have not deserved them, you may conquer the world and will die of starvation.

5. One very effective method for controlling not only jealousy but all other passions is to practise *Satsanga*, Discipline, Meditation, or SDM. *Satsanga* means to seek holy company, read good books, listen to devotional music, etc. Discipline means we must live a methodical life and should plan all our activities instead of living haphazardly.
   Meditation means watching thought flow exercise regularly, every morning and evening, as explained in Appendix II. Through this SDM, love for God will gradually increase and all evil passions, such as jealousy, will gradually drop away. Sri Ramakrishna has said that as one approaches closer and closer to God, one's passions and ego become more and more distant.
6. *Jealousy to curb jealousy:* try to concentrate on the feeling of jealousy and not on the object of jealousy. Suppose you are jealous of your friend. When the feeling of jealousy arises, try to analyse the condition of your mind. First the friend's face and body appear in your mind. Then the feeling of jealousy will arise in the mind. The friend is the object of jealousy. Learn to focus not on the object, but on the feeling. By concentrating on the feelings and not on the object, we will find that jealousy will slowly melt away. This may require a little practice initially, but it yields immense control ultimately. Just as a lever makes lifting a heavy weight much easier, this practice will be like a lever that will enable us to rid ourselves of jealousy.

It is important to realise that unless we voluntarily cure ourselves, nature will ensure that we are forced to make efforts to cure ourselves. Nature will give us several blows so that finally we are forced to accept the truth and follow the right path. This is analogous to what happens when a thief is caught by the police and is taken into custody. The police try to find out the truth from the thief. If he does not divulge the truth by simple questioning and threatening, the police reportedly use other methods like giving him a good thrashing, or electric shock, etc. until he tells the truth. The degree of torture goes on increasing till the thief is unable to bear any more and blurts out the truth.

Nature plays the role of the police when we suffer from jealousy or other passions. Unless we mend our ways, nature will keep giving blows to us in the form of tension, stress, etc. until we are unable to bear it and are forced to change our ways. The moment we start hating someone, we start taking the truth not as it is, but as we are. That means we are not accepting the truth. So jealousy starts to torment us and burn us. As the degree of jealousy increases, the degree of suffering also increases. A time will come, perhaps after one week, one month or one year, when such torture becomes unbearable and we are then forced to accept the truth and say: 'Yes he is better than me,' etc. This is nature's way of curing us. Instead of waiting for nature's blows to fix us, it is much better to accept the truth. We must awaken to the danger ahead of us and make all efforts to cure ourselves.

This must be taken as a compulsion and we must start practising right now. Most of us treat these things as optional and therefore suffer.

We say, 'There is so much time, why hurry? Let me live like this for a little while and then later I will cure myself ' In this manner, our entire lives run out and we fail to make any progress. Those who truly want peace will compulsorily undertake all steps to cure themselves. We have been asleep all these days and have been burning. Now, let us awaken and struggle to achieve that peace which we have been seeking for so long. We must try to change all evil habits. We live a bad life for six days and then on the seventh day when we sit to meditate, we expect to see visions!

It is only by curbing these small passions like jealousy and anger that we can truly expect to advance spiritually. Even the reading of holy books such as the Gita or the Upanishads is not going to help so long as we are in the grip of these passions. Just like a ten-year-old child reading a medical book, our eyes will only see the words, but our minds will fail to grasp the true meaning. We must purify ourselves through regular and sincere practice. Swami Vivekananda has said: 'Arise, awake and stop not till the goal is reached.' Let us follow in his footsteps to achieve the goal of our lives.

Appendix I

What is SDM?

S = Satsanga. It is true that our mind reacts at any particular moment according to the quality of our external environment. One can realise this fact by analysing the condition of the mind when one visits a holy place like a temple and when one visits a film theatre or a fashionable place like New Delhi's Connaught Place or Mumbai's Bandstand. The word '*Satsanga*' means a favourable environment, which takes our mind, without much effort, to a higher level from a lower level of worldly thought.

Satsanga can take various forms such as being in the presence of holy people, attending spiritual classes, reading good books, listening to good music and bhajans, etc. One should devote some time everyday for *Satsanga*.

D = Disciplined life or doing everything according to a set routine or timetable, not haphazardly. This discipline keeps us from reacting to all sorts of impulses and getting involved in unplanned actions. Our academic successes are the result of our strict adherence to the timetable of school and college. For example, we used to reach school everyday at 9 am sharp and not at any time according to our will. Similarly, one should make a timetable of one's day-to-day activities and strictly follow it.

M = Meditation or watching thought flow. There is a big difference between brooding over thoughts and watching thoughts. We are masters in brooding but find it difficult to watch our thought flow. We brood because of our identification with the thoughts and at the time of brooding, no other thought crosses the mind. Watching is possible only when we see our thoughts without attachment. For example, we can watch and count the patches of white cloud moving in the sky, but counting stops the moment we get attached to a specific white cloud and start brooding on it—such as when the shape of a cloud reminds us of a favourite sweetmeat.

Another example is surfing television channels to see what is being aired on TV at the moment, without any intention and without getting tempted to view a particular channel. Watching them just as if they are scenes flowing one after the other on a television screen, and getting acquainted with the kind of content currently being aired.

This is akin to our brooding on thoughts. One should practise watching thought flow daily for at least 10 minutes in the morning and evening. This is to be done in a sitting posture with the backbone held straight and eyes closed. Preferably, the legs should also be in a crossed position. Once it is ensured that apart from breathing no part of the body is moving, watch the thoughts go past, without reacting to them or, in other words, without brooding on them. Once this practice is established, the time of meditation can be gradually increased. This has been further explained in Appendix II.

Appendix II

Watching Thought Flow

How to Practise Watching Thought Flow

1. The primary requirement for successful 'Watching Thought Flow' exercise is correct body posture.
2. One has to sit straight with shoulders upright; spinal cord, back of the neck and head all in one straight line; without any backrest or hand-rest. The body should be relaxed and hands placed softly in the lap.
3. For the first few minutes, one should focus one's thoughts on the body to make sure that everything is relaxed and perfectly still.
4. There should not be any movement of any part of the body apart from breathing gently through the nose.
5. Once we have made the body absolutely still and completely relaxed we can start 'Watching our Thoughts'.

6. Now, we must simply watch the thoughts as they appear in the mind—just as we watch clouds float by in the sky or waves come and go at a seashore.
7. It is important that we don't react to any thought otherwise we will get lost in it and will start brooding on our thoughts, instead of watching them.
8. A simple analogy can be drawn with a watchman standing at a gate. He sees so many people come and go without reacting or talking to them. He is all the time perfectly calm and quiet. But the moment he sees his wife, he starts talking to her and so is no longer calm and quite. The watchman's talking to his wife is like our brooding on a particular thought. The moment we get engrossed in a particular thought, we stop watching and instead brooding starts—this has to be avoided.
9. Initially, one may find that the thoughts appearing in the mind are very foul and dirty. But we mustn't lose heart and should go on with the practice. It is like what happens when we wash an inkpot. As water is poured into it, at first it comes out deep blue. But as we persist in the washing process, gradually the water becomes clearer and clearer until it is absolutely pure. Similarly, we must keep on at this process and we will find that gradually our thoughts will become purer and purer until one day we find ourselves perfectly pure.
10. As mentioned before, the essential thing is regularity and sincerity. The practice must be done for at least 10 minutes every morning and evening.

Appendix III

Inspiring Words from Holy Mother Shri Shri Sharda Devi

- 'A person may have no relatives anywhere, but Mahamaya may make him keep a cat and thus make him worldly. This is how she plays!'

- 'A disciple asked if all men can get rid of desires. Mother replied: 'How can they? If they could, then creation would come to an end. The world is going on because not all can be free of desires. People with desires are born again and again.'
- As long as a man desires, there is no end to his transmigration. It is desires alone that make him take one body after another. There will be rebirth for a man if he has even the desire to eat a piece of candy. Desire may be compared to a minute seed. It is like a big banyan tree growing out of a seed, which is no bigger than a dot. Rebirth is inevitable so long as one has desires. It is like taking the soul from one pillow-case and putting it into another. Only one or two out of many men can be found who are free from all desires.'
- 'The Master used to say that the worldly person is like a spring mattress—sit on it and it goes down, but the moment you get up, it springs back at once. The regard and devotion for God of these worldly men is just like a drop of water on a hot plate—it evaporates in no time.'
- The whole world is a dream; even this (the waking state) is a dream. What you dreamt last night does not exist now. A farmer who had lost a son dreamt at night that he was a king and the father of eight sons. -When the dream had vanished, he said to his wife: 'Shall I weep for my eight sons or this one?'
- 'The happiness of the world is transitory. The less you become attached to the world, the more you enjoy peace of mind.'
- 'Everything depends on one's mind. Nothing can be achieved without purity of mind.' It is said: "The aspirant may have received the grace of the Guru, the Lord and the Vaishnava; but he comes to grief without the grace of the one". That 'one' is the mind. The mind of the aspirant should be gracious to him.'
- 'My child, this mind is just like a wild elephant. It races with the wind. Therefore one should discriminate all the time. One should work hard for realisation of God.'

- *Disciple:* 'I cannot concentrate my mind well during meditation. My mind is fickle and unsteady.'
- *Mother:* 'Don't worry! Restlessness is the nature of the mind, as it is of the eyes and ears. Practise regularly. The Name of God is more powerful than the senses. Always think of the Master, who is looking after you. Don't be troubled about your lapses.'
- Mother forbade a disciple to make pilgrimages without discrimination of time and company. Quoting from a song, she said: 'Pilgrimage and excursion are causes of misery. Oh my mind, don't be restless about them. You can attain more in your house, if you are really earnest.'
- Regarding weakness of the mind, the Holy Mother said to a disciple: 'Child, this is the law of nature. Have you not noticed the full moon and the new moon? Likewise the mind is sometimes dominated by good and sometimes by bad tendencies.'
- *Disciple:* 'I have been practising religious disciplines. I do not relax my efforts in that direction. But it appears that the impurities of mind are not growing less.'
- *Mother:* 'You have rolled different threads on a reel—red, black and white. While unrolling you will see them all exactly in the same way.
- *Disciple:* 'How many insignificant desires crop up in our minds! How can we get rid of them?'
- *Mother:* 'In your case these are no real desires. They are nothing. They are mere fancies that appear and disappear in your mind. The more they come and go, the better for you. So long as the ego exists, desires also undoubtedly remain. But those desires will, not injure you.'
- 'Whenever people discuss good or evil, all those who are present have to take a little share of the good or evil . . . . Suppose someone tells you about his good and evil deeds. Every time you think of that person you must perforce remember his good and evil deeds. In this manner his good

and evil deeds both must leave some impression upon your mind.'

- 'How can one's mind be healthy if one doesn't work? No one can spend all twenty-four hours in thought and meditation. So one must engage oneself in work; it keeps the mind cheerful.'

Swami Vivekananda

One of the Western disciples of Swami Vivekananda was keen to show him wonderful sights and sceneries. But Swami Vivekananda who was a worshipper of man, who always wanted people to develop themselves into comprehensive gigantic personalities, responded thus:

> 'Do not show me sights. I have seen the Himalayas!
>
> I would not go ten steps to see sights; but I would go a thousand miles to see a (true) human being.'
>
> 'The road to good is the roughest and steepest in the universe. It is a wonder that so many succeed, no wonder that so many fall. Character has to be established through a thousand stumbles.'
>
> 'Any thing that makes you weak physically, intellectually and spiritually, reject as poison; there is no life in it, it cannot be true. These mysticisms, in spite of some grains of truth in them, are generally weakening.'
>
> —*Swami Vivekananda*

Section 3

11

Physical Strength

If we give it some thought, we will realise that this body of ours is a great gift that Mother Nature has given to us. It is a wonderful instrument made of the five elements—space, air, fire, water and earth. Scientists have unravelled the mystery of the atom; they have theoretically conquered gravity and even been to the moon. But they have still not been able to determine all the details of this human body that is so close at hand. We still do not know how this human body is formed nor can we define the subtleties of the functioning of all its organs. This is the Age of Science. Many and varied are the fields of scientific study that have drawn the attention of man. The science of the human body is also one such highly developed field. As a result, man has been able to conquer most of the diseases that affect the human body and has been able to extend the human lifespan. But medicine and therapy alone are not enough for physical well-being.

Swami Vivekananda places before us the ideal of a perfect body. When we look at that ideal condition of the human body, we will realise the actual condition of our body, as it is now. Swami Vivekananda uses the phrase, 'Muscles of Iron, Nerves of Steel.' Our body must have these, so says Swami Vivekananda. In all probability, even an Army General may not have such a conception of the perfect human body! True, there is no second prize in a war; a strong body is a must if one has to win on the battlefield. Similarly, to be successful in the battle of life, one needs a strong body. To make the body strong, we must give attention to four main aspects:

1. Food
2. Exercise
3. Cleanliness
4. Worrylessness

Food

Nutritious food, balanced and regulated diet, tonic—these words and phrases are very popular nowadays. But the truth is, only the rich can afford-nutritious food or a regulated diet. But this class of people cannot digest the high-energy food properly because they do not indulge in physical exercise and all they gain from such food is fat and obesity. The poorer sections of society who burn calories by sheer hard physical labour cannot even dream of a nutritious, well-balanced diet because they cannot afford it. The middle class is ever trying to achieve the standards of the upper class and in this mad effort, they have no time to give due attention even to their food and exercise.

Be that as it may, now the youth will have to give sufficient attention to nutritious, balanced diet during their formative years. The food must be nutritious, no doubt, but one should not eat beyond his digestive capacity. This much common sense one must possess. There is a golden rule regarding eating habits:

(-) Means eating; (-) means pleasing; (-) means moderation; (-) means timely.

The food that we eat must be pleasing to the mind (that is, pleasing). If the food is half boiled, if it is stale and rancid, if it is producing a bad odour, it won't be pleasing to the mind. While eating, if the mind is not calm and pleasant, the food taken will not be properly assimilated into the body. If the food is not assimilated properly, how will the body get strength?

If the food must be pleasing to the mind, it must be prepared well and it must taste good. It is true that tasty food increases its palatability, but more importantly, apart from having a pleasant effect on the mind, tasty food enhances the production of various digestive enzymes, which help to digest the food properly and thereby enhance assimilation, increasing bodily strength.

We all know that Bhima was physically invincible. A lesser-known fact is that Bhima was a culinary expert too. King Nala also had great culinary expertise. Therefore, even today, we find that when a dish is exceptionally well prepared, they exclaim, "Ah! This seems to be prepared by King Nala!" We find it recorded in Swami Vivekananda's life that he could cook exceptionally well and, also, he would encourage others to cook well.

Today in the modern age, the art of cooking has developed significantly—especially in hotels; more so in the hotels of big cities. This is very good indeed. But imagine how many additional benefits can be derived in terms of our physical wellbeing when every home prepares such tasty food!

Now, what is this issue about taste? What is tasty food? There is a saying 'Hunger is the salt in food'. One must do hard physical labour. Hunger must be felt in the stomach; only then must one sit down for dinner. Then one can see for oneself the miracle of ordinary bread and water tasting like nectar! When we understand this, the whole point of view regarding taste changes. We begin to understand that *Hitabhuk* means we must exert ourselves physically; feel genuine hunger in the pits of our stomach and only then should we come to the dining table. This is true eating.

There is ample scope for deeper analysis of the term for enhancing our understanding of this question of food with respect to physical wellbeing. For instance, when we say 'pleasant', to what should this food be pleasant—to the tongue or the body? We have already seen that food should be pleasing to both the tongue and the mind. But we have to see how this element of pleasantness with respect to food affects the body too. In this regard, we would be wise to observe the eating habits of birds and animals. Good mangoes are very sweet. But dogs will not like them so much as they touch it. Why is this so? It is because, fruits do not suit their constitution. Lots of such examples can be seen in the animal world. Therefore, from the point of view of our physical wellbeing, it is essential to know the kind of food that is pleasing to our body and eat such food only.

So much for tasty food. Let us now look into the aspect of moderation regarding food.

Who cares for moderation when the food is tasty and the dishes are dainty! But those who wish to develop a good physique, increase, bodily strength and general wellbeing must give consideration to this issue of moderation. There is a saying: 'Avoid extremes in all respects' (or, 'with regard to anything and everything, moderation is the golden rule'). There is a difficulty here, however—in an effort to be moderate in eating, there is always the danger of under-eating, that is, in order to avoid over-eating, one might eat too little. This will lead to general weakness in the body. Therefore, one should set one's own limits about the quantity of food to be eaten so that one does not become weaker day by, day. Each has to find out his own limit. A general rule cannot be drawn.

Then there is the aspect of eating at the proper time.

This is a topic worthy of attention. Most of us do not seem to give enough thought to this issue. Most people eat whenever they feel like munching something. Their eating habits are, by and large, haphazard and random, especially the time and place of eating. This is a common observation in the present day jet-age society. Not so in rural areas, though.. We should learn from an expert physician the importance of eating at fixed times. Also, a lot can be learnt by comparing the physical health of persons who eat at any time, anywhere and those who eat at fixed times and at definite, places.

Exercise

Let us now consider the contribution exercise makes towards the development of our physique. The food we eat is no doubt digested quite naturally, without our conscious effort. It also gets assimilated into our blood quite naturally. Despite all this, even those who take no exercise would not venture to deny the role of exercise in digestion and assimilation of food! Of course, exercise may not be necessary in the case of those who do strenuous physical labour for at least three to four hours a day. For all others, exercise is mandatory for physical wellbeing.

To know what happens if one does not take regular exercise, we should look at the pot-bellies of such persons! Such people become objects of ridicule. Regular exercise is necessary not only to avoid facing such ridicule, but also for improving general physical health and being alert and enthusiastic throughout the day. For these reasons, it is essential to include exercise in our daily routine. However, the purpose of exercising regularly is only to be fit and fine, and not to become wrestlers or body-builders. From early morning till late in the night, no matter how much we work, how much we exert ourselves, how much we travel and move around, we must not lose our enthusiasm, we must not feel tired, fatigued or exhausted. To achieve this state of physical wellbeing we need a strong, flexible body, for which regular exercise is a must.

When we start taking exercise, in the beginning, our hands and legs feel pain. Initially, exercise seems to be a great exertion. Disheartened by this, many people will discontinue their exercise. But the fatigue brought on by exercise will not last. It will disappear soon and will be replaced by fresh vigour and enthusiasm. Observe the hands of a blacksmith! The hands that work on iron seem themselves transformed into iron. Whatever part of the body gets more exercise by means of regular work becomes stronger and stronger. This is a natural law of the body. Therefore, all the parts of the body must be properly exercised regularly. This kind of disciplined effort confers two boons—strength and relaxation; the body becomes progressively stronger and sleep at night will be deep and satisfying.

The need of exercise or *Yogasanas* may be a problem in old age, when it is no longer possible to take exercises briskly. Youth is the period when it is possible to exercise and perform *Yogasanas* and lay a strong foundation for that habit. But youths are seldom inclined to regular exercise. In old age, there is a felt need for exercise, but it is no longer physically possible! Therefore, today there is an urgent need to banish the lethargy in our youths and make them exercise regularly and make exercising a habit. Otherwise, our youths will rust. Swami Vivekananda has already given the motto for the youths—'Muscles of Iron and Nerves of Steel! Let them take up this challenge if they can.'

Now the next question is: should it be exercise? Or *Yogasanas*? Or martial arts? Which should we choose? Any one of these will do. They are all equally capable of increasing physical strength and thereby shaping an important facet of our personality.

However, it would be more beneficial for youths to give more importance to *Yogasanas* as it does not limit itself to physical development. *Yogasanas* develop the mind too. And not just physical and mental development, *Yogasanas* contribute to our spiritual development also.

Who is going to teach us exercises or *Yogasanas*? Vivekananda Kendra and Rashtrotthana Parishat and also Shantivana Trust, Dharmasthala conduct regular yoga camps at various places. One can join these camps. Similarly, in cities and towns it should not be difficult to find experts in exercise and in *Yogasanas*, who can be easily approached. In olden times, every neighbourhood would have a local gymnasium. Gradually they have all disappeared. Today, however, there is a resurgence of awareness regarding physical fitness and consequently well-equipped gymnasiums are coming up all over the country. This is indeed a good sign.

Cleanliness

When we say that cleanliness has a role to play in developing physical strength and wellbeing, it may sound surprising. When the body is not clean, it becomes prone to diseases and the mind is disturbed and distracted. A little thought will reveal the relation between cleanliness, body and mind. When we take regular bath and wear clean clothes, there is a feeling of elation, of wellbeing in the body and confidence in the mind. This too is a truth that can be easily verified. It is essential to ensure that every part of the body is clean, all the clothes we wear (especially the undergarments) are clean and tidy, and bed covers and bed sheets are clean and hygienic.

To see how cleanliness affects physical and mental health, we need to observe how rural people live. Rural folk have an abundant supply of fresh air and water, lots of sunshine on their skin and unadulterated food. Theoretically speaking, all villagers have a strong and healthy body. But reality is a different story. The majority of rural folk have thin, emaciated bodies. Why is this so? Added to their phenomenal ignorance about their own health, it is the horrible dirt and unhygienic conditions that are the reasons for their pitiable state.

Worrylessness

This is another aspect that contributes greatly to physical wellbeing. Here, one may ask, 'How can that be? Worrylessness is related to the mind. How can a mental attitude help to develop the physical body?' This question has been often made. But people who are aware of the deep psychosomatic relationship of human nature will not ask such a question. The state of our mind affects our physical health to a very large extent. This is a tested truth. When tormented by great mental tension, even the strongest of men become weak, the body becomes emaciated, the face is drawn and eyes lose their lustre. While bullets and cyanide kill a man instantly, worry and mental tension lead to a slow death. Nay, worry snuffs out the life in a man even when his body continues to live.

The importance of 'worrylessness' will become clear with this: I once asked a bodybuilder: 'What is the secret of your strong physique?' He told me a simple truth, but like all simple truths, this too carried a great philosophy in itself. He said: 'Swamiji, I never worry. I am always happy.'

This leads us to the important question: 'How to avoid worries and stay happy?' The answer to this question is not easy to find, because it is an extremely subtle issue; we are now dealing with ultra-sensitive mental forces, with the very nature of the mind itself. Suffice it to say that mainly, weak-minded, weak-willed persons, who cannot think rationally and deeply, fall victims to chronic worries and depression. Small things, trifling issues drown them in a sea of worries. Such persons should seek the company of strong-willed persons. Gradually, by their influence, these persons too will develop strength of mind, they, too, will learn to think rationally and deeply and learn to ignore the non-essentials and concentrate on the essentials of life.

One should not worry. But that does not mean one should not think deeply on the pros and cons of an issue. Worry is the misuse of imagination. There is such a thing as proper use of imagination too, as the bodybuilder said. In fact, one who does not properly use his imagination, who does not think deeply, will be forced to worry. Without giving due consideration he will take a wrong step; proceeding in the wrong direction, he starts piling up mistake upon mistake, and then gets into a complicated and uncomfortable situation. What else can such persons do except worry and moan! So, if we wish to avoid getting into the mental whirlpool of worries, we must cherish people with common sense. By staying in such company we learn the technique of thinking deeply, meaningfully, and profitably.

We must read good books and closely observe wise men. By doing so, we too will develop good qualities, which are commonly called virtues. Those virtues must enter deep into our personality. A virtuous man will never need to worry, for he will never take a wrong step. But he must be virtuous to the very depths of his heart, virtuous to the core, virtuous in the true sense of the term. Attempting to be virtuous, many just become do-gooders; many develop a feeble personality. Many people, in their attempt to be gentlemen, become so gentle that they become cowards. So, prudence, the queen of all virtues, must guide us here.

Thus, by giving due attention to food, exercise, cleanliness and 'worrylessness,' we can surely develop a strong and healthy body.

12

Intellectual Strength

The second aspect of a powerful personality is Intellectual Strength. K.V. Iyer, in his youth, was given to systematic exercise and had developed a strong and robust physique. He was in fact an expert in physical exercise. The great Kannada dramatist T.P. Kailasam was a genius. It is said that Kailasam once called the youthful Iyer aside and chided him:

'Hey, do you know what job you'll land up with if you merely develop a strong body like this?—grinding rice for idlis in a restaurant!'

That was the turning point for the youth. Iyer started to give more attention towards his studies. Today, Iyer is a renowned name in the Kannada literary world, immortalised by his novels *Rupadarshi* and *Shantala* which are masterpieces.

Of course, writing novels is not the only manifestation of intellectual strength. We must become self-reliant; we must be able to solve all the problems that arise in the course of life; we must be able to choose good books and develop the ability to read and understand them all on our own; we must be able to deal with the educated class on equal terms; we must be able to understand the affairs of our society, our country and the whole world; not just understand them but we must also be able to react appropriately in each case. All these become possible only when the intellect develops properly and the intellectual strength blossoms completely.

A man's life style, his standard of living, his fulfilment in life—all depend largely on the level of his intellectual development. Each man has a body. Even so, each man has a mind and intellect. Just as the body can be systematically developed, similarly can the mind and the intellect be developed. There is a limit to developing the body; but there is no limit to developing the mind. The mind can be made as deep as and as vast as infinity. Man has conquered the oceans. Man has conquered the skies, reached the moon and walked on lunar soil! Information technology and computers are another achievement that stands testimony to man's intellectual powers.

Now, is there a technique for developing this wonderful power of the intellect? Yes, there are time-tested techniques. But intellectual development can be achieved only through hard work, by relentless practice and by conscious effort. There are no esoteric, mysterious, magical shortcuts for the development of mind. Let us be very clear about this. The technique for developing the intellect has four major aspects to it:

1. Alertness
2. Deep study
3. Deep thinking
4. Prayer

Let us deal with them in detail.

Alertness

The ancient Indian sages said: The quality of your life depends upon the quality of your attention'. They have coined a technical term for this mental alertness called *Avadhana*: *Avadhana* refers to the attention we give with an alert mind to a thing or person or whatever is at hand.

Some students open their textbooks and start to read; by the time they come to the second page, they cannot recall the contents of the first page. Why does this happen? They do not read attentively with an alert mind. When you speak to some persons, you will observe that they seem to be all ears, listening to all that you have to say, but in the end, they ask: 'Eh? What was that you said?' Why is this so? It is because they did not listen attentively with an alert mind. Then, there are certain other persons; right in front of their apparently open eyes, a man passes by; but if you ask them if it was a youth or an old man who just went by, they cannot recollect! Why is this so? The eyes were open; but they see nothing. This is because the mind is pre-occupied. They are absent-minded. They were not mentally alert.

This shows that knowledge dawns in the mind only if the mind is alert. Alertness of the mind is a primary condition for intellectual development. Knowledge grows proportionally to our alertness, that is, the more attentive we are, the more we get to know, whatever be the subject. Therefore, whatever we read, we must read with attention. Whatever we hear, we must hear with attention. Whatever we see, we must see with attention.

Deep Study

Study, deep study, is of paramount importance in developing our mental powers. Every person has the faculty of intelligence but very few are aware that this faculty can be developed to unbelievable levels. Yet, each person's mind keeps growing without his being aware of it himself. The whole world is a university. Right from the protective bosom of a mother till complete self-enlightenment, eternal lessons are being imparted in this world. Joy and sorrow are very able teachers. Grief and failure teach one kind of lesson; joy and success teach another kind. Every experience in this world leaves us wiser by teaching us something valuable.

But there is a technique for expanding one's mental horizons, a technique that is quicker and more direct and certain. That is deep study. Basic literacy is a precondition for using this technique and books are also needed. By studying books attentively, we can learn by vicarious experience and need not wait to experience things first hand.

The present age has seen a deluge of printed literature. Millions of books on millions of topics! A question arises here—which topic should we choose for study and which books should we study? The answer is—we should choose that topic which appeals to us the most. Not wide reading but wise reading.

Intellectual power is an important tool. This tool can be made very efficient and versatile by disciplined study. Then, using this tool, one can achieve success in this world; using this tool, progress can be achieved in spiritual *sadhana* too. But what exactly does 'Disciplined Study' mean? What does it mean when we say that by means of disciplined study we can develop the intellect into an efficient and versatile tool? All these issues deserve our undivided attention and are by themselves fit topics for deep study. But, briefly, we can say this much—we must choose a subject that interests us greatly; then it must be studied over and over again, making one's own notes at relevant places; then we must discuss that subject with people who are experts on it and exchange ideas. Thus, we gradually get to know that subject in depth. The subject opens out to us, as it were, and we get to the heart of the subject. When we study in this manner, our intellect develops in a wonderful way.

Deep Thinking or Contemplation

We need to think deeply on this topic of deep thinking. In this whole vast world, man alone is blessed with the power of thinking. The faculty of thought is capable of freeing man from all the troubles and difficulties he faces in his life. The power of thought can be a cogent force in his life. The power of thought can force its way through to the very heart of existence and light up the spark of self-knowledge, making human life blessed, exalted and fulfilling. Many problems suddenly crop up in the course of our day-to-day life. It is this deep thinking that solves them for us. It is this deep thinking that breathes new life into our otherwise dry daily routine and dull existence. Finally, what frees us from the oppressive bondage of this manifested world of the senses and propels us on to enter the unmanifested world of spirit and live there in freedom and eternal felicity is this deep thinking.

Thinking springs from the intellect. Intellect grows by thinking. Only thoughtful persons know this secret. The role of deep thinking is very profound in developing our intellectual power. Physical exercises help to digest what we eat; deep thinking helps to 'digest' what we see, hear and read. Therefore, we must observe with an alert mind and think deeply about what we have seen; we must read with an alert mind and think deeply about what we have read. All that we see, all that we hear, all that we read, must be finely divided using the sharp knife of deep thinking and baked in the fire of our feelings; only then will they be internalised into our personality.

Man is a social being. It is impossible for us to avoid talking to our fellow beings. The whole edifice of interpersonal relationships is built on conversations. Speech is the bridge into the heart of our fellow beings. How many things we learn when we speak and interact with others! But if this learning is to become educative and beneficial to us, we must develop the habit of deep thinking, that is, we must think deeply before we speak; we must think deeply after we speak. We must think deeply when we are listening to others. After listening too, we must think deeply. The tremendous benefit of developing this habit will become self-evident as soon as we start practising this technique. As our thinking process gets subtler and more refined, certain wonderful new thoughts, of which we were totally unaware, start flashing in our mind like lightning. We will be wonder struck by this phenomenon!

Deep thinking also means contemplation. There is a very thin line dividing worry and contemplation. There are many who worry endlessly, in fact, who have made worrying a habit. But only a few can contemplate. Worrying drains us of our mental energy; contemplation increases and amplifies it. Worry never solved any problem for anyone. There is not a single problem that contemplation has not solved. Therefore, instead of worrying we should contemplate on the problems and solve them ourselves. This is not only simple common sense, but also most beneficial to us.

Prayer

When we say that prayer has the power of increasing our mental strength and capabilities, it may not be fully accepted. Many will even express scepticism. They reject the fact that prayer is a spiritual tool. Where is the connection between intellectuality and spirituality, for the former deals with the brain and the latter with the heart? But, if we analyse deeply, we realise that prayer is extremely important and useful for intellectual development, in fact it is more helpful than alertness, deep study and deep thinking.

'By the grace of God, a dumb man can get the gift of oratory, and a lame man can climb up the mountain. To that God, I offer my prayers.'

If we understand the spirit of this *sloka*, we will realise how potent God's grace is; Divine Grace can even make a born-dumb person deliver torrents of oratory. A common shepherd, Kalidasa, became the paragon of poets by the grace of Mother Kali. All this is not fiction. These things actually happened. Prayer has that power.

The *Taittiriya Upanishad* has a prayer: 'May Indra inspire my Medha'. Medha means intellect. Here Indra does not refer to the mythological king of heaven. Indra here refers to the Supreme Soul, whose symbol is OM. So the prayer means, 'May the Supreme Soul, (whom I try to please by chanting the *Omkara*,) inspire my intellect.'

There is another mantra, which is very famous, called the Gayatri Mantra. That mantra is: 'We meditate on the divine effulgence of the Supreme Soul. May He inspire our intellect.' The great sage Vishwamitra found this mantra in his consciousness after tremendous tapasya. It is not the creation of human imagination or a product of linguistic jugglery. In both these prayers—in the *Taittiriya Upanishad* prayer and in the *Gayatri mantra*—it is important to note that God himself is supplicated to strengthen our mind and inspire our intellect to make it brilliant and all-powerful.

This is a point that should make us think. Those sages were not strangers to thinking deeply, nor was it that they were not endowed with great mental alertness. Contemplation was their very life breath. Yet, they prayed to the Almighty Supreme Principle for the perfect unfolding of their mental faculties. Isn't it wise for us to follow in their path? Those who cannot chant Sanskrit *sloka*s can just as well chant a prayer in their mother tongue. God is omniscient and he can understand our prayers as long as there is sincerity and whole-heartedness. God looks not to the words we utter, but the depth of feelings we attach to our prayers. Have you observed how Saraswati Puja is performed in our schools and colleges? Is there any whole-heartedness in what they do? It is merely a social function. However we must be thankful that at least this much is done!

An objection may be raised here:

'What is the necessity of praying to God to develop our mental faculties? Don't we see tremendous mental development even in people who do not have any idea of prayer?'

But the answer to this becomes self-evident when we see the marked difference between the intellect that is inspired by Divine Grace and the intellect that is developed by one's effort. The intellect inspired by Divine

Grace makes a man engage himself in beneficial, positive and creative activities. It will help him to live a life of peace, happiness, contentment and charity. The intellect developed by one's own effort will inspire one to be selfish and to be engaged in all kinds of self-destructive activities. Egotism, arrogance, selfishness—all these are the manifestations of a destructive intellect.

Those who wish to develop their mental faculties must maintain intimate contact with persons who have already developed those faculties. This is very important, but we must have the common sense to discern whether those persons use their evolved intellect for positive things or for destructive purposes. The company we keep determines the direction in which our personality develops. While the benefits of good company are immense, the consequences of bad company are indeed terrible!

13

Intellectual Strength

Now, let us discuss how Moral Strength can be developed in our personality. Do you wish to know the importance of moral strength in moulding a powerful, all-round personality? If yes, just take a look at the lives of people in our society, our country, or for that matter, the lives of people in the whole world; you will see immorality and corruption of every conceivable variety flourishing everywhere. Immorality and corruption exist in uneducated as well as educated persons; it is present in youths and in senior citizens; it is present in Westerners and not less in the Orientals. It is present in men and also in women. Immorality, corruption and vulgarity cross all boundaries and barriers and have entered deep into every section of the modern world.

What is the reason for this rampant, almost all-pervasive immorality? This is really a meaningful question. But we need not seek a fresh answer to this question. The ancient sages of India had found an answer long back. Lust, anger, greed, attachment, arrogance, jealousy, egotism, selfishness, etc.,—are all naturally present in every human being; the *Bhagavad Gita* classifies these tendencies as demonic. It is said in the *Puranas* that Ravana, Kumbhakarna, Hiranyaksha, Hiranyakashipu, Kamsa, the Kauravas, Shakuni and others were all demons whose personalities were built entirely on these terrible propensities. But, come to think of it, don't we still find such 'demons' even in this jet-age society? Not only do we find them even today, but they are also more vicious and their number is rapidly increasing. It is not unusual to find vices among the masses. But what shall be the fate of humanity if immorality and corruption enter into monasteries, temples, mosques, churches, educational institutions and the leaders of society? It is today a common phenomenon that even these exalted places, beacons of society, are increasingly being sucked into the whirlpool of immorality and corruption. So, what wonder is there if our youngsters imitate their elders and imbibe evil propensities in their personalities?

But let us not understand from all these discussions that human nature is all demonic. Human nature has many divine qualities too in itself. Divine qualities such as non-violence, honesty, *brahmacharya*, compassion, sympathy, service attitude, brotherhood, love, faith, trust, humility, love of peace, etc., do exist. But these divine qualities are not self-manifest in our personality, nor is it easy to imbibe and radiate them in our personality.

On the other hand, demonic tendencies easily grow and develop by themselves. Why should it be so? We can resolve this riddle as follows: A farmer tills the land well and sows good hybrid seeds and waters and manures the farm abundantly. In time, seeds sprout and grow into healthy plants.

But, along with these healthy plants, we find that many weeds too take root. Now, when did the farmer sow the seeds for these weeds? He never did so! Yet, weeds generally outnumber the good plants! Why? Because it is a law of nature. But just because it is a natural phenomenon, will it be acceptable for the farmer to overlook the growth of these weeds and keep quiet? He will have to constantly keep removing the weeds in his farm. Just the removal of weeds will not suffice; he has to take care that sheep and cattle do not graze on his farm. He will have to put up a protective fence to safeguard the young plants. Of course, after the plants grow into huge trees, there will be no danger even if an elephant is tied to it.

Similarly, the heart of man is like a farm. Good plants, beneficial plants called divine qualities, grow there. Also, many weeds, that is, demonic qualities grow there. The intellect is the farmer which has to be constantly alert and keep on rooting out the 'weeds' from the heart, only then do the divine qualities grow there unhindered and can a man enjoy a wonderful harvest of peace and bliss in good time.

Morality is a small word. But the scope of its meaning is extremely vast. It is only when morality develops in man that every home, every nation, nay, the entire world will enjoy peace, harmony and prosperity. It is the moral strength that enables us to cultivate divine qualities in our personality. Neither mere physical development nor intellectual development can achieve this. Morality alone can do this.

What is morality? Morality means good conduct. Ethics, character and morality are generally synonymous. Good conduct is morality. Bad conduct is immorality. Morality and immorality have their genesis in the mind; they are manifested through speech. Therefore, if we wish to develop moral strength we need to culture our thought, word and deed. When we do this, our thoughts become pure, speech becomes cultured and our actions will be beneficial to others and ourselves. So, to develop the moral strength, we have to attain

1. Purity of Thought
2. Purity of Speech
3. Purity of Action

Purity of Thought

Purity of thought is the first ornament of our moral personality. Sit for a while silently with closed eyes and observe everything that happens in your mind. How many thoughts, how many feelings, how many impulses arise in such a short span of time! Now, we cannot safely say that all of them are pure and exalted. Some of them are good, some are base and some are useless. An untrained, uncultured mind generally entertains bad thoughts, which will be myriad. But we can safely say that bad thoughts arise largely from our passions. Lust, greed, anger, attachment, arrogance, egotism, and selfishness—these passions that are lodged in our mind ignite bad thoughts in us.

Added to this, there is that heavy burden of bad *samskaras*, that is, mental tendencies accumulated over many incarnations of bad deeds, wrong thoughts and base feelings. These tendencies keep surfacing again and again. For instance, lust. Life after life, this sexual impulse has accompanied the soul. It has become as natural as hunger and thirst in man. Fulfilling the sexual need has assumed a degree of necessity on par with eating and drinking.

But why does this sexual impulse in man become a terrible menace to the wellbeing of society? Why does it make a person forget his dignity and make him behave like a beast? To satisfy his sexual urge, man will go to any extent; why is it so? If sex is such a natural thing in man, why cannot it be fulfilled in a natural way, leaving an after-effect of peace and satiety? Here, lust is not to be blamed. The fault lies in man's mind. Man's mind belongs to one of the following three categories—cultured, uncultured and ill-cultured. There is no limit to the sexual perversions in uncultured and ill-cultured minds. But in cultured minds, lust stays well within manageable limits. Therefore, such persons are considered to be cultured and civilised.

So, the mind has to be trained and cultivated by conscious effort. By doing so, we can prevent the mind from getting perverted and immoral and make it flow along in the right direction. Good company and good books are indispensable for achieving this. It is only when we stay in good company and read good, elevating books that we realise what is meant by good thoughts, good impulses and good feelings.

Purity of Speech

Purity of speech is the second ornament of our moral personality. The manner of speech reveals the inner stuff of the person. It is only when a crow opens its mouth that we realise it is not a cuckoo! When a person starts to speak, we immediately judge whether he is cultured or uncultured or ill-cultured.

Man first learns to speak from his mother; then from his family members and later on from those around him. Those who get a chance to go to school or college for education, learn the next higher lessons from teachers and fellow students there. Thus, there are many factors that influence a person's speech.

It is in the midst of these influencing factors that one must achieve purity of speech.

The words we speak must soothe the ear, inspire the mind and touch the heart of the listeners. How many are there today who can speak like this? So, if we wish to achieve purity of speech, we must put in a lot of effort to refine and culture our way of speaking. Friends, colleagues and classmates might speak whatever comes to mind naturally, without any restraint. In spite of such influences to maintain the purity and dignity of our speech, we not only need to be alert, but also exercise a lot of self-control. Suppose our friends are liberal with bad words and generally do not care for the choice of their words while we continue to be dignified in our speech and choose our words with a lot of care and attention, it is interesting to notice the reactions that follow. Generally, these very persons who are of loose speech will recognise the qualitative difference and respect us for that.

He who knows the secret of speech will never get into a quarrel. Knowing the secret of speech means knowing the tact of what to speak, with whom, where and in what circumstances. So, if a person speaks the right words at the right time to the right person in a right context, we may safely say that his speech in cultured.

In the *Ramayana*, there is a scene of Hanuman meeting Sri Rama for the first time. He comes as the royal ambassador of King Sugreeva and is in disguise. His speech charms Sri Rama. Sri Rama tells Lakshmana: 'Look, this man here is a master of words. Only one who is highly learned can speak like this. He must have studied grammar and linguistics many times over, because even though he spoke for so long, not a single mistake did he commit nor one unnecessary word did he use. While speaking, his facial expressions and bodily movements were calm and poised. Not a single unnecessary wrinkle appeared in his countenance when he spoke. He was precise in his speech and did not leave any chance for vagueness. He has spoken only as much as the situation demanded, neither more nor less. Not one word to rouse suspicion or create confusion. He has clearly expressed whatever he wanted to express. Neither did he drawl nor did he eat his words. His words arose from his heart and came out of his mouth, amplified by the timbre of his throat and they were neither too loud to seem harsh upon our ears nor too low to seem inaudible. His words filtered and refined through the grammatical rules and syntactic regulations were well arranged and pleasing to the mind. He has spoken only auspicious words. His speech was perfect in every respect.'

'Who indeed would not be pleased with such words uttered in so mellifluous a voice! Listening to such wonderful words, even an enemy with a drawn sword is bound to be moved.'

Thus, a total stranger, Hanuman, endeared himself to Sri Rama and gained his confidence. He was able to achieve this through his purity in speech. People judge our personality first by our words, only later by our deeds.

Purity of Action

Purity of action is the third ornament of our moral personality. What goes on in a man's mind is difficult for another man to determine. It may be full of good thoughts or teeming with bad thoughts. Nobody can say what is there in another man's mind. A man may speak very sweet words. To judge how sincere his words are, one needs to know a lot about human psychology. But his deeds reveal his inner feelings. Words can be used to express as well as hide the inner feeling, but actions reveal the inner motive without fail.

What is purity of action? We have seen what purity means with respect to thoughts and words. Now what is purity with respect to actions? One who has purity of action

- will doggedly finish any job that he has taken into his hands;
- will give as much importance to the means as to the end in view;
- will be tremendously methodical in his style of working. Knows that enthusiasm is different from being unable to keep quiet;
- will work with enormous energy but won't be hasty or haphazard in his work;
- will give a lot of thought to his work; and
- will undertake only beneficial and profitable endeavours.

These qualities refer to purity of action. Dedication to work, dignity of work, work as worship of the Lord—these are some of the most wonderful ideas referred to by the term *purity of action*.

One may ask—are there really such persons who possess purity of action? It will be difficult to pinpoint and identify such a person immediately. But it is much easier to know persons who lack purity of action. Just go to a public sector office and observe the careless and deceitful officers working there; you will get any number of persons who lack all purity of action. However, don't linger and stay there for long; that impurity might infect you too!

Now, it is clear that Purity of Thought, Purity of Speech and Purity of Action form the primary aspects of our Moral Personality. It is no doubt good to know these things. But morality is such a subtle topic that one cannot imbibe it by reading books or listening to lectures. If that were possible, our nation today would have become filled with strictly moral persons and, as a whole, it would have had a palpable ethical atmosphere. This land has produced the *Bhagavad Gita, Ramayana, Mahabharata* and similar wonderful works. The moral culture and spiritual ideals taught by these classics should have by this time created thousands of exemplary personalities among the masses. But such things cannot be. Ideals presented in books can influence people only to a certain extent, not completely. For a root and branch transformation in personality, living persons who have integrated those ideals in their own personalities are required. If people do not see the ideals presented in our classic literature, personified in living examples, how will they be influenced by these ideals?—'as the king, so the subjects', 'like father, like son'—these proverbs are very true. Good conduct or bad conduct, whatever it be, the younger generation learns how to conduct itself only by observing how their elders conduct themselves.

Morality being extremely subtle, practising and realising it is extremely difficult. It is good to know that realizing moral ideals is difficult. Only then can we be prepared to face the difficulties that arise when we start realising those ideals. Only then will we be vigilant in times of moral dilemmas and avoid falling during our weak moments. We must be moral even when we live in society, amidst all kinds of people. The issue of morality does not arise when we are alone, cloistered away from others. Morality is always in the context of living and interacting with others. Hence, there is always a danger of falling, because of mutual influence of one on the other. We will have to be ever vigilant, ever on guard!

Morality has innumerable aspects. One of these aspects is *brahmacharya* or continence. Nay, *brahmacharya* is not just an aspect; it is a grand ideal! It is the king of ideals! *Brahmacharya* is the foundation of every single virtue. It is because of the lack of *brahmacharya* that great monasteries have lost their lustre and become remnants of their glorious past. It is because of the lack of *brahmacharya* that the grand temples of learning—schools, colleges and universities—have lost vigour, power, sweetness and most importantly their purity and have become mockeries of the ideal!

Most people are not even aware that there is an ideal called *brahmacharya*. Among those that know, most are scared even to speak about *brahmacharya* openly. Then, there are many who brush it aside as unnatural and as a perversion. This ignorance is due to lack of correct understanding regarding this grand ideal of *brahmacharya*. Nowadays, there is an attempt to impart sex education through radio and television. But this new, commendable experiment lacks the required intensity to reach the millions and millions of people in the nooks and corners of this vast country.

Moreover, the details incorporated in the programmes are extremely inadequate. Of course, the prevailing knowledge on the topic of *brahmacharya* itself is hopelessly insufficient. In fact, so much needs to be learnt about this most important topic. Therefore, there is an urgent need to develop a system of disseminating the significance of *brahmacharya*. The elders must make special efforts to know about it themselves first and then educate the youth about it in a dignified manner and with a heart full of faith in its efficacy.

Youngsters too should learn about it with faith, reverence and dignity; this moral dignity with regard to sex education is extremely important because sexuality has a tremendous influence on a person's mind, behaviour and the entire personality. Though sexual awareness is of paramount importance, society sees it as a taboo subject! People have classified the whole issue of sexuality as vulgar and turned a blind eye towards it. But just because they ignore it, the sex impulse does not die. Instead, it gradually makes the whole society vulgar! Ravana, Keechaka and other valiant persons failed to keep their sexual urge under control and that proved fatal to them.

There are records of many great sages and spiritual seekers who fell during the time of their austerity rites because of their ignorance in sexual matters. What to say then of the poor common man!

How can the masses survive the onslaught of the sexual impulse? In this regard, the *Bhagavad Gita* and other scriptures give us many directives. But if those teachings are not practised in everyday life, they will remain just as verses in bound books and studying them will be only an intellectual pastime.

As soon as we raise the topic of *brahmacharya*, the first question that is asked is: 'Then should everybody completely renounce sex?' No, not at all. This is an important question, deserving deep study and a detailed reply. But let us rather give a straight reply—the scriptures prescribe the time-tested path of marriage for giving a healthy outlet to the sexual impulse. Why don't people keep themselves bound within the precincts of this holy institution called marriage? Sri Krishna says:

'I am that lust which is bound within the precincts of the holy corridors of marriage!'

Speaking of students, it would be salutary if they can take a vow of *brahmacharya* at least till they finish their studies and get lawfully married. Even that degree of continence is not an easy thing. Hence modern-day students may take this advice lightly, many may even laugh at it. But there will be certain wise students even today, who will see the wisdom behind this advice, follow it and reap incredible benefits for themselves by developing a tremendously strong moral fibre.

14

Spiritual Strength

The central aspect of a completely developed, all-round personality is spiritual strength. All the three aspects of the personality that were elaborated in the earlier section find their fulfilment in spirituality.

What is spirituality? The Sanskrit term for spirituality is *adhyatma. Adhi* + *atma* = *adhyatma. Adhi* means 'related to'; *atma* means 'self', that is, anything related to the self. So, spirituality refers to everything concerning the Self. If we consider ourselves to be the spirit and not the body, then we can be considered as spiritual persons. If we consider ourselves to be this body and if we continually cater to bodily needs and desires, then we are to be considered as worldly persons.

Spirit, that is, consciousness, is our true nature. This Spirit is All-powerful and All-blissful. Therefore, to overcome our fears and weaknesses and to remove our sorrows, we need to know about our spiritual self.

Today's scheme of education has absolutely no place for spirituality. People in India claim, 'Ours is a secular country'. Ironically nobody knows what this secularism is, nor what it means. Our people have caught hold of this term 'secularism' and are fooling around for no good reason! 'Why bring in spirituality, are not the human values sufficient?'—this is another popular argument of the times. But it is not uncommon to see how inhumanly these people behave, who pretend to uphold 'human values' to the exclusion of spirituality.

Religion is the backbone of our country. And today, this nation has completely sidelined religion. Why is this so? There are reasons for this. Firstly, religion is the subtlest of the subtle subjects, and there is an acute dearth of people who have expertise in this field. But this has been the case through the ages; it is not a recent development. The *Katah Upanishad* says;

'Most people are not fortunate even to hear about Atman or the spiritual Self in man. And even if some get to hear about it, they cannot understand it.'

Spirituality is indeed extremely subtle. But it is not beyond the ken of human understanding as we ourselves are that spirit. Now, one may ask that if we ourselves are the spirit, then why don't we realise it? The answer lies in the question—can anyone see their own face? Don't we need a mirror to see our own face? Likewise, we need the help of meditation to see our own spiritual self.

Nature of the Atman

What is *Atman*? The Upanishadic sages have attempted to answer this question in a variety of ways. But perhaps, they were not satisfied by any of these attempts. Hence they said, The words went out trying to grasp the *Atman* in man, but they returned back along with the mind'. The idea is that even the mind, which is extremely subtle, could not grasp the *Atman* in man. How then could speech, which is very gross compared to the mind, ever reach the innermost self or understand it and express it clearly! We face the same difficulty when we try to explain about electricity! Who does not know about electricity? It has entered our lives in the closest ways, furnishing us every sort of comfort, lighting our bulbs and tubes, making incredibly huge machines work effortlessly, producing heat in the stove and iron box, producing ice in the refrigerator—yet, who can clearly express what this electricity is or how it looks?

Yet another example is the well known chocolate. Everyone knows chocolate is sweet. But if we ask what this sweetness is, who can explain it? Just because nobody can explain what electricity is, can we conclude that electricity is a fiction, a figment of the imagination and does not exist in reality? Just because no one can explain what sweetness is, should we conclude that there is no sweetness in this world, that it is quite intangible. Yet, its effect can be felt by one and all, and everyone benefits from the wonderful effects of this invisible electricity. Nobody can express in words what sweetness is. The quality of sweetness can be experienced but can rarely be expressed. Yet all it takes to experience sweetness is to place a piece of chocolate on our tongue. In the same way our own spiritual self is not visible to us. But, remaining unmanifest, it governs all our bodily functions and actions, it makes our mind and intellect think, feel and imagine.

There is another attempt of the ancient sages to describe the *Atman* in man. It goes like this—'The *Atman* never dies and was never born. The *Atman* was, is and will remain, from eternity to eternity. The *Atman* in man is purity itself; the *Atman* in man is knowledge itself; the *Atman* in man is ever free, having no bondage; nothing can bind it.'

Now, youths will invariably ask a question here: 'If we are the *Atman* as described above, then we must not have birth and death. But we are always seeing birth and death around us. How do you reconcile this?' The fallacy here is, birth and death are of the body and not of the *Atman*. Moreover, this transcendence of birth and death is a truth which we will know only when we ourselves realise that we are not this body and that we are the Spirit. Right now, all our knowledge is read from some book or heard from someone else. But we must experience this truth for ourselves. How exactly we can realise this in our own heart will be dealt with in the following pages.

The *Atman* is of the nature of light. It is self-luminous and resplendent. This is another truth concerning the *Atman*. The ancient sages ecstatically sing about the luminous nature of the innermost self like this:

In the realm of *Atman*, sun does not shine; so
also the moon and stars, and lightning even.
What then to speak of earthly fire!

Necessity of Meditation

Though we are actually this resplendent *Atman*, ignorance has made us blind, it has made us grope about in darkness. Our very nature is supreme knowledge. But since we do not know that our very nature is knowledge, we wallow in the mire of ignorance. Essentially, we are purity itself, yet, we seem to sink down day by day in thoughts of impurity Here comes the urgent necessity of developing our spiritual strength. Though we are children of the almighty, it has become our fate to feel that we are weak. In this connection, Sri Ramakrishna gives us a wonderful illustration:

Once a flock of sheep was grazing on a meadow near a dense forest. At that time, a lioness appeared there. It was extremely hungry. In order to catch a sheep that was nearby, it jumped on the flock from a small height. The strain of jumping on the flock was too much for the lioness. It gave birth to a healthy lion cub and died immediately. The shepherd took the orphaned lion cub and tended it with great care. The cub grew with the other sheep. The cub also ate grass like the sheep. Since they all bleated 'bya, bya, this cub also learnt to bleat 'bya, bya', although with a deep guttural voice.

Gradually, the cub grew big in size and became a full-grown lion. But it was only physically grown, mentally it was still a sheep. One fine sunny day, another lion jumped on this flock hunting for food. This lion was utterly surprised to see a lion eating grass with the flock of sheep! It caught hold of the grass-eating lion. The grass-eating lion started to bleat 'bya, bya', in fear. The lion of the forest said:

'Look here, you too are a powerful lion like me. How disgraceful of you to eat grass with those sheep! Come with me to the forest, let us be free in the wilderness.'

Then, the sheep-lion said: 'No no, you are mistaken. I am a sheep. Leave me alone, I beg you. Don't harm me. I will go back and join the flock and be happy.'

The forest-lion realised, 'Aha! I understand now. This lion is more than convinced that it is a sheep. What a terrible hypnotism! I must think of something to break this spell of misconception and bring him in touch with reality.' It dragged the sheep-lion to a nearby pond, and said:

'Look here, see how your face looks, reflected on the water.'

The sheep-lion meekly nodded. Then the lion of the forest said:

'Come on, now give out a roar like me.' Saying so, it gave out a roar that reverberated through the whole forest. After some effort, the sheep-lion too started roaring majestically. The lion of the forest was pleased. It went and brought some fresh meat and thrust it into the sheep-lion's mouth. The sheep-lion felt repulsion at first, but gradually it got the taste and then started enjoying the meat. Then the forest lion said:

'Good fellow, are you now convinced that there is no difference between me and you? Do you understand now that you too are a powerful lion and not a sheep? Come with me. Let us go into the forest.' And the sheep-lion found its true identity and lived independently in the forest.

Now, if we think deeply, this story tells us many things. Though the lion was, by nature immensely powerful, it imagined that it was a sheep. Because of the dense ignorance about its real nature, it became like a sheep and was terrified to see the lion of the forest. But, by the help of the forest-lion, it understood its real identity, lost its sheep-nature, regained the awareness of its real nature and became extremely powerful and free!

The same is the case with us: since we identify ourselves with our body, we forget our divine nature and feel we are the body! Just as that lion bleated, 'I am a sheep, I eat only grass', we too cringe 'I am this body, I need to enjoy sensual pleasures.' The lion of the forest broke the spell and made the sheep-lion realise its true identity. Similarly, a true spiritual teacher must come our way and open our eyes. But this world is too much with us. Body-consciousness is very deeply rooted in us. To remove this wrong notion and to establish our real divine nature will be a very difficult job. Some blessed spiritual teacher must exert his force and make us see our own true nature in the depths of our heart. We too must get a taste of Divine Bliss and revel in that joy just as the sheep-lion tasted the raw meat and started liking it.

Our real nature is Divine Bliss. In Sanskrit, our true nature is called *Sat-Chit-Ananda*. Sat means that which eternally exits. Since our nature is Sat, we must always remember that we are essentially immortal. Chit means the light of knowledge. Since our real nature is chit, no ignorance of any sort must torment us. *Ananda* means bliss, the supreme joy that is unalloyed by sorrow. No joy of this world can ever be compared with that Bliss. Since our real nature is this *Ananda*, we must never have long faces, we must always be beaming with a supernal joy welling up and overflowing in our heart.

Once in America, Swami Vivekananda was sharing some jokes with his friends and laughing heartily with them, making others also roll with laughter and joy. Seeing this, some orthodox people there asked, 'Swami, you are a monk. You ought to have a grave face and always be in a serious mood. Is it right of you to be so joyous?' Those orthodox people must have felt that the more grave a monk, the deeper his spirituality and greater the reverence he deserved. Swami Vivekananda replied: 'Why at all should I be grave-faced? I am the heir to Immortality! Bliss is my true nature! I cannot help but be joyful.' The *Upanishads* say the same thing—'Listen all of you, listen well. You are all heirs to immortality.' Here it means two things—firstly, 'You do not have any death, you are immortal.' Secondly, it means, 'Your very nature is Supreme Bliss!'

Spirituality means considering ourselves as *Sat-Chit-Ananda*. As we think, so we become. This is a universal law. Sri Ramakrishna says: 'If we consider ourselves as sinners, sinners we become. If we consider ourselves as exalted and pure, pure and exalted we become.' The *Vedanta* philosophy speaks of the 'parable of the wasp and the fly'. A wasp once caught a fly and brought and kept it ensnared in its niche on a tree bark. Then it went out to bring another fly. In the meanwhile, the first fly, in fear of its life, kept on thinking intensely: 'The wasp will be back and will eat me now; the wasp will be back any minute now; the wasp will be back . . . the wasp . . . the wasp'. Thus, so intensely did the fly think of the wasp that the fly itself got transformed into a wasp! When the wasp flew back to its nest with another fly, what a wonder! There was another wasp in the niche!

The *Upanishads* teach, 'You must first hear about your true divine nature; you must allow those thoughts to soak in through your ears and enter your mind. Then you must *think deeply* about it. Then you must *meditate* on the truth that you are that divine being and gradually become divine.' These steps are termed as *Sharavana, Manana, Nidhidhyasana*. This is systematic, graded spiritual practice indeed.

'I am the spirit, *Sat-Chit-Ananda*. I am ever existing, all-knowing, all-blissful.' When we can realise this to be true in our own consciousness, we become strong in the true sense of the term. It is indeed a great thing if we can systematically develop our physical strength. Even greater it is to develop systematically our mental and intellectual strength. Way beyond the purview of intellectual strength is systematically developed moral strength. Systematically developed moral strength can bear an invincible influence on other people. But the real source of all these strengths is spiritual strength.

Spiritual strength is the main fountainhead from which gush all the other strengths that embellish a complete, all-round personality.

How can we realise our own true nature as the *Atman*? By means of meditation. Now, how shall we meditate? There are many ways in which we can meditate. Let us observe a simple, but a very efficient technique of meditation here.

What exactly is meditation? It is to re-collect the mind and then to make it flow towards a particular subject continuously, undisturbed. We use the term 'flow' with respect to the mind because, a little reflection on the nature of the mind will show that it is always in motion. Generally, its motion is like that of a monkey or a sparrow, this moment here, the next moment there, and again gone elsewhere. Such a restless mind has to be tamed by regularly practising the techniques given below. To define the state of mind in meditation, the scriptures give a picturesque illustration of oil flowing from one container to another. The oil flows continuously, in one stream, without any break, in a perfectly smooth, streamlined manner. Likewise, our mind must 'flow' towards the object of meditation. Those who wish to realise their true spiritual nature must make their mind flow towards their spiritual self.

Meditation Technique

Let us now observe the systematic technique of meditation.

1. Choose a clean, silent place. Place a soft cushion on the ground to sit upon. Even if you sit for long periods at a stretch, you should not feel pain or discomfort. Hence the necessity of a soft cushion. If your legs hurt and you feel

discomfort, your attention will go towards the pain and not on the subject of your meditation.

Now, sit in any cross-legged position in Indian style (that is, *Padmasana* or *Ardhapadmasana* or *Sukhasana*). Keep your palms on your lap. Place the back of your right palm on your left and sit in a steady posture. Backbone must be in line with your neck. Body must be firm and steady but not stiff. Take care to ensure that your body parts, especially the muscles, are not tight, they must be free and relaxed. Make suggestions to yourself, 'my leg muscles are relaxed, my hand muscles are relaxed, my neck muscles are relaxed,' etc. Most people are ignorant of the subtle, but deep influence the nervous system bears upon the mind during the hours of meditation. It is very important to ensure that the nerves are relaxed during meditation. If muscles are stiff and tight, and nerves are high strung, body and mind get fatigued very soon. Moreover, various parts of the body will start paining, and it will become impossible to continue meditation.

So, it is essential to ensure that your muscles and nerves are totally relaxed and at ease during meditation. Not only that, in the course of meditation, there is every possibility of your muscles and nerves becoming tight and stiff, without your knowledge. If such a thing happens, you must divert your attention a little towards your muscles and nerves and give powerful auto suggestions to relax them. The main thing is that your whole body must be very steady and firm, yet relaxed and perfectly at ease, when you meditate. There should be no movement in any of your limbs. Initially, legs may pain when you sit like this. This is quite natural. Then you may interchange the lock of your legs at regular intervals. With practice, the legs and other parts of the body will come to tolerate some amount of bodily pain. No pains, no gains!

You may face another problem. In the daytime, there is the problem of flies. In the night, there is the problem of mosquitoes—a perennial source of trouble to those who wish to meditate. You cannot swat them or shoo them away because there is the instruction that the body should be kept motionless! But if you don't swat or shoo them, the flies tickle you and the mosquitoes pester you! So, the best option is to sit inside a mosquito net and meditate.

2. Now that the place and posture are taken care of, you may next give your attention to the mind. After all, it is the mind that has to meditate, is it not? At least for the time being, you must forget the hundred thousand thoughts that occupy your mind. You must ensure that you don't remember anything related to your work and activities. But this is easier said than done. Thoughts have a wonderful knack of entering into the mind; somehow or other they rush in. Memories keep on rising to the surface. To counter them, you need to keep chanting some meaningful *slokas* and prayers. You may chant the *Omkara* for a couple of minutes. You will clearly observe how the mind quietens down all by itself when you do this.

You must however, tell the mind sternly, like you chide a mischievous kid, '0 mind, now you must get ready to meditate. You can look into your other affairs later. During the period of meditation, you must do meditation and meditation only. The joy that you get by meditating on the *Atman*, you will get from nowhere else, from nothing else. Do you understand me?' Telling this once to the mind will not be enough. Each time you sit for meditation, you must instruct your mind with these words. If the desire to meditate is sincere, very soon the mind will start accepting your instructions with great seriousness and will start to co-operate.

Now, you must offer your heartfelt salutations to the Guru. The grace of the Guru is the only secret of spiritual success. He, who has met his true spiritual teacher, must remember him and chant this sloka inside his mind:

He who has not yet met his true spiritual teacher must imagine his own inner Guru, his conscience, as his Guru and offer him his salutation. Sri Ramakrishna says: 'The actual Guru is one—the inner consciousness is every being, which is *Sat-Chit-Ananda*. When this

Guru Vandana is properly done, the mind becomes fit for meditation; it gets into the correct mood for doing meditation.

3. You must now do *Pranayama* for a couple of minutes. Well, *Pranayama* is not the correct term for what you do now, it would be better to call it 'deep, rhythmic breathing'. *Pranayama* is a highly technical exercise, needing the constant, watchful guidance of an expert teacher and tremendous amounts of physical and moral discipline. *Pranayama* requires tremendous practice. It is a separate branch of spiritual practice by itself. Anyhow, you won't attempt actual *Pranayama* here. Deep, rhythmic breathing is more than sufficient for the purpose of meditation, as this itself is highly beneficial. A simple technique for deep, rhythmic breathing is given below.

Firstly, take as deep a breath as you possibly can, as deep as you can. Then you must exhale out all of it. This is called deep rhythmic breathing.

Secondly, inhaling and exhaling must be neither too fast, nor too slow. It must be natural, smooth and comfortable on the lungs, muscles and nerves. The respiration during sleep has those qualities. Here, you should mark the word 'natural', because any attempt to force your respiratory system to lengthen the duration of breathing. ould be harmful.

Thirdly, while exhaling, that is while letting out your breath through the nostrils, imagine intensely like this, 'I am throwing out all weakness and impurity'. Similarly, while inhaling, imagine intensely, 'I am drawing in right thoughts, right feelings, strength, purity, spiritual brilliance and all these divine qualities are being assimilated into my personality'.

Continue doing this for about five minutes. You will yourself see how calm, composed and comfortable the mind will become. You will yourself see how pure, strong and energised the mind becomes. It is important to feel that your mind is becoming pure. Because it makes your meditation more effective.

4. You must now pray for the peace and wellbeing of the whole world. From time immemorial, the Vedic Rishis have

composed and chanted *mantras*—*Shanti Mantras*—for peace and harmony of the whole world.

You must however remember one thing here. In spite of your best prayer for the welfare of the whole world, war and disharmony may take their own course. But this prayer will certainly calm down the turbulence within your mind—this much is certain. Whatever thought-waves you send out from your mind, they travel the whole world and will one day come back to your own mind—the place of its origin. This is a universal law related to mind and thought. Moreover, when you pray sincerely for the welfare of others, your own mind will lose its narrowness and short-sightedness and become deep and expansive. To realise the infinite God, you need a mind that is as expansive as the sky and as deep as the ocean.

How to pray for world peace? You may pray like this: 'May all beings in the northern direction be contented, peaceful and blissful. May all beings in the southern direction be contented, peaceful and blissful. May all beings in the western direction be contented, peaceful and blissful. May all beings in the eastern direction be contented, peaceful and blissful. May all beings residing above be contented, peaceful and blissful. May all beings residing below be contented, peaceful and blissful. May all beings everywhere be contented, peaceful and blissful.'

While praying like this, you must feel that you are sending out waves of contentment, peace and bliss in all directions. You may ask what this sending of waves means. You know very well that the mind has the nature of roaming all over the world. Wherever your mind goes, there goes your feeling. You may be seated on your chair in your small room in some remote corner of some small town. But the moment you think of Delhi, your body is left behind in that room, while your mind is already roaming the streets of Delhi; and along with the mind, your feelings too. So, when you think of the four directions, it is certain that waves of feeling arising from your mind also reach there. However the results will be proportionate to the intensity and sincerity of your feelings.

5. Next, you must offer prayer to all the gods, goddesses and *avataras*. Your must then offer prayers to all the *jnanis* and

bhaktas, men of realisation and men of God from all parts of the world. The benefit of doing this is tremendous. The success in spiritual endeavour depends as much on your self-effort as on the grace of these gods, goddesses and men of realisation. But the inquisitive mind of the modern day youth will logically raise the question: 'Just because we salute them and pray to them, what certainty is there that their grace flows down to us?' The gods and goddesses and *avataras*, men of realisation, saints and seers don't need your money and wealth. What they value most is your trust, devotion and love for them. If you trust them, if you show your love and devotion to them, they immediately and wholeheartedly accept you as their own and draw you into their protective fold. A hearty salutation is the symbol of trust, love and devotion. When you whole-heartedly offer your salutations to the gods, *avataras* and saints, they feel pleased. When they are pleased their grace flows down on you automatically.

In this world, nothing is more difficult than directing your whole mind towards *Atman*—the spiritual Self. There are two main reasons for this. Firstly, the mind is fickle, hyperactive and restless. To find out how fickle, hyperactive and restless the mind is, you must attempt to meditate! You will then know. Secondly, the mind has neither seen nor heard of nor experienced the unmanifest, invisible *Atman*. The mind does not know your spiritual Self. It is totally unfamiliar with your spiritual Self. It is true that the spiritual Self is shining resplendent at the core of your own personality. But until the mind reaches this core, it has to sail on dark, unknown waters. No one in this world can protect you in these dark, unknown waters, in this inner voyage to your spiritual Self. It is only the grace of the gods, *avataras* and saints that can keep you safe from the dangers involved in the adventure.

It is good to know the philosophical rationale behind offering the prayers to all gods, *avataras* and saints. All gods, goddesses and *avataras* sprang from the same infinite supreme spiritual principle—*Parabrahman*. So, if you offer salutations to only a few gods and *avataras* and ignore the rest, it is as good as showing disrespect to

Parabrahman itself. So, it is good and correct in every way to accept all gods, goddesses and *avataras* as saints equally and pray and please them without being narrow-minded and dogmatic. Moreover, what do you lose by saluting them in your mind? Instead, you stand to gain in every respect.

6. Now, we come to proper meditation. In which centre of the body should you meditate? Some say that we must meditate in the *Sahasrara*, that is, the centre of consciousness located in the crown of the head. Others refute saying that the seat of the mind is located in between the eyebrows. There is another argument that it is safe and also natural to meditate in the *Anahata Chakra* located in the region of the heart. These are all endlessly controversial. All the hair-splitting arguments and counter-arguments regarding these centres of consciousness need not confuse you. You can meditate on any one of these regions. But, it is a safe advice for the beginners to meditate in the *Anahata Chakra*, that is, the heart region. The *Upanishads* and the *Bhagavad Gita* too recommend this centre as being most suitable for meditation. Therefore, it would be better to meditate in the region of your heart.

The moment you hear 'heart', the picture that comes up in the mind of the modern-day educated youth is the fist-shaped muscular blood-pumping organ. That is the physical heart. But what the Yogis mean is not this heart. At the base of the spinal column, there is the *Muladhara Chakra*. A little above that is the *Svadishtana Chakra*. Above that, in the plane of the navel region coincident with the spinal column lies the *Manipura Chakra*. All these *Chakras* lie along the spinal column. Though these *Chakras* or Centres of Consciousness do not have any physical location in the body, the reference is made to the parts of the body such as navel, heart, etc., only to make it easier to learn about these *Chakras* or Centres of Consciousness.

Thus, the *Anahata Chakra* lies in the centre of the spinal column at a place which is coplanar to the heart. This is what is called in the yogic language as—'Lotus of the Heart'. This is the spiritual heart. It is from this region that all our feelings arise. Since this is the residence of the effulgent spiritual self (Atman), you are required to meditate in your heart, you must intensely imagine this heart. Yes, imagination is the only resort in the beginning. But you must keep in mind that here you are imagining about what actually exists, but is right now not in the purview of your experience. This imagining, when done intensely and strongly, for a long period of time, will lead to a revelation of the Truth. Even in the day-to-day mundane existence, everything depends on your mental conceptions, your imagination and your feelings. The same is the case in your spiritual practice too.

It is at this stage that you feel the need of a mantra. Using a mantra, it is easy for the mind of move towards the Atman. By contemplating the meaning of the mantra, people are rescued from ignorance and misery. *Mantra* indeed is that which rescues.

For those who meditate on the *Ishta Devata*, there is the *lshta Mantra*. For those who meditate on the spiritual Self, *Pranava Mantra* is prescribed. *Pranava* menas *Omkara*. Generally, a mantra has to be given by a guru. But the *Upanishad* says:

'Chant *Omkara* and meditate on the spiritual Self. Banish darkness and perceive the effulgent Atman. May all success be yours in this endeavour.'

Very true indeed! Atman does not have any other name to represent it except for *Omkara*. Now, chanting this *Omkara* means that you should think deeply on its meaning; the mind should be made to meditate on the self-effulgent, brilliant Atman, your own spiritual Self. But in the beginning, no light will be seen. It will be dense darkness all around! So, instead of thinking about the Atman, the mind may start moving towards something else that it already knows, the memory of that which is strong and vibrant in the depth of the mind.

This is the nature of the mind. It always gravitates towards the persons and places and things it already knows. Or else, it starts daydreaming about the future, building castles in the air, about the 'immense projects' it wishes to undertake.

So, except for dwelling on the innermost Atman, it will do anything and go anywhere and think and dwell on whatever catches its fancy. If you know this nature of the mind, you won't get despondent when the mind starts to play all sorts of tricks and mischief. Instead, you will take the necessary steps to control it, break its will and train it to go inwards and dwell on the Atman. What are those necessary steps? Sri Krsna says:

> 'That is, this mind, that goes here, there and every where, has to be brought back slowly and steadily by the intellect that is coupled with a "special" kind of courage called *Dhriti*. Then the mind is to be made to meditate on the innermost Atman; and all other thoughts must be neglected and forgotten for the time being.'

Dhriti is a kind of courage that comes to the intellect after intense study, thinking and discussion on the scriptures.

It is interesting to note that you are asked to bring back the mind 'slowly and steadily'. The mind is extremely subtle. Not only that, for ages upon ages, it has been spoilt by over-indulgence. You have pampered it by giving it all that it asked, allowed it to do as it wished. Now, all of a sudden if you ask it to forget everything and dwell on the innermost Atman, it will give a hundred reasons for not doing so and go its own way. It might even revolt and go to sleep if you exert extra force. So, wherever it goes, you too must go there and coax it to come back to the innermost atman. See what a wonderful hint this is!

Here, you are instructed to bring back the mind using the 'intellect that is coupled with a special kind of courage called *Dhriti*. Let us go a little deeper into this point. Here you are dealing with your own mind. To bring back your own mind why do you need courage? If you examine this a little, the incredible, alluring power of passion will be clearly felt. Then you will understand why your intellect should be coupled with courage. So all-powerful are these passions, so all-embracing is their hypnotising power that even ascetics of great repute have fallen prey to them. The king of gods Devendra, served by the most beautiful nymphs, was smitten by the charms of Ahalya and had to relinquish heaven. Now, where does an ordinary man stand in front of such seemingly insuperable power! Ordinary intellect will be simply powerless to deal with the mind against the incredible power of the passions. It is only a specially cultivated intellect, an intellect coupled with *Dhriti*, that can face this onslaught and come out victorious.

So, now you have seen the how-and-why of bringing back the turbulent, self-willed mind from roaming in the external world using your intellect coupled with *Dhriti*. The question that arises is: what to do after bringing the mind back? It has to be made to dwell on the innermost Atman.

At this, the modern-day youth, with hot blood coursing through his veins, is apt to say, 'What benefit is there in making the mind passively sit in one place, while it should be kept active and engaged in beneficial activities?' It is very good that such questions arise. That will provide an opportunity to clarify issues. How can these youths know the blissful nature and the glory of the Atman? It is this ignorance that gives rise to these questions. In the preceding discussions, the glory of the Atman has been described. But man has a very strong tendency to forget. So, in spite of knowing so much, he tends to forget, ignorance regains its strong hold on him and reigns supreme in his life.

Come to think of it, the intensity of mental alertness of man is very low; consequently his mental activity is also very limited. This intensity that he has at present will serve no higher purpose. Compared to the minds of saints, a layman's mind is gross and stupid. The minds of saints are supremely powerful, because they would have touched the innermost Atman as a result of deep meditation. Their minds are completely awakened, alert and full of consciousness. It is meditation that has made their minds so perfect. Whatever work they undertake with such a perfect and supremely efficient mind will be equally perfect and efficient.

It is quite natural that in the beginning you may find it difficult to direct the mind towards your innermost being. That is because the mind is completely ignorant of the supernal bliss of the Atman! Happiness is the only motive of the mind. It is always in search of happiness. So, you have to educate the mind about the supreme bliss of the Atman. 'O mind, you have tasted sense-pleasures till now. Have they ever satisfied you completely? Could you get permanent happiness from any of them? Could you get pure happiness from any of the sensual pleasures? Now have faith in the words of the realised souls, in the words of the saints. Go to the Atman, which is right there in the innermost self. There lies permanent, unalloyed joy, supreme contentment and eternal bliss. There you will get all that you have been searching for—power, knowledge, wisdom. And more importantly there is security and permanence. There you will come face to face with the Infinite!'

You must not overlook another hint given by Sri Krsna for making the mind dwell on the Atman, that is, when you sit for meditation, you must not allow the mind to think of anything else. But this is totally against the nature of the mind; the mind is habituated to roaming about. It keeps dwelling on past memories. Or it will project itself into the future and keep building castles in the air. All of a sudden, how can it break this habit? In such a situation, how does one free the mind from activities detrimental to meditation? The answer is: Practice/Everyday, again and again, the mind has to be told and trained and educated. Come to think of it, nowhere in the long history of mankind has the mind been obedient to anyone at the very first attempt. Every saint, every prophet has had to wage a relentless war with his own mind for long periods. Eventually their efforts came to fruition and their minds obeyed them and they could experience heavenly joy. It is a great irrefutable truth that the mind definitely yields through constant practice.

Keeping this truth in mind, we must constantly direct the mind towards the Atman, the abode of supreme bliss. Thus, everyday, the Atman should be meditated upon at a fixed time. As this habit becomes established, first of all, we achieve *Asanasiddh*, that is, not a single part of the body will move unnecessarily; the whole body will sit still like an idol. This is a great achievement and it comes to us as the first milestone. As one goes on further, meditation deepens. As meditation deepens the next thing we achieve is victory over the sense organs. This is another wonderful thing because this further strengthens the triumph of the spirit over the flesh. All our senses will then come under our control and they will not hanker any more for sense-pleasures.

This second milestone ensures our supremacy over the senses. As we progress further, greater achievements lie on the path for us. After *Indriyajaya*, as our meditation matures, we attain an invaluable state called, *Shamasukha*. The joy associated with this state is a true indication of *Shamasukha*. Etymologically '*shama* means the serene state of the mind. Sages, who were masters in psychology, have considered the mind to be the sixth sense, of the same category as the other five senses. Just as the five senses always run behind their respective sense objects, the mind is also always on the run to enjoy sense pleasures.

Thus, even as the senses are turbulent, the mind also is constantly under a state of tension and disturbance. This craving of the mind to enjoy the sensual pleasures is the root cause of all misery, all unhappiness, all sorrow. The mind that has become steady in meditation on the Atman, the mind that has gained the grace of the Atman by intense, continued meditation, loses this sensual hunger. This state of mind is an extremely pleasant state, associated with indescribable joy, a truly enviable state of mind. This state of mind is called *Shamasukha*.

But this is not the goal of meditation. This is just another, although an important, milestone. Meditation must deepen further, mature further. The mind must become merged in the Atman. Meditation itself must stop; and *Samadhi* must ensure. Only then the Atman is seen face to face, the supreme bliss of the Atman is experienced firsthand.

But attaining this unique state of *Samadhi* is not in our hands. We can only meditate sincerely, regularly, intensely, for any length of time. But attainment of *Samadhi* and the consequent firsthand experience of the supreme bliss of the Atman is something that happens only by the grace of the Atman. Sri Ramakrishna gives a wonderfully apt illustration to drive home this point. A small child has a sweetmeat in his hand. All the people around this child are asking him to give them the sweet, '0 dear, will you give me that sweet?' That child keeps laughing and playfully looks at everyone. But he does not give it to anyone. Among these people, there sits one who does not ask him for the sweet, but gazes at him lovingly. Ignoring all these persons the child goes straight to this person, gives him the sweet, and goes his way, laughing with his childlike naturalness.

This illustration may confuse us, even frighten us. If the Atman like that child, cares only to listen to those who don't ask anything, then what need is there for meditation with strenuous efforts? Here lies the key point: all those persons, no doubt, asked the boy endearingly for the sweet. But, that man, not caring for the sweet, just poured out his heart in love. He was simply gazing at the child with intense love, engulfing the child in waves of love and affection. The pure heart of the child felt this marked difference in attitude and, as a mark of his love for that strange man who was interested in him and not in what he had, gave that sweet to him.

So, when by means of meditation we direct all our loving attention towards the Atman, waiting with the greatest eagerness to see the Atman face to face, then the Atman, our own innermost self, feels pleased. The Atman shows its true nature only to such sincere aspirants. The Katha Upanishad proclaims it like this:

'Atman is realised by those who sincerely wish to realise only the Atman; and to such intensely sincere persons, the Atman reveals its true nature.'

This is a unique experience. There is nothing known to man, which can be approximated to this experience. This is the state of existence called *Samadhi*. Words fail to describe the intense bliss we enjoy in this unique state. The mind is rendered speechless when it tries to express the intense bliss. In this state, we get merged in our own innermost Self, totally identified with it. We become thoroughly intoxicated with the bliss of the Atman. We start to get intimate with the Atman and interact lovingly, playfully with it.

Thus, our spiritual strength increases as we continue to meditate on the Atman. But we should not be under the impression that all this is possible in a matter of a few days or a couple of weeks. The idea that we are the body is a very deep-rooted one. It has been our confirmed conception for many incarnations. To shake off this notion that this body is our true self and to replace it with the idea that the Atman, the inner consciousness, is our true self, takes continued effort for a long period! But, what if it is? Considering the tremendous gain that will be ours at the end of this struggle, of what concern is a few years dedicated to this effort?

A question may arise at this juncture: is meditation the only way to increase our spiritual strength? The answer is no. There are other ways too. There are four major systems of Yoga namely Karma Yoga, Bhakti Yoga, Raja Yoga and Jnana Yoga. We may choose any one of these, get acquainted with details of that particular system, go deep into it, gain intellectual clarity and then sincerely practise them in everything in life. Spiritual strength is increased only by sincere practice. Sri Ramakrishna says that it is possible to increase our spiritual strength even by adopting a combination of all the four Yogas. But a great deal of detailed knowledge is essential for harmoniously blending all the four yogas to increase our spiritual strength.

This is a stupendous challenge before the youths today—how to develop a powerful personality. It is the primary duty of elders to direct the attention of our youths towards this responsibility and challenge of developing their personality. And it is the sacred duty of the youths to walk along the path shown by the wise elders.

References

Bar-On, R., 'Emotional and social intelligence: Insights from the Emotional Quotient Inventory', in The Handbook of Emotional Intelligence, eds. R. Bar-On and J. D. A. Parker. San Francisco, USA: Jossey-Bass, 2000, pp. 363-8.

Boyatsis, R., Goleman, D. and Hay-McBer, Emotional Competence Inventory, Publishes: Name Millennium Press, 1991 Edition.

Carless, S. 'Gender differences in transformational leadership: An examination of superior, leader, and subordinate perspectives', Sex Roles, Vol. 39(11¬12), 1998, pp. 887-902.

Cherniss, C. et al., 'Bringing emotional intelligence to the workplace', Technical report issued by the Consortium for Research on Emotional Intelligence in Organizations. Available online http://www.eiconsortium.org/ research/technical_report.htm

Cross, S. and Madson, L., 'Models of the self: Self-construals and gender', Psychological Bulletin, Vol. 122,1997, pp. 5-37.

Dayananda Saraswati, Swami, Talks on Emotional Maturity, Rishikesh, India: Gangadhareswar Trust.

Eagly, A. H. and Johnson, B. T., 'Gender and leadership style: A meta-analysis', Psychological Bulletin, Vol. 108(2), 1990, pp. 233-56.

Eagly, A.H., Karau, S. J. and Makhijani, M. G., 'Gender and the effectiveness of leaders: A meta-analysis.' Psychological Bulletin, Vol. 117(1), 1995, pp. 125-45.

Eagly, A. H., Makhijani, M. G. and Klonsky, B. G., Gender and the evaluation of leaders: A meta-analysis', Psychological Bulletin, Vol. 111(1), 1992, pp. 3-22.

Goleman, D., 'What Makes A Leader?', Harvard Business Review, November-December, 1998.

Goleman, D., Working With Emotional Intelligence, New York, USA: Bantam, 1998.

Kathleen, Cavallo, Emotional Competence and Leadership Excellence at Johnson &Johnson: The Emotional Intelligence and Leadership Study, PsD, Corporate Consulting Group.

Landau, J., The Relationship of race and gender to managers' ratings of promotion potential', Journal of Organizational Behavior, Vol. 16(4), 1995, pp. 391-400.

McClelland, D. C., 'Identifying Competencies with Behavioral Event Interviews', Psychological Science, Vol. 9(5), 1998, pp. 331-40.

Osborn, R. N. and Vicars, W. M., 'Sex stereotypes: An artefact in Leader

Behavior and Subordinate satisfaction Analysis?', Academy of Management Journal, 1976, pp. 439-49.

Ragins, B., 'Gender effects in subordinate evaluations of leaders: Real or artefact?' Journal of Organizational Behavior, Vol. 12(3), 1991, pp. 259— 68 .

Robert, Emmerling, The Consortium for Research on Emotional Intelligence in Organizations', Web Master Emotional Intelligence: A critical Analysis. Psy. D., 2004.

Importance of Emotions

http://www.learningtoforgive.com/san_jose_mercury_news.htm from the site by Stanford University Prof, Frederic Luskin: http:// www.learningtoforgive.com/

http://www.forgiving.org/campaign/research.html. I feel skeptical and cynical about their pleas for five million dollars in donations though!

http://www.psyc.leeds.ac.uk/research/hlth/arp/forglinks.htm There is also lots of stuff on forgiveness on the net. I recommend a search in goggle.com

Cindy Wigglesworth, President Conscious Pursuits, Inc. Spiritual Intelligence & Leadership: www.consciouspursuits.com

Danah Zohar and Ian Marshal, Spiritual Intelligence. The Ultimate Intelligence, Reviewed by Ian Bullock.

R. Venkatesh, 'Spiritual Intelligence', Times of India, Wednesday, January 24, 2001.

`Spiritual Intelligence', Financial Express, Tuesday, July 25, 2000.

Index

D

E